CHINDIT

www.penguin.co.uk

CHINDIT

RICHARD
RHODES JAMES

PENGUIN BOOKS

This book contains descriptions and words which readers of a modern sensibility may find offensive but reflect the realities of the times in which this book was written.

TRANSWORLD PUBLISHERS

Penguin Random House, One Embassy Gardens,
8 Viaduct Gardens, London SW11 7BW
www.penguin.co.uk

Transworld is part of the Penguin Random House group of companies
whose addresses can be found at global.penguinrandomhouse.com

First published in Great Britain in 1980 by John Murray (Publishers) Ltd
Reissued in 2022 by Penguin Books
an imprint of Transworld Publishers

Copyright © Richard Rhodes James 1980
Introduction copyright © Al Murray 2022

Richard Rhodes James has asserted his right under the Copyright,
Designs and Patents Act 1988 to be identified as the author of this work.

Every effort has been made to obtain the necessary permissions with
reference to copyright material, both illustrative and quoted. We apologize
for any omissions in this respect and will be pleased to make the
appropriate acknowledgements in any future edition.

A CIP catalogue record for this book
is available from the British Library.

ISBN 9780552178945

Typeset in 11/13.75 pt Van Dijck MT Pro by Jouve (UK), Milton Keynes
Printed and bound in Great Britain by Clays Ltd, Elcograf S.p.A.

The authorized representative in the EEA is Penguin Random House Ireland,
Morrison Chambers, 32 Nassau Street, Dublin D02 YH68.

Penguin Random House is committed to a sustainable
future for our business, our readers and our planet. This book
is made from Forest Stewardship Council® certified paper.

To Rachel

CHINDIT, the name given to Orde Wingate's two Burma operations and the men who took part in them, is a corruption of the word 'Chinthe'. This is the mythical animal, half lion and half flying griffin, that sits at the entrance to Burmese pagodas to ward off evil spirits.

CONTENTS

INTRODUCTION

The Chindit expeditions of 1943 and 1944 are mythical and controversial in equal measure. Heroic, punishing excursions behind enemy lines in the harshest of terrain, how could they be otherwise? The earliest embers of Allied success in Burma, elusive proof that the jungle could be tamed and that the Japanese could be beaten. And at the centre of the saga: their instigator, the enigmatic, mercurial Orde Wingate, who continues to cast the spell he exerted on his men as well as some, though by no means all, of his superiors to this day; he glares out of photographs, his charismatic gaze trying to fix you from beyond the black and white. The Chindit expeditions have the glamour of being near-impossible, audacious and unambiguously heroic. Or it is argued they have the notoriety of being a needless waste of materiel and well-motivated men at a stage in the war when they could be ill afforded, the bitter cost of entertaining a charismatic genius. This controversy continues today with less urgency and bitterness than at the time – although the distance time affords us looking back now makes the Chindits' feats no less awesome.

Richard Rhodes James' account, written up from his notes while he convalesced after Operation Thursday, is a visceral reminder of why the Chindits and their quixotic leader still grip the imagination. Rhodes James captures the hardship and the horror, the slog of marching through the jungle, the hypnotic grind of following the man in front in the stifling heat and humidity, the struggle of cajoling mules across the Irrawaddy River, the balm and comfort of brewing the military elixir that was tea, the sweat and effort of Long Range Penetration of the most unforgiving landscape imaginable, malaria, dysentery, leeches, jungle sores, as well as the bitter business of fighting an opponent able to take his time against the stranded and exposed Chindits. He questions why he is there, what they are doing, and the man who brought them to this hellish place – 'the strange man we followed'.

Born in Mandalay in what was Burma in 1921, Richard Rhodes James was the second son of five children of an Indian Army officer, Colonel William Rhodes James, and his wife Violet – and in the style of the son of an Indian Army officer he was sent back to Britain to be educated at Sedbergh School in Cumbria, going on to Queen's College, Oxford, to read history, returning to India in 1942 to join the Gurkhas. Writing was in the family: the ghost-story writer M. R. James was a cousin of his father, and Richard Rhodes James's younger brother Robert went on to become an MP and historian, writing about Churchill's pre-war political career and sweating out the uncomfortable business of being a One Nation Tory with Margaret Thatcher in charge of the party. Putting his experiences down on paper was a natural thing for Richard Rhodes James to do, and we are fortunate he did.

Richard's style is vivid and personal, he has an eye for detail and an understanding of character that brings his fellow Chindits to life. He intimately describes how he keeps himself together through the hardship. At the book's core is his Christianity – in moments of extreme stress in the jungle and in combat he refers to his faith, it gives him hope, furnishes him with endurance – and it was through his Christianity that I came by my copy of

Chindit. An old school friend of mine, Gavin, had met Richard at his church in Cambridge, they had struck up a friendship, and though Richard had mentioned his service he preferred not to speak of his time in the Chindits. I like to think he felt that in writing the book he'd said what needed saying. Out of curiosity Gavin bought Richard's book, read it and passed it on to me – 'You have to read this, it is truly extraordinary.' He wasn't wrong. And, as coincidence would have it, I later discovered I had studied history at university with Richard's daughter.

Rhodes James took part in Operation Thursday, in the opening months of 1944. Thursday was intended to draw on the lessons learned the previous year in Operation Longcloth, as well as to expand from one brigade to a divisional scale of operations. Longcloth, which began on 8 February 1943 and ran for three months, had been a qualified success, disrupting the Japanese, blowing up railway lines, winning the Chindits plaudits in the press and offering the British and Indian Armies some good headlines after their ignominious start in Burma. The columns had marched into the jungle and endured the appalling privations they found there, as well as trying to take the fight to the Japanese – the Chindits were active rather than passive. In 1943 this in itself constituted a win. Although the Japanese soon learned to keep an eye on Wingate's roving columns, and gradually shut them down, the Chindits were able to disrupt Japanese communications by attacking the railway scores of times.

Wingate's erratic command style, changing his mind unexpectedly, bawling out officers he felt had let him down – often after changing his mind – further burnished his legend as a man living on the edge of genius or madness. Some of his decisions do seem peculiar: at the end of Longcloth Wingate marched his headquarters out of the jungle ahead of the rest of the Chindit columns as the operation wound down, rather than seeing to it that everyone else got out. Men were lost in the jungle, marched into China, were captured. But on reaching India, Wingate felt he had proof of concept: you could take the fight to the Japanese and you could endure the jungle.

Looming over the perceived success was the cost. Some of the wounded men had been left in villages, abandoned to fate and the possibility of Japanese capture and reprisal. And almost certain death. Of the 2,182 men 77 Brigade had taken into the jungle more than 600 of those who returned were left unable to participate in any further active service because of jungle sickness or the injuries sustained during the operation. These losses and consequences were something everyone involved in Long Range Penetration had their eye on in 1944; when Thursday was planned, reassurances about the treatment and evacuation of the wounded were central to the question of establishing morale – reassurances which did not amount, in the clinch, to promises, causing considerable bitterness. In the wake of Longcloth, the unsentimental Wingate rebuilt the Chindits, taking the men who he felt had done well on that first expedition, returning the rest to their units. Wingate's ambitions were grander for his next sally into enemy territory.

By the beginning of 1944, the Allies were pretty much in the ascendant in all theatres bar Burma. With North Africa and Sicily falling in the summer of 1943, the bomber offensive proving its gruesome power with the firestorm in Hamburg in late July, American dominance in the Pacific and the Soviets' implacable defence at Kursk, it was clear that the war was headed in one direction only: Allied planners were looking well ahead to the invasion of France in the summer of 1944. But in Burma the British and Indian Armies had failed, so far, to land a decisive blow on the Japanese forces. Training and morale in both armies had not yet caught up with the theatre they were expecting to fight in against a keenly motivated enemy seeking to overthrow British rule in India. The British imperial effort, multinational, multilingual and with a whole host of motivations, some of them contradictory – British soldiers fighting to defend the Empire, Indian men fighting to defend their homeland in the hope of then leaving it, African soldiers pressed or paid to be there, and so on – was united in its loathing of Japanese brutality, but had staggered from disaster to disaster, most notably the expedition to the Arakan in 1943, a shambolic attempt to encounter the Japanese in Burma that reflected poorly on the leadership and the men. Wingate's methods seemed – to some, especially those not as up to speed on the difficulties of the Burma campaign – to offer a short cut to success. However, Bill Slim, commanding 14th Army, had become convinced that the way to beat the Japanese was to be resolute in defence, to get the Japanese to come to him and destroy them from solid air-supplied positions – the antithesis of Wingate's roaming columns. Yet Wingate got his way, and Operation Thursday was given the go-ahead.

In its conception and in practice, Longcloth's successor Thursday relied on air supply and air delivery – two of the three Chindit brigades would be placed behind enemy lines in gliders, saving them the grind of a long jungle march forward, using American WACO gliders that would land the men and their supplies in the jungle. Once up and running in the jungle, the columns would be resupplied by air, finding or creating suitable spots for aircraft to drop or land rations, ammunition, medicines. Pulling off this kind of resupply required cheek-by-jowl cooperation between army and air forces, flexible planning but within realisable parameters. Nevertheless, when the Thursday glider landings began on 5 March 1944 – a whole month after the land-borne footslogging component had set off through the jungle, which gives some indication of how difficult getting through the jungle was – they got off to a rocky start. Wingate had been so desperate to maintain secrecy that none of the landing zones had been recced properly; he had forbidden over-flights for fear of tipping the Japanese off – and they had to be switched at the very last minute. It was in the swirl of this kind of mercurial leadership and decision-making that the Chindits toiled and fought. So it is that no account of the Chindit expeditions can ignore the man at their centre and the drama that he courted and, as a consequence, surrounded him.

At the heart of *Chindit*, the sixth chapter does what it can to get to grips with Orde Wingate. Rhodes James writes:

> *I remember considering seriously with my fellow officers the question Is he mad? He would approach you staring straight at you with his piercing eyes and in a hard monotone fire off a string of questions. He seemed to want to wring everything out of you and you were conscious that your answers, however prompt, would always be inadequate, for his standards were unattainable. He was living in the clouds and inattentive to the ways in which he clothed his spiritual self. As you looked at him – it was difficult to stare back into those eyes – you saw at first a Bohemian who didn't mind how he looked. You felt: 'He doesn't look much like a soldier'. His appearance compared oddly with other great men of arms.*

Wingate's larger-than-life presentation of himself to his men, his confidence in confidence as an end in itself – regarded by plenty as a completely unrealistic understanding of what men could achieve in the jungle – are depicted first-hand. He was, no doubt, a difficult man; Rhodes James makes clear how he was hard to digest, even for those he sought to inspire. Orde Wingate's eccentricities – not washing, eating raw onions, taking orders meetings in the nude, his attempted suicide (possibly a reaction to malaria medication) – are often used to dismiss him and his achievements, but if he was anything, Wingate was an incredibly effective lobbyist and organiser, his ability to find the ear of the powerful and get his projects on their feet perhaps unrivalled in the British Army. His time in Palestine before the war, where he had become deeply sympathetic to Zionism, had given him a taste for irregular warfare, for stepping outside traditional military structures. He took these ideas to the limit with the Chindit operations, Operation Thursday being the grandest irregular campaign ever fought. Having bent Churchill's ear at the Montreal conference, he was granted more men, twenty-three battalions for the spring of 1944, with air resupply to match. These were resources jealously guarded in the Burma theatre, and for that reason alone Wingate made enemies. But Wingate's life was cut short in a plane crash three weeks into Thursday. At the very moment that he could have triumphed, seen Operation Thursday succeed and his Long Range Penetration concept come to maturity, Wingate left the scene. If the Chindits were the one-man band they were accused of being, proof of *that* concept was on hand. As the columns marched around the jungle looking for their objectives and doing their damnedest not to engage the enemy, the question of what the Chindits were there for was raised again, and never quite answered. Perhaps it was just as well in a way, as after his death his men struggled. Was this because those who took over lacked Wingate's vision, or because the concept itself was essentially flawed?

Rhodes James was a signals officer, so he knew everything that was going on. Requests for resupply went through his radio set, orders to move on, regroup, disengage, withdraw. He was present when his brigadier Joe Lentaigne received the news that Wingate had died. Lentaigne had had a tense relationship with Wingate. They had disagreed profoundly about how Lentaigne's men should deploy and fight in the jungle. Lentaigne was every inch a conventional soldier, so a strange fit in the Chindits. Arguments continued throughout Thursday about command and Lentaigne's style, and in May General Slim – who had been one of Wingate's disbelievers in 14th Army command – handed over the Chindits to the Americans, and General Joe Stilwell. Stilwell, advocates of the Chindits will tell you, had no idea what the Chindits were or what they were capable of, but they had been in the jungle for months, had fought closely against the Japanese and were pretty much worn out.

How Rhodes James felt about his time in the Chindits and whether it was worth it – well, I shall leave that to the reader to discover and consider. It is our good fortune that someone with such a keen eye, steeped in the cool compassion that came from his faith, was able to record the experiences of the man in the Chindit column. Richard Rhodes James does omit some of the grimmer aspects of the battle at Broadway, he resorts sometimes to the language of gallantry to describe how men fought and died, and he isn't inclined to judge his fellow officers in the decisions they made. But given his understanding of the bond of mutual hardship that the men had endured, I understand how the suffering of men in battle and the chaos of the retreat from Broadway was something he felt the need to draw a veil over.

As the war for Burma turned in favour of the British in 1944, so the Chindits were disbanded, their operations eclipsed into irrelevance by 14th Army's epic and destructive battles at the Admin Box, Kohima and Imphal, battles which excite none of the controversy that the Chindits inspire. Without Wingate the Chindits had neither a champion nor a leader – his commanders and rivals no longer had to address his demands for irregular warfare. The war had changed. Bill Slim's emphasis on 14th Army as a cohesive force had no room for personal commands and buccaneering expeditions. In these pages Richard Rhodes James takes us right to the heart of the Chindits and, with modesty, depicts their superhuman efforts.

Al Murray

FOREWORD

I commend this book as an authentic and moving recollection of the atmosphere and high tension of the second Wingate expedition into Burma behind the Japanese lines in 1944. It has recalled to me much that I remember and much that I had forgotten. It is beautifully and sensitively written: the more effectively because it eschews the melodramatic, and allows the story to unfold in its own way.

Richard Rhodes James was cipher officer at the headquarters of III Brigade, the formation commanded by the redoubtable Brigadier Joe Lentaigne, until the death in an air crash of General Wingate, when in circumstances of great difficulty Lentaigne was extricated and flown out to take over the command of Wingate's Special Force. A cipher officer in such a spearhead formation as a Chindit or Parachute brigade leads no sheltered life, and is especially well placed to observe. He knows the contents of the messages that are passing; he is aware of every crisis, and of every clash on views between superior and subordinate commanders; yet he remains very much a participant in the operation. Not for him are the comforts of a French château, an Italian palazzo, or even a caravan in the desert. The bullets whizz about him (or even through him); the mortar bombs burst around him; he shares the mud and the hunger; he carries his pack like everybody else. He is accorded no immunity from the mosquitoes or ticks or leeches; he helps to succour the wounded, and to bury the dead. And his duties, like those of the signallers, are most exacting at the midday halt and the evening bivouac, when others are able to relax and to rest. The spectrum of his experience includes all colours, and stretches farther than most.

I am sure from my own knowledge that Richard Rhodes James is correct in his surmise that Wingate and Lentaigne were antipathetic from the outset, and remained so. About this, I can say only that, different though they were, I greatly admired them both. A considerable and conflicting canon has built up around the personality of Wingate, who was so inspiring to his men and so abhorrent to some of the orthodox. The first expedition was small enough in numbers for every man-jack to feel that he knew Wingate personally, and also to feel the magic of his impact in full; not so the second, which comprised six brigades. For much of the training period, Wingate was sick, and unable to make himself known throughout his expanded force as he would otherwise have done. Yet Rhodes James conveys how his electric influence pervaded it nevertheless: even the large Gurkha element, of whose tongue Wingate knew barely a dozen words, recognised him as an inspiring Bahadur. This matter has puzzled the historians, whose job it is to seek chapter and verse. The author does not seek to account for it; but his testimony to the manner in which Wingate inspired the force like an injection into its bloodstream glows from his pages.

I would make one comment on the principal task imposed on III Brigade. It was a major mistake to try to repeat the brilliant exploit of Brigadier Michael Calvert's 77 Brigade. A few weeks earlier, he had virtually garrotted the northward Japanese lines of communication by establishing his block across their road and railway at 'White City', near Mawlu. He speedily made it impregnable before an adequate force could be built up to dislodge him, and 'dislodged' he never was: he held it triumphantly against several times his strength for two months; and only moved out, at a moment of his own choosing, so as to adjust to the changed strategy of the campaign. It was an error of judgement at a higher level to think that such a coup could be repeated: the Japanese were the last soldiers in the world to be caught out that way twice within two months and 100 miles. Hence the foredoomed catastrophe at 'Blackpool', so vividly described from the commander's level in Brigadier John Masters' *The Road Past Mandalay*, and here, from a lowlier level, by his cipher officer, who witnessed and endured the whole costly drama.

I knew some of the characters whom he sketches; and here they are, exactly as I remember them after thirty-five years, drawn in a few deft lines. Others whom I did not know spring equally to life: many, alas, only to die in action in the course of the story.

This book does not really need any commendation from me. It will surely stand on its own merits, both as a piece of writing and as a memorial to that grim ordeal of long ago. Every word of it rings true.

Bernard Fergusson

AUTHOR'S NOTE

The original manuscript of this book was written shortly after the events that it records. I started it during illness and convalescence after the campaign. I wrote much of it on board a troopship sailing between Bombay and Malaya on the operation to dispossess the Japanese of Malaya, and I finished it in Kuala Lumpur.

A short time ago, encouraged to believe that a worthwhile story was contained in its pages, I took it up again and looked at it afresh. It has been a strange experience to relive those laborious nights and days, to catch again faint echoes of fear and exhaustion and to recollect the companionship of men now grown old.

I have cut out bits that were clumsy or superfluous, or which might cause hurt – truth is both stranger and more wounding than fiction. I have added other bits to explain to today's reader the background to the events of 1944, and I have corrected some facts. I have amplified the passage in which I assess the character of Orde Wingate. But it is essentially what I wrote in 1944 and 1945, and it is my hope that some of the mud is still clinging to its pages.

Those wishing to understand the story of the whole campaign – and a pretty tangled tale it is – should read Brigadier Shelford Bidwell's recent book *The Chindit War*. I have set out to show what it was like to be there and to take part in this extraordinary adventure.

A writer incurs many debts. I am especially grateful to two of the brigade commanders on the operation: Bernard Fergusson for his very kind words on my behalf, and Lieutenant-Colonel John Masters, who took time during a brief visit to England to read the typescript and make some very percipient comments. Jim Macpherson has also kindly read it through and made some suggestions. The errors that remain are, of course, mine.

I must thank Gill Sayer and Brigadier Bidwell for both playing a key role in getting this book through to publication; and my publishers for their skill and care.

Mrs Hedley, Dr Desmond Whyte, Squadron-Leader R. J. Jennings and Major Frank Turner have been kind enough to lend me precious photographs and help in other ways, and Mr R. Moffatt, late of 14 Brigade, has allowed me to see some of his collection of Chindit photographs. I would particularly thank Squadron-Leader Jennings for cherishing a historic aerial photograph of 'Blackpool' through all the hazards of the campaign.

Mr R. W. A. Suddaby, Keeper of Documents at the Imperial War Museum, and his staff have given me most courteous service whenever I asked for it.

Finally, I must thank my wife for valuable help with the proof reading.

The formal dedication of this book is to my wife. I would also like to offer it to the memory of those Chindits who, having landed behind the enemy line, did not return.

R. R. J.

CHAPTER ONE

BEGINNINGS

I got out of the train at a desolate little wayside station in the Central Provinces of India, a miserable shack and a tiny platform with the jungle closing in on all sides. It was July 1943 and the rains were in full swing. There was a layer of rich brown mud over the road which led to the camp. I felt in all my finery like a man coming from a party who had lost his way and stumbled into a farmyard. I had come straight from an office stool, having rashly asked to be given a strenuous outdoor job. This was outdoors all right, and I was soon to discover how strenuous it was.

The camp, or that part of it that contained brigade headquarters, was perched on the side of a steep muddy slope. Small tents were dotted about in an air of abandon, and fit young men were walking around on their daily tasks, stripped to the waist and bronzed by the weather. The Intelligence Officer, John Hedley, boomed a greeting to me. I was to accustom myself to that boom in the next few months, the cry of an Old Etonian to whom the whole world is a friend. We retired to the mess, a most inadequate little tent with a table made of dried mud and bamboo, a symbolic piece of furniture. There were the officers, with whom I was to share much in the months ahead. First, Brigadier Lentaigne, who was known during the day for his unflagging energy and at night for his after-dinner stories. 'Briggo' Briggs, the Signals Officer, who in more peaceful days used to sniff out illicit whisky stills in Scotland. Major Beaumont, the animal transport officer, complete with long cavalry bush-shirt. The 'Wingco', our RAF officer, who in the First World War had acquired most of the decorations awarded by the Army, and in this war had joined up in the balloon branch of the RAF, was a man of astonishing vigour for his years who had the unique privilege of owning a house in Timbuktu. And finally the Brigade Major, Jack Masters, who could out-think anyone by five clear minutes and was equally at home discussing the company in the attack or American railroads. We never really found out what he did not know. A brilliant, aggressive, thrusting mind.

I settled down to the task of operating the ciphers, which were in a state of disorganisation bordering on chaos, and toiled long hours with hieroglyphics. Closeted in the tent I had little time to notice the procession of mules and men which plodded up and down the muddy road; nor those groups of men huddled over their fires after an exhausting day's march, the rain fighting with the flames. But when we gathered round the table at night by the light of the solitary hurricane lamp, I began to imbibe the philosophy of these strange men who took apparent pleasure in living uncomfortably and eating only a trifle more delicately than pigs. In three months the brigade was to plunge into Burma as Wingate had done before.

In February, Orde Wingate had led 77 Indian Infantry Brigade into Burma to operate behind the enemy lines. A man of striking character and highly unorthodox views, he had persuaded the authorities to allow him to try out what he called Long Range Penetration, roaming at large in enemy territory, supplied entirely from the air, and harassing the enemy's lines of communication.

His force emerged two months later. It had achieved few tangible results – some bridges blown, some stretches of railway damaged, some Japanese killed – had suffered fearfully and had sustained considerable casualties. But the operation made an enormous impact: through its sheer audacity, through showing that the British could operate in the jungle at least as effectively as the Japanese, and through the exciting possibilities it opened up for air supply. For a defeated and jaded army, it was a wonderful shot in the arm.

And now III Indian Infantry Brigade was to carry out a similar operation. Only this time we would profit by his mistakes and would bring to perfection that branch of warfare which he had conceived. Our name, like his, would be blazed across the headlines of the world's press; we suffered from no false modesty. Wingate's expedition had returned to India a month previously and strange tales were drifting about, tales of hunger, exhaustion and isolation; no wounded could return. This was strong meat, and for those about to follow in the pioneer's footsteps it was disquieting. The result was a strengthening of our feeling of gallantry and a heightened resolve to see the matter through.

It is not always easy to foresee the troops' reactions to conditions such as these, and the Brigadier thought it advisable to insert in the training instructions a denial of the rumour that a man would lose his taste for beer after three months on short rations. Malnutrition was another bogey, which we persuaded ourselves would be overcome. Often at night the conversation would turn to Wingate himself and we scrutinised this strange man closely. The verdict was unfavourable. We could not understand a man who worked his troops mercilessly, continually changing his orders and willing to publish scathing comments on his officers. I say we could not understand, but then I have met no one who did. We learnt later to respect and admire him when we were his troops and our interests came before all else. Now we were a chosen people and felt justified in surveying critically anyone who did not reach our self-imposed standards. But in our criticisms we were sobered by the thought that the lessons of the campaign had been learnt at great cost.

And so we talked far into the night with the little tent shaking under the lashing rain and the hurricane lamp flickering lower. Briggo, an ardent Yorkshireman, became the butt of the Brigadier's humour and defended his native county with a fervour granted only to Yorkshiremen. The Wingco would come out with the most impossible statements and take on all comers. Jack Masters would continue to demonstrate his amazing fund of knowledge. It was rumoured that he could tell you the timings of all the trains between Chicago and St Louis. I sat in a corner and listened. This strange new life exhausted but enthralled me, and the Great Crusade became as much a part of my life as of those who were arguing before me in the ill-lit tent.

There was one part of our philosophy which for the want of a better word I call 'the cult of the scruffy'. Our living quarters, our dress, indeed our whole life was one of disorderliness. We made the mistake of connecting 'scruffy' with 'tough'. The connection is a false and dangerous one which we did not realise at the time. We were so imbued with the notion of the jungle life that we seemed almost to assimilate ourselves to the jungle animals. But, as one commanding officer remarked, 'Any fool can be uncomfortable in the jungle,' and on this reckoning we were indeed fools. Our object, of course, was to harden ourselves to the jungle life, but we made the mistake in our excess of zeal of imagining that hard training meant bad quarters and indifferent food. It was fortunate that the high morale of the men was sufficient to overlook, or at least to tolerate, a serious defect in our training.

While we scratched our pens – we were the 'paper boys' – the troops marched, sweated and slept in the surrounding country. It was a rough country holding little promise for anything but hard training, and yet in its wild way it was beautiful. In peacetime few sahibs frequented this part of India; it was away from the military north and the commercial centres of the east and west coasts. To me it will always be a place of physical stress, but even on the long marches I had time to see that the country was green and the hills attractive in their sudden jagged outlines. The thick jungle would rise up abruptly into a rocky slope, as if pushed up by the whim of a powerful hand. Perhaps the geologists would say that it was a 'young' country and had not been weathered into symmetry. If so, I wish it not a day older. The rock slopes would give way to sudden vistas of jungle stretching in broken shapes towards the horizon. It was here that Kipling chose the scenes for his *Jungle Books*, and he chose them well. It was primeval, unfrequented and for the most part unknown. The year before, Wingate had chosen it because it resembled central Burma, and this year we were treading the same paths and scrambling up the same rocky slopes. There was a feeling that we were the direct heirs of that first great adventure and we would be tried by the same physical standards as they were.

Our brigade at that time, two months after its formation, consisted of only two battalions: the 4th Battalion 9th Gurkha Rifles and the 1st Battalion The Cameronians. One a set of Jocks, grumbling, joking, sweating and cursing, the other – just Gurkhas. By which I mean a cheery, carefree, soldierly crowd, not over-particular about their living conditions provided there was a plentiful supply of water and good officers. It is often said that between Gurkhas and Scots there is a connection which links all true highlanders. The link, if it exists, is forthrightness and broad humour. The Gurkha has no inhibitions and his thoughts express themselves freely in words and action. He reacts naturally to the stimulus of everyday life. These attributes have shielded him from many of the vices of civilisation and the Army is careful to maintain this guilelessness. His faults are easy to see: wine and women. The Gurkha will drink for the joy of the feast, chanting round the fireside, and he will desire women undisguisedly. To this may be added a third vice, the love of gambling, which comes from his open-handedness and lack of forethought. These three defects the Army seeks to control without fettering the Gurkha's free expression. In my opinion it has succeeded brilliantly.

The Jock I did not know so well, though I got to know him far better in the dirt and fatigue of the column. Grumbling and grousing on the line of march and through the long weary days of training, he will shatter the silence of suspense in battle with a rich joke. I had one of them with me at headquarters and I got to know his quality.

When I arrived we were just finishing the initial training before setting out on our first long trek. Long Range Penetration is a mode of warfare not easily learnt except by those who are willing to dispense with certain deep-rooted conceptions of war. So we learnt and unlearnt. There were plenty of weak points and we were by no means ready for battle. There were untrained mules which delighted in tossing off their loads at 5 a.m. and careering away into the jungle. We had not mastered the art of controlling the long column 'snake' or of reacting quickly to an emergency. Above all we were not hardened to the daily grind of ten, fifteen, twenty miles a day carrying a load of fifty pounds. This was our goal; indeed it was the essential minimum for our operation. Silence, which was the golden rule of the column, was a hard lesson to learn. And perhaps we overdid it, for silence is a strain on the mind and in danger the troops need a safety valve. For the present, however, we were eager to restrain the natural volubility of the Jock and the constant, cheery chatter of the Gurkha. A wilful mule must not be shouted at; it must be coaxed with gentle words and soft touch. On seeing a deer cross the path you do not give a whoop, as the enemy may be close at hand. On reaching night harbour you do not make the jungle ring with the sound of chopping, nor do you sing over the fire as the water boils. These were hard lessons to learn, both for townsmen and countrymen.

To march in silence is unnatural, besides adding to weariness. To live in silence over a long period is like adding the discipline of the monastery to that of the Army. It was our first big obstacle in the process of orienting our minds to a new idea in war.

This, then, was the background for our future efforts, the starting-point for our long trek, our growing confidence and our final pitch of readiness. The troops were beginning to shake off their natural distaste for discomfort and hard living. They were beginning in a faltering way to regain some of the qualities of which they had been deprived by their own civilisation.

'Get a move on, Beaumont, your mules are half an hour late!' They were indeed, but then we were starting on our first big trek, and the other columns were worried with far bigger problems than half an hour's delay in loading up mules. Briggo went round to help coax wireless sets on to the backs of the unwilling animals. If there is one thing a mule really dislikes it is an object that rattles, and wireless sets suffer from this defect more than any other load. A bountiful harvest of wireless equipment scattered round the countryside was proof of this. The sets were slowly retrieved, one by one, by a crowd of blaspheming signalmen and the mules were recaptured. I collected my ciphers and packed them away in my haversack; my office was highly mobile, consisting as it did of a couple of field service notebooks and a plentiful supply of pencils and rubbers. Jack Masters was supervising the packing and loading of the office boxes. These were meant to contain maps and equipment for the issuing of orders in the field. On this occasion, however, there were precious few maps and very little other equipment. Instead we had a large kettle and an ample supply of tea and sugar; hardly a good start for a life of hardy abstinence, but we did like our tea.

Ken Beaumont, the animal transport officer, known to us as 'Beau', had provided each officer with a charger. But, lest any misunderstanding arise, it must be explained that the animals were not for the use of officers who felt in need of a rest. They were needed to carry in their saddle-bags certain extra items of kit and for the purpose of reconnaissance. On column an unmounted horse was a tantalising sight, but as the march went on more and more of them were carrying men who had fallen by the wayside. We learnt to look on them as one of our most precious possessions, for it was they who carried our wounded.

We formed up outside the camp, shouldered our packs and moved off. We felt for the first time the full weight of our operational kit, and we loathed it. Never through all the long training marches or the muddy scrambles over the Burma hills did we accustom ourselves to the enormous weight we had to carry. The modern soldier expects to have a vehicle for the heavier items of kit; and his demands are just. For us there were no vehicles. Our food, spare clothing, ammunition, blankets and personal belongings were crammed into that preposterous mass of webbing that hung about us, tearing at our shoulders, bending our backs and rubbing our sides. The sweat clotted on our backs and chilled us at the end of the day. We longed to throw the stuff away and be able to walk out with a light step. We rejoiced to get rid of it at the hourly halts and cursed as we dragged it on to our backs again and staggered to our feet. The very effort of getting up thus attired was a feat and left us momentarily breathless. I pitied most of all those who had to carry service rifles, and those thrice wretched men whose turn it was to carry the Bren gun. Having carried one for only short periods I marvelled that anyone could survive under such a load.

It did not take long to find these things out as we walked out of the camp on the eighty-mile march to the town of Jubbulpore. Four columns were advancing on different axes to converge on Jubbulpore and defeat the local troops who were guarding it from the north on the line of a fast-flowing river. After a long but fairly easy day's march we reached the camp of one of the columns which was to accompany headquarters and provide protection. If we had lived like pigs, it would be hard to find an adequate description for the caveman existence of the Gurkhas and their officers. This state of affairs was caused to a certain extent by a breakdown in supplies and a period of very short rations. This is not good soldiering, though perhaps they felt at the end that it was all to the good. I enciphered a message, tore it up and did it over again. My office feet were complaining loudly and I felt apprehensive of the following day's march.

The days that followed in that first exhausting trial of strength were not pleasant, even when viewed through the flattering haze of the past. The morning would start very early, cheating the night of its last fleeting moments. A hasty snack from our hopelessly inadequate rations and a delicious mug of tea. The rations were indeed deplorable. They went under the title of 'Indian Light Scale'. It was aptly named. They consisted of biscuits, raisins, dates, bully beef and cheese. The raisins and dates were almost invariably weevil-ridden and we had to content ourselves, as sustenance for one day's hard march, on a small tin of bully beef, cheese and a few biscuits. We were saved by our daily brews of tea. For the soldier in the field drink means just one thing – the soothing, warming, invigorating mug of tea. We found this out soon and we rediscovered it daily with fresh delight. Wingate's men had lived on this sparse fare – when they got any food at all – and it had been proclaimed inadequate. Perhaps this is why we were charged 'extra messing' for consuming it.

My Gurkha batman, Birbal, would be preparing a fire when I awoke, and at the appointed time he would put a light to the little pile of wood neatly arranged to catch the draughts of the early morning breeze. The officers in British regiments always envied us in this respect, for the Gurkha batmen were far more knowledgeable of the ways of the outdoor life than their British counterparts. So when my mug was steaming to the brim my less fortunate brethren would still be fanning the flames or striking a succession of damp matches. We would linger for a few precious minutes in the growing light and think the world a better place, knowing that soon we would be cursing it. For there were mules to load.

At about 7.30 came that dread signal, 'Packs on,' and we shouldered our gargantuan loads, feeling again the creases and bruises of yesterday's march. That first hour was by no means the worst of the day. With the sun not properly risen and one's insides aglow with the tea of a few minutes back, we could march with ease and confidence, silent and settled, hearing only the clink of mule harness and the rattle of a badly adjusted load. The rise and fall of the equipment of the man in front had not begun to irritate and served only to emphasise the rhythm of the march. There is leisure to look around before the weight of the pack has bent the back and fixed the eyes in a weary gaze at the boots of the next man or the hooves of the mule in front. There is enchantment in this early hour more clearly defined in its contrast to the toil ahead and the troops, after they have overcome the depression of the early rise, are ready to face the day.

The enchantment is short-lived, and especially in our case with unaccustomed bodies and soft feet. The sun mounts and sheds no kindly light but a merciless glare on the column. The sweat begins to collect under the pack and flows in great salty streams from the forehead through the eyes and down the chin. All the aches and pains of yesterday appear again, to be joined by the peculiar discomforts of today. The ill-adjusted pack, the rubbing of the water bottle or haversack, that place where the belt fails to coincide with the contours of the body, the place you long to scratch but cannot reach. And then the boots, pinching, slipping, rubbing, the socks sliding down the foot and collecting in an abrasive bundle at the heel. Having very unaccommodating feet I fared badly on that first march and suffered the extreme indignity of travelling for a whole day on a horse.

The first sign of weariness is easily recognised. It is the furtive glance at the watch, first occasionally and increasingly frequently until we glance every few minutes in a desperate hope that time has passed and the hourly halt is due. The hour seems longer and longer as the day lengthens, and woe betide the commander who dares to trespass one minute across the boundary of that time of rest. Impressed immediately with the great monotony of the march we sought to evolve a means of keeping our minds occupied. When the hypnotist tells you to 'make your mind a blank', he is asking the impossible. And we found that our minds craved an outlet from the prison which our physical activity imposed on them. The Gurkhas, having not reached, by our standards, a very high state of mental development, did not seem to find much difficulty in sustaining interest; the noises of the jungle and the sight of game satisfied them. For the British troops the problem was more difficult and no one but the individual himself could tell how successfully he overcame it. For myself, I used the method of the marching tune, and prided myself on my ability to convert any tune into the rhythm of the march. Conscious thoughts were less easy to arrange. They varied from a pride in physical achievement, which lasted only a short time, to nostalgic memories of physical comfort. There was always a special place reserved for anticipation of the midday halt or the night's bivouac, but it was not wise to encourage these thoughts too early in the day.

The first big moment of the day has arrived and after four or five hours' marching we disperse for the midday halt. Jack Masters gives instructions: 'Signals under the big tree over there with a set one hundred yards to the right.' 'Command post under this tree.' (Selecting the choicest position.) 'Transport along the line of the trees fifty yards off the track.' 'Medical, half left by that bush.' 'Orders in twenty minutes' time.'

Each man barely reaches his allotted station before he hurls off his pack, slumps down and surveys the scene wearily. But the rest is short-lived. There are mules to unload, fires to prepare, water to fetch and blistered feet to inspect. I take up my position by the wireless set and enjoy the supreme luxury of having my pack removed by Birbal. The world is acceptable again. The Brigadier is already removing his boots.

Orders are issued in a very informal fashion. We stroll up to the command post, trying to appear fresher than the next man. John Hedley strides up; he always took a delight in his rude health and became rather overpowering with his vast strides and booming voice. Beau turns up late, having been round all the animals and inspected them for galls. His report is bad and he complains bitterly with some justification that the mules have been under load for too long. This is their first real test and they are being unfairly treated. The animal transport officer on a column is fated to be continually at loggerheads with the commander: it seems strange how few commanders in this type of warfare take into consideration the endurance of their mules. Sometimes of course we may have to wear them into the ground. Briggo has a grumble about the siting of his wireless sets, and he has a right to be heard, for he is responsible for our only contact with the outside world. The Wingco for all his years is taking it very well and regales us with sundry observations on anything that enters that agile, eccentric mind of his. Jack Masters issues orders for the lighting of fires, time of starting and order of march. No questions, only a few facetious comments on the hardness of the march and the desire for a soft bed.

For a delightful hour and a half – sometimes it is as much as three hours – we laze about in the shade. The fire is lit with the same skilled hand and I sit back against the trunk of a tree, the steaming brew held in both hands with an occasional bite at a Shakapura biscuit. The dates and raisins I leave well alone. My feet are hot and throbbing, but I leave them too. I have learnt not to touch them in the middle of a march. Usually I am halfway through my mug of tea when a message arrives for enciphering. I summon my unwilling sergeant and we start in on the figures. The troops are sprawled around the trees welcoming this brief respite from the rigours of the march. They lay their arms and equipment beside them, stretch out their legs and take their ease, dreaming of I know not what. They are conscious of their physical needs and their other requirements matter little. They are tired and hungry but are not especially aware of the lack of women. They think not of parties and cinemas but of food, drink and sleep. And I believe a man like this is happy. His horizon is limited and he learns not to expect too much. Life is very simple.

'Load up. Packs on.' The pack settles down on my back with a thump and I stagger off. Those first few minutes are torture. All the sore parts of the feet send up a wail as they are set down again on the track and it is some time before they settle down in their boots. The afternoon march is trying, and for those who have lunched too well – which on our rations was quite an achievement – it is additionally exacting. It took time to regain the rhythm of the march and for this reason we sometimes cut short our midday halt, preferring to arrive early at the night bivouac. There were many theories on when you should stop and for how long, but no definite rule was ever established.

Finally, as the sun is going down, we reach our night harbour, sited near enough to water for convenience, but not so near that the enemy may spot us. Again we disperse and once again the packs roll to the ground. It is wise in the chill of the evening with the sweat still on you to put on a jersey, and it is a wonderful rest to get into gym shoes. There is a lot of delicate treading on very hot feet, but many do not care to walk around, content to relax on the ground until the limbs cool and the body returns to normal. For the signallers there is no peace. They have time only to rid themselves of their equipment before they unload their mules and start erecting their sets. The aerials are flung over the neighbouring trees, sometimes missing their mark and landing with a thud beside a recumbent soldier. In a few minutes everything is fixed and an operator sits at each set with the sweat of the march still on him. They have a hard time, and they deserve the thanks and praise of us all. They have no time to relax or even enjoy the advantage of sitting by a fire watching the food cook or the water boil. Briggo goes round the sets and checks up on the progress, repeating the same three words, which were to be our theme in the future, 'Are you through?' Jack Masters comes up to Briggo and asks, 'Are we through?' The Brigadier turns to Jack Masters, 'Are they through?' And the only man who can do anything about it is a signalman (the lowest rank in the Royal Signals) on whose ability depends the maintenance of the whole column. So that, while majors swear and brigadiers fume, the man on the set carries quietly on with his job, perhaps a little amused but always conscious of the vital nature of his work. A pal hands him a mug of tea which he gulps between messages. Briggo makes another enquiry. 'Trying, sir,' comes the answer, 'but there's a lot of interference, and the operator at the other end . . .' An awkward feature may interrupt the waves or a badly placed aerial limit the range. The key hammers away, and at last there is an answering call. Briggo crouches over the set from behind. His reputation depends on those few minutes, and he is longing to say confidently to the Brigadier, 'We're through, sir.' His moment has arrived and he hurries away.

With the last fade of light and duties done we gather round the glowing remnants of a fire and though exhausted by the day's march have enough strength to carry on an idle discussion. Jack Masters as usual dominates and scintillates, having a crack at a particularly weary officer or starting an argument on the relative merits of Bix Beiderbecke and Harry James. The Brigadier, listening in the background, comes out with a choice Simla story; perhaps that tale of the impecunious subaltern who absconded with the regimental funds. The moral of these stories, if any, is dubious, but they are richly embroidered with Irish whimsy and compel us to laugh more loudly than our training allows. John Hedley, who in peacetime was in the Bombay Burmah Trading Corporation and had stayed in Siam for some time, is particularly engaging with his stories of horse-racing in Bangkok. His booming voice is somewhat hushed on this occasion but there is still that gurgle of delight as he recounts how one famous race never finished owing to the determination of all the jockeys to lose. Or the one about the Australian horse which was smuggled in, raced as a 'country-bred' and carried off every prize for which it was (not) eligible. He does not tell us that in Rangoon life as a sahib did not prevent him from looking after the welfare of a large number of orphans. This side of his character I came to know only gradually, when things were going against us. Briggo continues to extol the qualities of the Pontefract cake, the Yorkshire cricket eleven and the West Riding with the same apostolic fervour. The rum is produced, a drink I find nauseating, but which the others find acceptable. Finally we disperse to our posts and drop onto the welcome ground, falling asleep to the sound of many snores and the rustling of mules in their standings. Life is sweet, brother.

The second day of that first wearisome trek brought us to a huge plateau of thick jungle. We wandered along it seeking a way down to the plains below but found to our astonishment that we were apparently cut off on a lost world. After hours of searching we found a steep rocky defile down which we slid, our best mule spiking its belly on a rock. That night we were too exhausted to talk.

On the fourth day we reached the fast-flowing river which the enemy was supposed to be defending. There was no enemy, but the river was formidable enough. It was just shallow enough to wade across, the water surging round one's chin. The Wingco, a small man, stood in the middle of the stream waving us on; I expected him to disappear at any moment. On the far bank we dried ourselves, scraped off the mud and decided to call off the battle. The enemy was apparently some distance upstream. We had unwittingly deceived him as to our intentions; and there remained the fifteen-mile march along the road to Jubbulpore.

I arrived with tattered feet and presented myself to the MO, Major Whyte. He had just arrived, and I had my first glimpse of a remarkable man, tireless, fearless and infinitely assuring in time of trouble. It was a pity that we could not think of any more significant name for him than 'Doc'.

We were due to have ten days' rest in Jubbulpore, having capitulated to the idea that troops cannot go on training indefinitely under extreme conditions of discomfort. But for most of the officers it was a time of feverish preparation for our next venture, a 160-mile march north to an uninhabited locality between the military stations of Saugor and Jhansi. Beau had the worst time, as the mules had suffered very badly in the first trek and needed constant attention. The saddlery and loading equipment was unsatisfactory and needed redesigning. Briggo's wireless sets caused the most trouble, as they always did, and that battery-charging engine of his which only the strongest mules could carry. Long hours were spent at the local garage whose enterprising proprietor had contracted to make the new equipment. Jack Masters sat in his office all day and most of the night writing rude letters to GHQ; the Brigadier used to say that our letters always commanded respect in the halls of the mighty as the sweat of the march was still on them when they were opened. Anyway he usually got what he wanted, though our demands were sometimes outrageous.

The troops accepted this brief pause in training. Indeed the thought of the 'big city' ahead kept men going who, without such an incentive, might well have fallen by the wayside. But they were due for a disappointment. The camp was a collection of tents sited on one of the muddiest spots in the area, and the continual downpour, which had kept off during the march, turned the place into a quagmire. The city itself was neither big nor especially attractive. In fact the British soldier was experiencing just one of the many disappointments which appear to be his lot and which do little to him except inculcate a dour pessimism. The Gurkhas cared little and wandered down the streets staring curiously at the shops; they were due for some rum and the world was good.

The march to Gona was a different affair to that first hectic scramble. It was in fact merely a method of getting from A to B – B being our new training ground – and for the most part it was a route march. The only thing to watch was our feet, which did not thrive on continuous road marching. The second day was long and exhausting, but after that it was just a case of covering the miles before bedding down for the night just off the road. We acquired a strange complex about this question of mileage. It became imperative to cover the maximum distance every day, not to fulfil any tactical plan but to prove to ourselves that we were indeed the chosen race. Along the road this becomes a farce and tests nothing except the soles of one's feet, least of all the qualities required for Long Range Penetration of enemy territory.

Perhaps the troops themselves did not share these feelings with the same vehemence as the officers. Indeed I can imagine no one to equal the pure physical delight of John Hedley as he covered the ground with his long raking strides and a shout of welcome for all and sundry. The men had less of a stake in the adventure, certainly less in the training, and if they covered twenty miles in a day that was due to the persistence of the officers. This feeling expressed itself clearly in the earlier stages of training, but later on there developed a new feeling which bound up the men in a great cause, the cause which the officers had already embraced. While they were now covering the miles with a certain dumb resignation they later developed a most un-British enthusiasm for strenuous work. The cause of this change was Wingate.

The march to Gona was interrupted by a day's halt at Saugor, an unattractive enough place in normal times but to us as we flogged along the road it seemed a pleasure ground. The last day into Saugor was one of torrential rain, so heavy that you could barely see through it. Strangely enough I liked it. It reminded me of my schooldays at Sedbergh among the Yorkshire fells when I used to run along the high ridges with the rain lashing against my flimsy shirt. In Saugor there were bathtubs in abundance and for sheer physical pleasure I can think of nothing to equal that first glorious plunge into the steaming water. We had all the next day to indulge ourselves in supreme idleness, an art that is easily lost unless it is hardly gained.

At Gona we were joined by another battalion, the 3rd Battalion 4th Gurkha Rifles. Here we reached our first climax in training. All was well. Our date of readiness had been changed from October to November, but we were not unduly worried by the delay. There were plenty of matters to put straight before we were finally ready for war, and we could well occupy our time in the intervening three months.

Things started happening outside. Churchill had read Wingate's report on the operations of 77 Brigade. Comparing it with what he regarded as the stagnant caution of the other commanders in the Far East he was determined to know more. He summoned Wingate home, met him and was attracted. Then and there he invited him to the conference of the Allied chiefs of staff to be held in Quebec. At this conference Wingate sold his ideas with total conviction and telling assurance. It was an astonishing achievement for a brigadier.

He got most of what he wanted. The idea of Long Range Penetration had been greatly enlarged to include several brigades with American air support; Wingate had captured the imagination of the Americans and they were prepared to supply air support on a huge scale. Wingate was now a major-general and was promoting his old column commanders to positions of responsibility under him. 70 Division was turned completely over to the new force, three British brigades and a reconnaissance regiment.

Wingate had triumphed and his new warfare had been given the seal of approval. But for us in Gona the news was not altogether good. We had lost our exclusiveness and become one element of a large force. For three months the brigade had been stimulated by a feeling of uniqueness. We had endured the discomfort and fatigue because we felt that we alone could endure it. When these discomforts were shared by four or five other brigades they lost the element of adventure and became an ordinary training programme.

For the troops this period was a sort of psychological interim. They were leaving behind the gay adventure of those earlier hardships and had not acquired the new and broader loyalty to the force as a whole which was only developed when the presence of Wingate made itself felt. At present the General was away conferring with the mighty and his force was beginning to assemble for its task. We regarded the new brigades with a certain uneasy patronage, though we had not yet met them. One of them was 77 Brigade, which had gone in with Wingate only a few months before and had been entirely re-formed. There were a few veterans left with strange tales to tell, but we regarded them with suspicion and carried on with our training determined to prove to ourselves and to the world that III Brigade was 'the tops'.

Colonel Fergusson joined us for a short time as second-in-command. His name was rapidly becoming a legend, as a result both of his recent exploits with Wingate and of his outstanding personality, which was a rare gift to the press in those humdrum days. His appearance was dominated by his monocle, which gave the clue not only to his assurance and magnificent flow of words but also to that gay insouciance which now we tend to link only with the knights of the past. To hear him talk over the mess table was an experience which will always have a special niche in my memory. An Old Etonian, like John Hedley, with the pride of race belonging to the great families of Scotland, he could yet eliminate in five minutes that appearance of supercilious superiority which was his immediate front to the world. He talked at length on the incredible hardships and many mistakes of that first campaign, but he prefaced each story with an apology: 'I apologise for thrusting 77 Brigade down your throats the whole time, but you might as well learn by our mistakes – we made enough of them.' In his work he would consult everyone, drawing on their opinions and leavening it with his own experience, dictating their thoughts to no one but ready to query an obscure statement or a hasty argument. He left us after a few weeks to command a brigade of his own, but in that short time he left a lasting impression.

Perhaps for our future history the most significant event during our month's stay at Gona was the arrival of Frankie Baines. He came to us for attachment as G III Camouflage for no particular reason, and so firmly did he attach himself to us that we eventually managed to smuggle him into Burma when no one was looking. He took delight in running down his own job. 'I come from the Camouflage Pool,' he would say, 'where the sedge is withered and no birds sing.' His life was a defiance of all convention, from the time that he ran away to sea to the time when, in need of a cheap leave, he dressed up as an Indian and travelled third class to Darjeeling. His Urdu was superb and he almost got away with it. He could pour out words of great eloquence for hours on end, and his last job as assistant Conservative agent for Wimbledon must have been good training. But he was hampered in his speech by no inhibitions, and his frankness about everything, especially his own defects, was at times embarrassing.

He was perhaps the greatest contributor to our fund of story tellers, and even the Brigadier had on occasions to take second place to his rich yarns. A sailor's life does not appear to add refinement, and some of his tales of foreign ports had to be reserved for special occasions when the drink was flowing freely. His outrageous and spontaneous comments were an easy target and Jack Masters, when feeling provocative, used to arouse him to fierce protests over some very trifling matters. Life without Frankie would have been a much duller thing.

The troops were now at the climax of their training with hard bodies and high morale. They had earned their fitness by the sweat and toil of the march, their morale they had gained by the vision, a trifle hazy at times, of a great adventure.

The rot set in with a march to the Betwa River, and here again we followed blindly the principle of physical exertion which had led us through our training. The previous year Wingate's men had trained in the same place and at the same time; and they had been decimated by malaria. The lesson was lost on us, as were most of the lessons of moderation, and we set out on a period of intensive training in the sticky heat and malaria of September. The Brigadier even conceived the idea of living by the Betwa without tents, but he was compelled to change his decision by the unanimous protest of COs and medical officers.

The march to the Betwa was seventy-five miles across country, and what country! After marching one mile one of my sergeants collapsed and declared his inability to go any further. I do not know whether this was real physical exhaustion or lack of willpower; I believe the latter played a big part in his decision. The march lay across heavy cotton soil, and the heat was of a peculiarly oppressive nature. In the softer parts we had to unload the mules and manhandle the loads until we reached firm ground. By the end of the second day I was well and truly 'on my knees', as were we all. And that night a strange thing happened. We were harboured in the middle of a muddy field through an error on somebody's part.

It was neither tactical nor comfortable, but we were all in and it did us well enough. Suddenly at midnight all the Gurkha mule leaders let out a weird cry. Every single mule uprooted his stake and came charging down on us. By the light of a full moon this was inexpressibly uncanny, and the incident remains unexplained to this day. The Brigadier, a Gurkha officer, advanced the theory that Gurkhas when they are exhausted give vent to strange cries; but that still leaves the action of the mules to be explained.

The next day we marched eighteen miles in the blazing heat. Men were dropping out right and left with heat stroke or malaria, and even the gallant Wingco had to declare himself beaten. He finally collapsed halfway up a long hill. Frankie Baines, who had recently been injured by a mule, found his arm suppurating and went off to hospital; he very nearly lost the arm. To cover these eighteen miles we had to flog ourselves and again John Hedley showed his imperviousness to fatigue by carrying quantities of extra arms. We halted three hours in the middle of the day by a small lake and drank until we could take no more. The temperature was around 100 degrees and the humidity was about the same. I have sweated many times in my life, but never as much as I did on that blazing day. We sank down in our night harbour in a kind of stupor.

When we arrived at our new camp we found we had lost a quarter of our personnel, and the final casualty occurred about a mile from the camp when a Gurkha suffering from malaria suddenly gave way and ran amok. The camp was the usual collection of tents arranged in disorderly patterns by the sides of the River Betwa. Brigade headquarters, true to tradition, had selected the worst possible site. The mess was the usual hovel with a table so uneven that a visiting general was compelled to ask if it had been used as a sand model for tactical exercises. With the end of the rains and the arrival of the post-monsoon heat the surrounding jungle began to lose its greenery. It became parched and carpeted with a layer of dead leaves which crackled as you waded through them. The heat got steadily worse and more oppressive and the fine edge was slowly worn off the men.

Then the malaria started. I became an early casualty and swore in the midst of my fever that I would never carry a pack again. Men were being carried off dozens at a time to Jhansi hospital twenty-five miles away. Battalions were left with barely enough men to look after their mules and training came to an abrupt halt. An air of depression hung over the camp combined with a listlessness of movement which transformed every little act into a great effort of willpower. We were due to start on our final big scheme and apparently the Brigadier intended to go through with it. He was finally dissuaded by one of our medical officers who came into the mess one day and railed at him for about an hour. It was a remarkable performance, though somewhat embarrassing to us as we listened, and he won his case. Plans were scrapped and we sat back to rest ourselves.

Eventually, the higher command acquainted itself with the situation and was horrified. General Auchinleck himself wrote to enquire why 77 and III Infantry Brigades, which were due to enter Burma in two months' time, were in such an appalling condition. General Wingate was at this time himself desperately ill with typhoid, having apparently refused with true Wingatian obstinacy to be inoculated or to refrain from drinking unsterilised water – or so the story reached us. Perhaps it was symbolic that he who always shared the discomforts of his men should now be like us on a bed of sickness. There developed what the Army describes as a 'first-class flap'. Daily we were visited by doctors of renown, feeling our pulses, examining our eyes, appraising our bodies. Nutrition experts examined our food and were not impressed. Malariologists took one look at our camp and raised their hands in hygienic horror; we conceded to them by moving one battalion away from the river's edge. What had been a fine fighting force was now a collection of convalescents.

Convalescence is a trying period. We were taken in hand and given everything that the medical profession had to offer. Crates of food came down to us, and there was a rumour that green vegetables were being flown down from the hills. Iron tonic was dispensed daily to the troops, while the final stage of medical ingenuity was reached with the introduction of shark's liver oil. All ranks were made to drink this nauseating medicine. John Hedley for once turned mutinous and refused to touch the stuff, and it was tacitly agreed in the end that perhaps it was better to do without a few vitamins than to suffer constant diarrhoea. Rather belatedly we went through a course of Mepacrine, which if it had been given to us a month earlier might well have prevented ninety per cent of the malaria. But it was a new drug and could not be squandered. At least that was the only reason we could find for this parsimony.

A new officer arrived at headquarters to replace Beau, who could not see eye to eye with the commander on the treatment of mules. And so we got Frank Turner. You could tell his origin a mile off. He spoke with a rich Gloucestershire brogue which surprised until it delighted you. He had been born among horses and he had spent his life among them, teaching others to acquire that mastery of man over beast that he so obviously possessed. Frank was a very accommodating fellow with a polite, 'Yes, zir' to every request which did not interfere with the welfare of his animals. All his mule leaders were Gurkhas and to meet emergencies he evolved a strange brand of Urdu, consisting of a few memorised sentences and spoken with a slow, methodical Gloucestershire accent. His vocabulary enabled him to deploy his mules off the track, halt and advance; the more complicated manoeuvres were somehow interpreted by his Gurkhas as the occasion arose. These Gurkhas took an extraordinary liking to him. I think it was his slow, fatherly manner which surmounted the barriers of language. In their more mischievous moments his men used to mimic his laboured Urdu. Frank added a touch of honest-to-goodness England to our strangely assorted gathering at headquarters.

Meanwhile, the men were slowly regaining their strength, and wondering where all the magnificent food was coming from. They got used to expecting the worst and when something appreciably better turned up they were curious and not a little suspicious. But it became clear to them that the 'brass hats' had a real interest in their welfare, if only for the reason that they were shortly for operations and unhealthy men do not make good fighters. The training creaked into motion again as the hospitals gradually emptied. We spent days endeavouring to persuade mules to cross rivers, beating, cursing and threatening them. We tried different types of bank and widths of stream, catapulting the animals into the water with ropes or standing on the far bank making tempting noises and holding out bags of grain. But usually we had to resort to riding the animals across ourselves. This was hectic, though not as dangerous as it might sound. Mounting a mule which is lashing about in shallow water in company with several others is not easy, but the water seems to absorb much of the power of their kicks. Having been mounted, the mule would try to unseat the rider by rearing up backwards. This was a bit alarming, especially if the two of you fell over backwards, but I never knew of anyone who was badly hurt.

This is perhaps an appropriate moment to introduce Maggie, the 'pin-up' of brigade headquarters. She was a huge, broad animal with an exceptionally thick neck captured from the Vichy French in Syria, or so the story went. Maggie was the perfect mule. She carried the most fearsome loads without complaint and had the gentlest nature of any animal I have known. She would look at you with her big, soulful eyes as if longing for a chat and taking a quiet but real interest in everything that went on. The Gurkha who was chosen to lead her had a special place among the mule leaders and would delight in introducing newcomers to his

Maggie. Not even the mightiest of the long succession of visiting generals could be allowed to leave without an introduction to Maggie. And Maggie, realising the importance of the occasion, would respond magnificently.

The mules had by this time been 'de-vocalised'. Having been deprived of their ability to breed they were now deprived of their voice, that magnificent bray in which they took so much pleasure but which used to frighten us not a little as we crept through the jungle. All that could be heard now was a hoarse rush of wind like the sound of a mighty bellows; or perhaps it could be better described as whooping cough. Unfortunately, some of the animals began to get back their voices, and we received a message from a column which read, 'One mule braying *sotto voce*.' The chorus was gradually taken up until the last state was worse than the first. We were considerably annoyed and felt we had been cheated by our vets, but I had a sneaking feeling of satisfaction that the mules had defeated our foul designs.

Perhaps the most energetic of us in the water-training period was the Wingco. He had been released from hospital after his collapse and had insisted on walking the last seven miles into camp with full marching orders. He spent hours floating about in the river testing various types of equipment. Balloon fabric was a big sideline of his and he sold it to us very successfully. There was the empty pack made waterproof by means of a balloon fabric lining which was the climax of his inventions. An apprehensive soldier attempted to pull him out one day when he had been floating about for several hours on the assumption that he might be in difficulties. But difficulties existed for the Wingco only to be surmounted. Poor man, he was told a short time later that he was too old for the column. He never came with us.

At this stage of our training we first met the Burma Rifles. This battalion, for there was only one of them, built up a tremendous name for itself. They were very enterprising and utterly reliable, so that the troops began to regard them as an assurance of a smooth day's march. I met one second lieutenant, a Kachin, whose map reading, initiative and, above all, jungle sense would have shamed many a field officer. These men were doing only what they did in their daily lives before the war, and they did it with the ease and efficiency which could come only from long practice. And they enjoyed perhaps the greatest compliment that can be paid to troops, the confidence of the British soldier.

The period of convalescence was over and General Wingate was reported to be out of hospital. The force was feeling its way towards cohesion, though we as the original brigade still did not find it easy to digest ourselves into the larger whole. We were now known as Special Force, which appeared to us to be odd for a force whose special nature it was imperative to hide. But it satisfied our pride, and at this stage our morale was even more important than the dictates of security. The outlying brigades were getting to hear of each other, which may sound rather an elementary stage of cohesion, but we were scattered over India and it took some time to get a sense of unity.

Our date of readiness had again been changed, this time to January 1944, and the final trial of strength was arranged for December. It was to be an exercise on a grand scale, though they could think of no more exciting code-name for it than 'Thursday'. A similar exercise the previous year had laid out half of Wingate's original brigade, and there was a feeling that we would require all our strength to pull us through. Frankie Baines had returned by now with a large scar on his arm, but his arm was still there, and life was assuming its former irresponsible cheerfulness. Frank Turner looked over his animals, tended them, healed their sores and took pride in them. Certainly they were improving. Continuous hard work had worn the edge off their rebelliousness and their backs were hardening well. John Hedley gathered in the officers and the little mess echoed as he described the hills, rivers and towns of Burma. 'That man seems to have a religious fervour,' one of the intelligence officers said to me afterwards. Jack Masters, who in the temporary absence of the Brigadier was running the brigade, was bringing his weeks of toil to a climax in a vast series of orders, instructions and memoranda. Equipment of a kind we had never seen was issued out and there were rumours of a new ration called 'K', rich in every possible vitamin and very acceptable to the palate. Out of the long months of training had at last risen that feeling of expectancy that was so vital to our morale.

Then we set off.

The approach march was seventy miles, flogging along the roads with the same passion for speed and distance that had us all through our training. Only this time the speed was greater. Our feet wailed and our bodies sweated, while at night we shivered in the chill of a north Indian December. Indeed one of the coldest nights out I can ever remember was on this march. The foot problem assumed rather alarming proportions and there were long lines of men strung hobbling along the road. But this time we did not drag our feet wearily towards the next bivouac. There was a feeling of adventurous tension in the troops that spurred them on. Our ability to achieve success in Burma and the confidence of our leaders in us depended to a large extent on our showing in this exercise.

The days that followed were hard ones. We reached the concentration area on the third day and after a brief rest swung across country. On the first night there was weariness and on the second exhaustion. The third day we covered twenty-three miles. We had left the jungle and were marching through a sandy, sparsely cultivated country. Our midday halt on that memorable third day was a small rise completely without shelter and blazing hot. We crept under some tiny bushes and lay breathless, stirring only to make ourselves tea in the stifling haze. Then on again, until we reached harbour in a thick patch of jungle, proud of our day's achievement, but very, very tired.

On the fourth night after another long march we replenished our rations from the air. Our only model for this operation was Wingate's first expedition, for the troops defending the Burmese border had as yet had no experience of supply dropping. We watched enchanted as the parachutes floated down and alighted with a slight jolt beside the flares. The thing worked and we were satisfied. Then next morning we examined our new K-rations. We tore open the double packing, excitedly like children, and gaped in wonder at the neat little tins and cellophane wrappings. Beside our previous rations this was a feast. We ate it with relish.

Then on the sixth day we saw General Wingate.

He came upon us as we were about to launch the final attack, accompanied by General Sir George Giffard and wearing a peaked cap with a strap under his chin. We stared at this odd man and wondered why he fell so far short of our expectations. We learnt later that until he spoke or acted he was ill at ease and presented a gruff and awkward front. Wingate in repose was essentially a contradiction in terms. The introduction was unfortunate. For the troops it was an awkward moment and I think the reaction was one of uneasy surprise. This was especially so with one of my NCOs who turned to me and said, 'Good gracious! The last time I saw him was when I stood guard over him in a Cairo hospital.'

It was an allusion to a sad episode in Wingate's past. He had made a striking contribution to the reconquest of Ethiopia from the Italians in command of an irregular body of troops called Gideon Force. But when it was over, ill and confused, believing that men of malice were operating against him, he attempted to take his life. And he recovered in Cairo Hospital. It was a painful glimpse of a man of genius feeling too deeply for his ideas.

The post-mortem on the exercise was held in Jhansi cinema. It was something more than a conference; it was a gathering of the clans. For the first and only time in the history of the force every officer who called himself a Chindit was gathered under one roof. The old warriors of the first expedition, beribboned for the most part and exchanging talk with the second generation, while through them all moved the figure of Wingate, silent, preoccupied, curt with the thin, untidy wisp of a new beard on his chin. On the stage sat Wingate and General Giffard, taking tea from a splendid silver service as if it was the opening scene in a drawing-room drama. 'The Barretts of Wimpole Street,' I whispered to Frankie Baines.

Several officers got up to speak on the lessons of the exercise, but it was a one-man show. The moment Wingate got up to speak, he had us. His eloquence was of a strange brand, requiring a large audience, yet with only a thin, rasping voice as its instrument. He did not search for words, for they were already formed on his lips. He knew exactly what he wanted to say and was convinced that he alone could say it. It was this complete confidence that impressed us most, as he spoke of 'the form of warfare that I have perfected' and outlined to us the measureless possibilities of Long Range Penetration columns. Then in the middle of an oratorical passage he would switch to a damning criticism of whatever or whoever incurred his displeasure. On this occasion he outdid himself and launched into a bitter indictment of one particular battalion. He described their performance as more befitting to holidaymakers than soldiers, declaring that their officers were directly responsible for this lamentable state of affairs and threatening to expel them from the force. We were amazed at this ruthlessness and what appeared to us a lack of the most elementary form of decency. It was just another lesson to us in the ways of that inexplicable character.

I said it was a one-man show, but there was one very prominent supporting star, a man whom only the United States could have produced: Colonel Philip Cochran. This dashing figure – the inspiration for 'Flip Corkin', the leading character in a well-known American strip cartoon – was in charge of the remarkable private air force that Wingate had won for us. He got up onto the platform to apologise for not having given us air support on the exercise; he sat down having convinced us that whatever the future held Colonel Philip Cochran would deliver the goods. He would supply us with 50 Mustang fighters, 30 Mitchell medium bombers, 100 light planes and 100 gliders.* (Wingate looked uneasily round the doorways as this astonishing information was given.) If we wanted any help, just 'Dream it up.' This phrase became a catchword, and came to stand for that feeling of security that was the foundation of our operation, the knowledge that our wounded would get out. Cochran spoke for about fifteen minutes and in that time he had us at his feet. And he fulfilled his promises. American air support did in fact make the whole operation possible. It was our close tactical support, our heavy artillery, our lifeline.

The last few weeks before we set off for Assam were wild and irresponsible. There was an air of 'eat, drink and be merry, for tomorrow we die.' Christmas came and for three days we went berserk. Wingate attended our Christmas dinner and sat between two ENSA girls who were there to entertain the troops, feeling more ill at ease than ever, while in the corner our second-in-command talked Russian to another ENSA girl who could apparently speak no other language. Jack Masters concocted some fearful rum punch which he sold with great persistence and no little success. Frank Turner threatened in a moment of unusual

---

* The Americans also contributed a large force of Dakotas: all the glider tugs, and many others for troop transport and for supply dropping, which they shared with the RAF.

exuberance to 'slap our ears back' if we did not join more fully into the spirit of Christmas. John Hedley alone was unwilling to lose his self-control for the sake of Christmas.

Equipment came rolling in and we prepared for war, having barely recovered from the wild scenes of the New Year. As we fitted up our packs and stuffed our haversacks we had a growing conviction that in operations we would be asked to carry far more than in training. We debated whether to dispense with a grenade or a water-carrier or mosquito cream, until we decided finally that everything was essential and prepared to turn ourselves into coolies.

We acquired a new RAF officer, Squadron-Leader M ———, 'Mad M', a gallant and unorthodox fighter pilot who sprinkled commands excitedly about him. And Luke, an American Air Force officer hailing from Portsmouth, Ohio, who was attached to us on training. He was big and friendly and good to have around.

Those last few days before we got on the train were unreal. We were continually trying to think about the future, yet we could never bring ourselves to understand what we were in for. It seemed like something out of the story books. Wingate gave a final talk to our troops, of which the theme was 'Life is fleeting'. It was most depressing, but I think the troops appreciated it in a grim sort of way. We had trained together for seven months and achieved a sense of unity that I have never seen before or since. There was a feeling of nostalgia as we were about to leave our familiar haunts, though we hated them enough at times. The process of mental and physical adjustment had been completed for which we had strived, and the troops were as near perfect instruments of war as we could hope.

As we marched to the station the Gurkhas broke into a song, a rather bloodthirsty one about attacking the Japanese with their kukris.

CHAPTER TWO

APPROACH TO WAR

The train journey took us six days. It was our train and we took our time, stopping when we felt inclined, and for the rest taking a long, last, gentle look at the Indian countryside as it passed slowly by. Breakfast was taken by the side of the line and hot water for shaving could be obtained from the engine. Brigade headquarters occupied a first-class compartment and shared it with a large crate of 'comforts'. In a carriage nearby one of my sergeants, a quiet cultivated man who had been in the consular service, was attempting to command a bunch of Cameronians. He succeeded by being so transparently nice that the Jocks felt they ought to obey. In our own carriage Jack Masters unwound in ways that were at times spectacular. On the last stages of the journey, after we had crossed the Brahmaputra, the officers took it in turn to drive the train. It was a splendid week.

We detrained at the little town of Sylhet in Assam, a small community of tea planters in one of the poorer districts in the south of the province. It was a curious change from the heat and sandy scrub of central India with its green countryside, scattered bungalows and little 'small town' stores. To the east stretched the massif of the Manipur Hills, which stood for us as the dividing line between the past and the future. Before us there was war and we strained to catch an echo of the guns, though the attempt was futile. Behind was the past to which we would never return and the countryside that not everyone would see again. These were morbid thoughts, but the suddenness of our irruption into war produced reactions which did not trouble troops who came to the line for a more normal tour of duty.

There was a mass of baggage to unload, orders and counter-orders, until we moved off to our camp a little nearer to the hills. We had no form of shelter but contrived some bamboo huts which the Gurkhas put up with lightning speed and in which the sahibs relaxed luxuriously. We spent a fair amount of time speculating on the future, which according to the latest reports did not look too bright. It was planned that we should march south from Imphal into the Chin Hills through Tiddim, Fort White, Falam and Haka (all held by the Japs), then cross the Chindwin and strike north to the town of Pinlebu in north central Burma. Our job was to disrupt communications between the River Chindwin and the south. 'Smithy', our Burma Intelligence Corps officer, stated categorically that the country through which we were to go was quite impossible for a brigade operation, if any but a small proportion of exhausted troops were to arrive at the destination. The more obvious difficulty was the fact that we were supposed to go through centres of Jap resistance which the 14th Army had failed to overcome. This was certainly flattering to us, but small comfort. Fortunately the troops did not know all this.

We cropped our hair, actuated I think both by the desire for cleanliness and a sense of separation from the past. Frankie Baines, true to his nature, went the whole tonsorial hog and had his head completely shaved allowing only a small tuft of hair to remain. He had long since given up all pretence of being a camouflage officer and had taken over command of the two Gurkha defence platoons, the little men regarding him with awe and wonderment as a sahib who conformed to none of their preconceptions. To the British officers, until they got to know him, he was equally an enigma and he remained unique.

We scanned our maps and studied the 120-mile track to Bishenpur in the Imphal Valley, which was our immediate destination. The track ran from west to east and the rivers from north to south, so that the journey was a series of long climbs until we finally dropped into the Imphal Valley. The contours looked frightening and there was the absence of that rich green which so delights the eye of the weary map reader. The track itself was marked 'Jeepable in dry weather', which I believe is the lowest classification permissible. And, as far as I know, we were the first infantry to march the entire length of the track since the stragglers of 1942 had stumbled up the muddy hillsides on their nightmare flight from the Japanese. A few months later it was to be the scene of bloody and vital encounters between the Japanese invaders and Slim's 14th Army.

The second day took us up to the foot of the mountains, and we gazed up at them rather doubtfully as we bedded down in the paddy. Then we climbed. The track wound up in a series of sharp curves, the edge giving way to a sheer drop into a jungle of thick bamboo. Below us stretched India and above the track wound up and up into the sky. As we reached the 1,000-foot mark the bamboo started, masses of it clinging in dense folds along the sides of the hills like stubble on a giant's chin. The air got cooler and we breathed more freely than we had in the valley below, but the path got steeper and then our breath began to come in short gasps. The mules needed constant attention, as the steep slope tended to thrust the load onto their rear quarters, and the breast collars had to be continually tightened up. Men and mules began spreading out as the climb continued and I spent a large part of my time marshalling stragglers. It was strenuous work, but it afforded an occasional rest as I waited for those behind to come up, with a fleeting glimpse of the Assam plains through the clearings in the bamboo. 'Jeepable in dry weather' – just about, and fortunately the weather was dry, though a recent spell of rain had given the track a muddy, treacherous surface. On average one jeep a day went over the side – we saw one lying far below in the valley – but the drivers were seldom hurt as they had acquired considerable skill in leaving their vehicles at the right moment, and a jeep is in fact remarkably easy to bail out of.

On large-scale maps it is possible to see place-names along the track at scattered intervals, but for us there existed merely mountains and villages, each mountain representing a day's march and each valley the site of a night's bivouac. The third evening we dropped into one of the narrow valleys, so narrow that there was barely room to site a bivouac. After our first day in the hills our bodies were showing entirely new symptoms from those we got to endure in our headlong training marches in the plains, and we showed up rather badly in this slogging sweat over the hills. The first sight of camp came when we reached the brow of the hill. The track seen in patches through the bamboo wound down until it ended far below in a small patch of flat ground by a small fast-flowing stream, which cut its way with difficulty through the steep defile.

Our rations were brought up by jeep, this concession resulting in lighter packs, but the rations themselves were a throwback to the bad old days – bully, biscuits and a few dried apricots. We were expecting something rather good on this trip, but the supply services – which I'm afraid we never regarded with any great measure of confidence – fell down badly. The troops, quick to react to any slight on their stomachs, growled.

On the first night in the hills Jack Masters made an unexpected request to me. He suggested that every evening I should read a passage from the New Testament. I was surprised as Jack Masters rejoiced in a robust worldliness, and it was even stranger that his request should be backed by the other officers in advanced head-quarters. It was the clearest indication yet of our apprehension about the future. Were we using God as a kind of blood transfusion to be used only in cases of emergency? Still, I was glad to have the opportunity to read, and the priceless truth and beauty of the words came over as effectively in the Manipur Hills as anywhere else. Jack Masters had originally asked for a rather bellicose passage from the Old Testament, but I had only a New Testament, so we listened to St Paul. I read a few verses from Galatians, feeling a little embarrassed, and stopped. Frankie Baines asked me to continue, Frankie the roistering ex-sailor and man of the world, and I did: that splendid fifth chapter, 'The fruit of the Spirit is love, joy, peace, patience, kindness, goodness, faithfulness, gentleness and self-control.' And here we were marching to war, intent on killing. Our trials were physical, but the assurance we sought was something much deeper. It was a reading party of a particularly memorable kind. We had readings on other evenings, and I determined not to be separated from my New Testament.

Each day we climbed 2,000, 3,000, 4,000 feet and each day we dropped into the narrow valley, vowing we would never again take pleasure in Snowdon or Sca Fell. Planters were scattered along the track maintaining its surface with very few resources and we used to encroach rather heavily on their hospitality, enjoying the luxury of bread, butter and jam in their little shacks. In the general welter of recriminations regarding the civilian war effort in India, the planters alone have come out with a completely untarnished reputation. Their hospitality was not only boun-teous, it was gracious, and the soldier on leave was able to capture far more of the spirit of home than in other and more consciously 'Europeanised' parts of India. The planter is a lonely man and he longs for company instead like others of finding excuses for shunning it. He lives in a green country which has little of the dust and glare of the rest of British India, though it can be very humid, and his efforts to transplant his homeland are less obvious because they are less necessary. The result is that he is not so defensively engaged in shutting out the influences of the country in which he has found himself, and is able to live naturally. The lives of thousands of soldiers struggling out of Burma in 1942 were owed to the efforts of these planters in providing roads for them and caring for them; the goodwill of many other thousands was won by their gracious and generous hospitality when these men had safely arrived in India.

There was one thing to be thankful for in this march and that was that the signallers were able to get some rest. There were no communications to open up, in fact there were no wireless sets. It was the first and about the last time they were able to get away from the fatigue and drudgery of operating, a task that enslaved them throughout the training and was to play them out to the finish in Burma. During the marches they were haunted by the thought of the long night watches and looked enviously at their fellows brewing up in the dusk. And when the morning came they had to put on their packs with the others and march those long hard miles. So they were glad – and I think we all were – when as they marched over the Manipur Hills they were able to sleep soundly and wake refreshed.

And so the days passed. The early start, the long weary trudge up the hill, the brief halt and panorama at the top and then the march down to the night bivouac. One day when we had reached the top of a long hill we were confronted not with the usual steep drop but with a village a short distance below, a surprisingly broad valley that looked like a sort of lost world. I often wonder how many people have visited this remote valley. That night Maggie went off her food and there was consternation at head-quarters. It was the first time she had shown any signs of ill health and she was obviously not well. There were volunteers willing to sit up with her during the night, but fortunately next morning she was greatly improved and our minds were eased.

There was, too, that delicious river towards the end of the march, a swift, unexpected stream which flowed south, washing its banks with cold, clear water. We stayed there some time and vowed we would return again in happier days, idling with no war to compel us to sweat on. We thought often along these lines. But they remained just memories.

Strange news reached us on our last night in the hills before our final climb over into the Imphal Valley. It was brought to us by the Administrative Officer and reached us at a rather depressing time when the rain was just starting in the growing dusk. He referred darkly to the 'Risorgimento' and we, the more junior members of the headquarters, were afraid to ask more. Later that night Jack Masters gathered us round and told us the news. We were to fly into Burma. That briefly was his message, the 'Risorgimento', but we could not at once grasp it. We were aware that the flying of troops to battle zones was a common operation; we were aware also that these planes frequently went right up to the fighting line, but what we found hard to understand was that we were going to land in the middle of Burma over 100 miles behind the Japanese lines. Was such a thing possible? We left it to the experts to think out, feeling a vague thrill at this new development but hardly daring to stop and think out the details.

Next day, with this startling information to chew over – the troops had not yet been told – we started on the last and most gruelling climb of the whole march. The track rose from the valley to nearly 5,000 feet before it finally dropped into the broad valley of the Manipur River at the head of which stood Imphal. Jack Masters, who had gone ahead to fix up our future, warned us to take it easy, and we took his advice. We swung steadily up the winding track which was mercifully gradual in its gradient, doubling back in long curves round the sides of the mountain. Near the top the track made a sharp turn to the left rising steeply as it did so, and here as we rested for our hourly halt we got our finest view. To the north-west were the slopes of the mountain we had been climbing and we marvelled at our achievement; to the west a succession of giant folds waving on to the horizon, sharp, rugged and inhospitable; to the south the mountains and valleys running parallel in clearly defined rows on to the Lushai and Chin Hills, the Arakan Hill Tracts and so on to the Bay of Bengal just south of Akyab. These Manipur Hills that we had climbed appeared to us now majestic and wild; later on they became sinister.

We reached the top of the pass, shivering slightly as the damp mist settled on our perspiring bodies, and passed a monument to the memory of 'Chapforce',★ a handful of anti-tank gunners who had in a few months converted an overgrown path into the track along which we had just passed 'because', ran the inscription, 'those who knew said that it was impossible'. Below us was the valley of the Manipur River, a sudden rift in the circle of mountains. There were miles of paddy with an occasional copse and at the southern end a huge lake in which great quantities of game could be shot. We were now looking down on the 'forward areas' and I half expected to see the flash of a gun or hear a rattle of machine-gun fire. I heard neither, only the sighing of the wind driving the mist over the pass. We descended rapidly; it had started to rain and we did not feel like dawdling. The track left the bleak scrub of the pass and came through clusters of bamboo into the highest row of paddy fields which clung precariously to the side of the hills. Then into the outskirts of the small Manipur village of Bishenpur. There were some welcome sheds in which we would have liked to dry ourselves, but we were rather sharply reminded of the tactical requirements of concealment and were led to a tiny bamboo copse on the side of a small hill which

---

★ An independent force that operated during the retreat from Burma in 1942.

could only be reached along a very muddy track and which itself became a quagmire after a shower. We built some bamboo shelters – entirely inadequate as it turned out – and after a welcome mug of tea settled down to await further developments.

We had arrived and were ready for war, eager to prove our mettle and to satisfy our commander that we were worthy successors to that first gallant body of men who had fought, dragged and starved their way through Burma.

Then we had to wait.

The two months that followed were very trying. The troops did not know the reason for the delay, which was caused by the change of plans, and even we who knew felt the edge taken off our enthusiasm. The process of mental acclimatisation and gradually mounting effort was stopped abruptly and there was a sort of vacuum into which crept dissatisfaction and disappointment. One of my sergeants, who I am afraid was only too willing to complain, expressed his thoughts rather bitterly; he had been engaged in East End politics in peacetime and had acquired a rich vocabulary of sarcasm. At one time he earned his living as a member of a dog-track betting syndicate, and then when he got bored with this he went to Spain to fight in the civil war. He was a quietly bitter man, over whom hung a grey uncertainty about his parentage. My Glaswegian corporal, accustomed to disappointment at the Labour Exchange, accepted it all philosophically and started in on his next task. Most found it less easy. The southern end of the Manipur Plain is no place for British soldiers to hang about. There were no amenities for after-duty except the canteen, the occasional film and from time to time a concert party; there was certainly no big city. The troops thought reasonably that they had arrived here to fight and that, oddly enough, is what the British soldier is happiest doing. His morale slumped considerably. The Gurkhas, who demand little of life except adequate food, good water and sound officers, appeared to be content.

The site of our camp was thirty-three miles south of Imphal on the road to Tiddim, a name that was to mean much to the 14th Army in the next few months. It was at a point where the broad Imphal Valley narrowed down so that it was just wide enough to accommodate the Manipur River. We were on the west side of the valley perched on the lower slopes of the hills we had just crossed and looking across to the east at the hills which stood between us and Burma. The camp itself was a short distance off the road, sprawling without shape or order over a series of small pimples jutting out from the main range. A river flowed conveniently through the area, which solved a lot of our problems, while there was sufficient wood to build ourselves shelters. We had no tents so that some form of construction was essential. The Gurkhas applied themselves with their usual skill to the task of building *bashas*, small huts for sleeping in. My orderly, Birbal, was already recceing a site before I had removed my pack, and appraising the local vegetation. These little men seemed to know the peculiar qualities of every tree, its suitability for building material, the edibility of its fruit. The huts were already up when the last troops were marching off the road, and the kit laid out in piles on the grass floors or perched on neat bamboo trays to escape the ravages of the white ant. The British troops passed by and scowled many curious comments.

Brigade headquarters got together, examined its resources and started on the task of building a mess. It was to be a choice work in Assam bamboo built to seat fifteen officers in comfort and more in some considerable discomfort. If the mess did not live up to all our hopes it was certainly adequate and a palace compared to some of the hovels we had put up with in central India. We were learning to live well. The Brigadier was still away and Jack Masters presided. There was Frankie Baines, loud and unrestrained; Briggo recounting his difficulties and exploding occasionally with his hoarse, civil service laugh; Luke delighting us with his reminiscences of the Deep South; Smithy tall and vast; John Hedley still brimming over with the joy of life; Mad M drinking and spilling some very 'duff gen'; Doc Whyte ready with words of cheerful wisdom; and 'Mac'. 'Mac', or Major Macpherson to give him his full name, was our Burma Rifles officer. He had been on the first expedition, distinguishing himself, and had come out of Burma by the long north route to Fort Hertz. He was thin and did not look at all strong, but that was his way, and he was indefatigable. His stamina, I think, was as much an effort of willpower as anything else. He worked himself mercilessly, patrolling, recceing camp sites, navigating the column. He just carried on, dressed in his natty jungle scarf and carrying the map he knew so well how to use. Mac always managed to retain his smart appearance, a real 'jungle gentleman' who knew what he was about and did it unsparingly.

Then there was 'Chota'. Chota was our mess waiter, a Gurkha from Darjeeling, very small and incredibly podgy. We had tried him on a march, but alas! those little legs just buckled up. He seldom spoke, but he had a sort of wry cheerfulness which endeared him to us. He would approach us and whisper in our ears, afraid to speak louder but very conscious of his duty to his sahibs, and his little eyes would twinkle with merriment as we tried to goad him into further speech. Chota was an institution and was always introduced to guests of honour. I am afraid he did not realise the greatness of some of these gentlemen, for to him the hierarchy of sahibs was rather puzzling, but he could tell red tape when he saw it. On festive occasions he would be hauled in to join in the fun, as we felt that a party without Chota lacked something. I am afraid this shy man suffered rather at our hands, but his eyes never stopped twinkling and I think he must have had some interesting tales when he returned to his family in Darjeeling.

Training was in the form of a stop-gap, as there appeared to be nothing we could do with profit that we had not done already, and there was a feeling that we should reserve our energies for the real thing. Strange new weapons started arriving and these formed the only real kind of training. Anti-tank projectors called PIATs in heavily boarded boxes, common enough in England but as yet unknown in this theatre. 'Lifebuoys', portable flamethrowers which Wingate had got for us only after long skirmishes with the War Office. He told us this and asked us to take full advantage of what had been so hardly acquired. We built miniature bunkers and roasted chickens in them; I wondered if the poultry world had any Hague Convention of its own. The sticky oil bursting into flames as it shot through the air pleased us and satisfied us that though our weapons were light they were certainly lethal.

All along we were very conscious of the lack of heavy weapons, having nothing bigger than the Vickers machine-gun and the 3-inch mortar. These were splendid weapons, but against the Japanese 75-mm and 105-mm they seemed a trifle inadequate. The need was partially filled by our magnificent air support, but only partially, and the troops were glad of any weapon which would strengthen our firepower. Our hitting power was conditioned by our mobility, and the two were constantly at loggerheads.

One of our first tasks was to build a strip to take the light planes that were due to arrive. Luke chose the only suitable spot which lay between the road and the camp. It was 375 yards long but by no means flat, and we spent many weary days levelling it by hand. Fortunately it had a perfect approach – provided you were not too particular about the wind. It was not our first strip, but it was the first from which our private fleet of planes would operate, and we eyed it a little dubiously, wishing we could have made a better first impression on our American sergeant pilots. We watched anxiously as the first two planes arrived, a small L 5 and its larger but slower brother, the L 1. They started the approach a long way off, coming in low and dropping neatly over the boundary. 'A rugged field, but good practice,' was the comment of Captain Taylor, the Squadron Commander. Soon we had half a dozen of these planes parked by the camp and there started a long and happy partnership with our 'mercy pilots'. With the exception of Taylor the pilots were all sergeants, big-boned men who lived, ate and slept by their little planes. A partnership of mercy between the men in the forward columns and the Yanks who brought them out was being born in these days of waiting.

We initiated the sergeants into the mystery of Long Range Penetration and caught them up in the spirit of our cause, telling them the tales of the past and the hopes of the future. We explained to them the system of columns, the wireless layout, the possibilities and limitations of our work and above all the vital necessity of getting our wounded out; this they understood well enough. John Hedley 'preached' to them on the characteristics of the Jap and showed them how to fire our weapons, long bursts coming every day from just behind my *basha*. Jack Masters, who knew America like the palm of his hand, would challenge them to name the forty-eight states and beat them every time. They came on occasion to our mess and filled the small hut with their huge forms, answering our questions on America and asking as many more on the saga of the Chindits.

Then they started training on the little strip, taking up intelligence officers on reconnaissance flights up and down the valley and swooping down to pick up messages. One demonstration on message-picking nearly ended in disaster owing to a strong crosswind on the take-off and I was once caught by a down gust of wind when about to drop over the boundary one evening. I was flown to Tamu on the Burma border to visit a detachment of our light plane force and to explain the ciphers. I saw the kind of country that we were originally planning to march through, and I was mightily comforted that we would not now be marching. Our RAF officers appraised everything critically and were not entirely satisfied. It seemed to me that the RAF assumed an attitude of settled superiority to the USAAF. They were quick to label workmanship as shoddy and fliers as inexperienced. What they did not fully appreciate was the enormous *élan* of the Americans. There were rough ends, but there was also a tremendous drive that tackled everything with the minimum of fuss and red tape. 'Come on, fellers, let's go.' And they did.

Our sense of isolation was somewhat diminished by the continual entertainments supplied by the welfare staff at Imphal. Films in the open, which could be seen from either side of the screen, and to which the Gurkhas as well as the British came, dazzled by the brilliance though somewhat puzzled by the sequence of the story. The Gurkhas dearly enjoy slapstick, and should a man be so unfortunate as to fall over or receive a custard pie in his face, a yell of delight would go up from the little hill men. We too had our Road Show, made up of men from the force and better than any of the offerings of ENSA. The camp area resounded to the trumpet, saxophone and drum, the troops whistling noisily to anything that faintly resembled a tune. Jack Masters came to the microphone and gave a spirited rendering of his favourite, 'Casey Jones', which he used to sing in the mess on gala occasions and which never failed to bring the house down. Those were joyous times and not, we hoped, funeral rites.

To help feed us came the WAS(B), Women's Auxiliary Service (Burma), and we were introduced to the finest women's service of the war. Many of these women had come out on the first dismal retreat from Burma, and all of them since then had spent their time in the forward areas, dispensing food and refreshment as well as a sight of English womenfolk. They were no glamour girls but they had the indefinable charm that comes from loyal and cheerful service. The men of the 14th Army worshipped these women in green. They were of Burma; their duty was to be as near Burma as possible and by their ministrations to assist our troops in the hard journey back to that country. We met them only for a brief period before going into Burma, but we loved them.

One day the Brigadier returned and gathered the officers round to tell us officially of the plan to fly into Burma. 'When I left this brigade,' he said, 'it was at the top of its form. I return to find it in a completely different state, and I am concerned. The reason I know is that the men don't like hanging about. Nor do I. You can tell your men now what we are going to do without, of course, mentioning dates and places. We are waiting for the March full moon for this operation . . .' He carried on with a brief outline plan. There were three sites chosen for landing fields, and in these areas gliders were to land troops and equipment to build air strips. The following night the Dakotas were to come with the remainder of the troops. Further details would be given later.

We were glad of the opportunity of telling this to the troops and certainly the reception was excellent. John Hedley apparently put it over very well to the other ranks in headquarters, as my sergeant, the gloomy one, came up to me wreathed in smiles, breathing fire and destruction. My Glasgow corporal, Jock Yuille, accepted it all and hardened his resolve. Everywhere the news was greeted with amazement and delight, and it began to dawn on the men why we had been sitting down so long apparently doing nothing. Gone was the old gloom and apathy which had struck them when they had come over the hills. In its place was a sense almost of inebriation. They went round the camp shyly exchanging congratulations, with just a thought at the back of their minds as to how all this would come about. They had envied the brigade which was already marching in from the north, Fergusson's brigade, but that envy changed to superiority. We were unique. This had never been done before and it had taken a man like Wingate to put it over. He was very good in our eyes. We would surely go down in history, a different breed from those who had to stagger through the jungle on their feet. The cry was taken up and there were many happy hearts round the camp fires that night. The officers, too, caught the spirit of the men's new vision. We had known this all along, but we now felt a surge of expectation, and the future training was carried on in a sense of impatient adventure. We had been saved the fate of those many army formations who had been trained up a blind alley.

In those last few weeks we felt a gradual acceleration of effort. Our training was now devoted to solving the problems of our new air warfare. A few miles from the camp we scraped out 800 yards of paddy, entirely by hand, and on this two Dakotas landed, dropping beautifully over the hedge and pulling up in 600 yards. We spent days getting in and out of these planes and pushing mules up the bamboo ramps, coaxing, swearing, threatening. For the most part the animals were quite amenable provided it was all done in an orderly manner. The pilots of these planes came into our mess and provided us with some magnificent fun. They had been through their entire training together with some 2,000 hours apiece and had volunteered for Cochran's force because they thought the authorities had said 'Berlin' and not 'Burma'. They came from California, which, of course, was the greatest place in the world, though one of them, Ben, would get nostalgic over the girl he had met at the Brass Rail in Chicago, reading us extracts from her letters.

Then we saw our first glider. I remember watching it break away from the tow at about 500 feet and come down in slow flat circles, turning steeply to drop onto the paddy strip; it seemed a long time coming down and very fast in landing. So we had another Yank in the mess – a quiet, likeable fellow whose accent I could not place. The Gurkhas eyed the glider with suspicion. It suffered the outstanding disadvantage of having no engines and they could not understand it. They eventually took it to be a 'demonstration pattern' like those weapons that are made only in order to be taken to bits at schools of instruction. Still, they practised assiduously at getting in and out of this rather frail thing, not being over-particular as to how they treated the less robust parts of its structure.

When the time came for the glider to be returned to base a Dakota arrived to snatch it up. We watched from the top of the hill as the big plane came low over the ground, engaged the tow-rope and pulled the glider off the ground in a few yards, going into a steep climb with full revs to gain a safe altitude. A lot was said in the press about the way in which gliders were snatched up in France, but we were doing this many months before, and we were shortly to do it under conditions which were never approximated to in Europe.

Great men came to visit us in those last three weeks to wish us good luck in our unusual adventure. General Slim, the 14th Army commander with that look of a very wise bulldog and very much liked by all. He came to see us at a time when our forces in the Arakan had been surrounded by the Japs, and I remember being particularly impressed by his confidence in the issue, as he talked to us over a rather-better-than-average lunch. He was one of the few commanders in the East who never lost the confidence either of the higher command or of the troops. The visit of General Giffard, Commander 11th Army Group, was less fortunate. He lacked the impressive appearance and powerful voice of Slim, and his efforts to address the troops were hampered considerably by a fire which broke out in an ammunition store and which sent bullets whistling about a few yards from where he was speaking.

Lord Louis Mountbatten, immaculate in the middle of a strenuous tour of the front, visited us and transmitted to us some of that charm of personality which was so much more than a drawing-room manner. When he arrived Wingate was there to meet him, dressed in that hideous Wolsey helmet that he so dearly loved. Lord Louis got out of the car, took one look, and murmured, 'That hat!' Many people had to put up with

Wingate's foibles for the sake of his greatness, but none did this more graciously than the Supreme Commander. His talk to the troops seemed to the officers a trifle forced and hearty, but it was not for our consumption and when he turned to us he spoke to each one of us at considerable length, being able in some remarkable way to share in the experiences of us all.

But for us the interest did not lie in these great men who came from afar; it was centred on our leader as he expounded his plan to us. Wingate had evolved a new theory – his mind was never content to rest at any one particular place – and he came down one day to tell us about it. It was the theory of the Stronghold, the establishing of a position strong enough to withstand all minor attacks and so placed that the enemy would not be able to deploy any of his major weapons. 'Make the enemy attack you where you are strongest.' It was a solution to the problem of how Chindits were to kill without themselves becoming completely disorganised. We sat round a sand model near the airstrip and heard him pour out his soul, for he did no less when he spoke. Again the same exquisite fashioning of words, the same vehemence and above all the same supreme confidence. 'The form of warfare that I have perfected.' One day in the mess we got him to smile, a shy concession to our gaiety which wrinkled that untidy little beard of his. We got him arguing and felt some of the eccentric brilliance of his mind. I remember him propounding a theory that all ball games are unnecessary and harmful, beating us down with some astonishing statements. We were beginning to learn more of him.

We began to spy out the land from the air, going over in B25 Mitchells – that is, the more privileged of us – and searching out broad acres for landing strips amid the surrounding jungle. The specifications were rather difficult to fulfil. The sites had, of course, to be of sufficient length to take Dakotas and with an adequate flying gap at each end, but they had to be in remote areas so that time would elapse before the Japs could bring up troops. One area we already knew, as it had been used the previous year to evacuate some of Wingate's casualties; this lay north-west of Katha near the Irrawaddy. The second and almost ideal site was picked a short distance to the north in the valley of the River Kaukkwe between the railway to Myitkyina and the Irrawaddy, while a third was chosen across the Irrawaddy south of the junction formed by the Irrawaddy and the Shweli, which flowed into it from China. We often wondered during those flights if the Japs were growing suspicious at the repeated sorties of single B25s over the same areas, but our suspicions were not confirmed. The navigation of the planes was done by the intelligence officers who had to read their maps rather more quickly than they had been accustomed. The recce sorties returned well satisfied. 'It stood out like a sore thumb,' said Jack Masters, referring to the site across the Irrawaddy, 'but the Mitchells are infernally noisy.'

The March full moon was rapidly approaching and about a week before the first wave flew in the officers of the brigade went into Imphal for briefing. The operations room was covered in maps along its four walls and on the floor, with huge photo mosaics extending the entire length of the room showing stretches of the Irrawaddy and the Mandalay–Myitkyina Railway. We removed our boots and padded into the room. John Hedley started off with a short but typically sharp dissertation on the topography of Burma, pointing out the towns, rivers and above all the dry spots, which had caused so much trouble to Fergusson's column the year before. He concluded, and the Brigadier took over to give us the detailed plan.

Three brigades were engaged in the initial operation: 16 British Brigade and two Indian brigades, 77 and 111; 16 Brigade had been in Burma for a month and had just crossed the Chindwin in its upper stretches, having overcome tremendous difficulties of weather and terrain in its march south from Ledo across the Naga

Hills; 77 and III (that was us) were planned to fly in starting on the night of 5 March. We were then to operate in different spheres to cut Japanese lines of communication to their troops facing Stilwell in the north. General Joe Stilwell was the American commander of the American and Chinese troops operating in north Burma; 77 Brigade was to establish a road and rail block near Mawlu on the railway running north from Mandalay while we were to operate south of this in a mobile role, blowing bridges and blocking communications as we saw fit; 77 Brigade was providing the spearhead of glider troops to land on the two strips west of the Irrawaddy, code-names Broadway and Piccadilly, and the balance of the two brigades less one battalion was to be landed by Dakota there. The remaining battalion, the 4/9 Gurkhas, was to land across the Irrawaddy by glider and Dakota at Chowringhee, named after an area of Calcutta. They were to strike north-east to operate along the roads leading to Bhamo on the upper Irrawaddy. A further brigade, the 3rd West African, was allotted to us at the last moment and it was split up to provide garrisons for the strongholds we were to establish. In reserve for the present were two more British brigades, the 14th and 23rd. It was indeed a mighty force, and surely never before in the history of British arms had a major-general commanded so large a body of troops, to say nothing of its private air force.

'This operation, unlike the last, will be undertaken in conjunction with regular troops. Our job is to help Stilwell, who is coming down from the north with his Americans and Chinese. We will create chaos on the enemy's rear. We will have him guessing and keep him guessing. We will give him the fright of his life and we will kill him.' The Brigadier finished his outline and gathered the commanding officers together to discuss some points of minor tactics. The rest of us filed out of the room, collected our boots and went off in possession of the most startling news in Asia.

CHAPTER THREE

INTO BURMA

Wingate came down to give his final address to us. It was a queer mixture of high rhetoric and worldly wisdom. One moment he would be exhorting us to acquit ourselves like men and be strong, the next advising us how to keep our weapons clean. No point was too big that it could not be enlarged, none so small that it should be omitted. This was our leader's swansong, for it was the last time we should see him. I remember him standing up in the middle of a small amphitheatre in the camp expounding with the same fluency but this time more conscious of the impending trial. He always seemed to feel deeply with his men and he told us quite bluntly what we would have to endure. 'But,' he said, 'you will go down in history.' We felt sure we would and were well contented. And then he made reference to Providence.

Wingate, it was said, always carried his Bible with him, and has been pictured as a sort of Cromwell. He certainly quoted from the Scriptures freely. On our copy of the Force Operation Order he had written in his own hand the text, 'He is able to save by many or by few.' In him were none of the Christian graces that we can recognise and admire, what the Americans call 'winsomeness'. His God was the God of the Old Testament, a preserver, strengthener and deliverer in battle who defended the Righteous

53

Cause but insisted that His soldiers be worthy of His cause. In Wingate there was a constant attempt to attain this worthiness by all means. He was confident about his job, yes, but he himself I think he judged harshly.

He finished his address and having received the cheers of the troops he turned back to bid us good luck. Then he stalked off down the path, preoccupied as ever, not noticing the men beside him but thinking out the problems of the future. He reached the strip, got into his plane and disappeared west to visit some more of his troops. We never saw him again.

There was a final reallocation of personnel. Mad M was transferred, as he was not considered psychologically suitable for this form of operation. We felt that the headstrong fighter pilot would not take well to the grinding monotony of the column. This question of psychological stability was always cropping up and the reinforcement authorities used to complain bitterly when we rejected a man who appeared to be a perfect physical specimen. But we realised very early on how much depended on the psychological make-up of the individual and stuck to our point, though we were forced to concede it later, owing to a shortage of reinforcements.*

M's successor was 'Chesty' Jennings, so called because of his rather overpowering physique. He was tough, and his life was a record of hard knocks. In peacetime he used to race on motorcycles, having regularly one crash a year, a large dent in his forehead showing the marks of a particularly heavy fall. He had joined the RAF as a gunner. He rose to the position of master-gunner and operated for some weeks as rear gunner in a Blenheim

---

* This was how it appeared at the time, and it was certainly an element. But M tells me that there was a clash at the final briefing when he expressed views that were not acceptable to his superiors. His fearlessness was never in doubt.

day-bomber, surely one of the war's most hazardous assignments; until some shrapnel received in a daylight raid over Le Havre put him in hospital. Since then he had been in flying boats. Chesty was very brusque and to the point. If doing could effect more than saying he acted rather than spoke, and he judged other people's actions by his own standards. He did wonders, always completely composed and sure of himself.

Jack Masters completed his masterpiece, the Brigade Operation Order, a bewildering series of appendices and loading tables. Planes could not be used as elastically as ships and each small item of kit had to be considered. Someone was even detailed off to weigh a toothbrush, though he was unsuccessful, as the scales failed to respond. The animals presented a big problem, and we finally gave up any attempt to weigh them, contenting ourselves with grading them into three classes: ponies, large mules and small mules. Our solitary clerk typed far into the night; he was a great-hearted fellow and quite impervious to fatigue. This vast document must have cost him many sleepless nights.

The mess got steadily noisier as the night approached. Americans would pop in and out, leaving behind a trail of irresponsible gaiety. Jack Masters asked Jackie Coogan, the ex-film star and glider pilot, to a party, but he was engaged on more important matters and could not get away. We called for 'Casey Jones' and heard once again that epic of the American railroad. Frankie Baines opened to us the less beautiful chapters of his life. John Hedley produced his masterpiece, 'A mother was bathing her baby one night', the sad story of Alfie and the plughole, rendered in raucous music-hall cockney. We were always so convulsed by the opening bars that the rest of the tragedy was not easy to follow.

The night of 5 March was slightly cloudy. The moon was dodging in a staccato of black and white between the racing clouds. It was a full moon all right and as it emerged it lit up the whole of the Imphal Valley, until the hills in the distance were just visible.

It was slightly chilly, or so we thought. A wind was coming over the valley, whispering through the camp and ruffling the under-growth in a murmur of expectation. There was the occasional trudge of feet, a man going to his *basha* for the night, and the muf-fled stamp of the animals in their standings.

We were sitting in the mess, waiting and listening. The dinner had been cleared away and we were left with our thoughts. We made one or two attempts to sing, but stopped, afraid that we would miss the sound of the engines as the planes came over the hills. We looked at our watches. We did not know when they were due, but we thought it would not be long now.

'They must be taking off about now.'

'Poor devils, they can have their gliders.'

'What about a game of poker? No?'

'I think we'll remember this night.'

'I reckon the fellows up there won't forget it easily.'

'If they return.'

A long pause. And then, 'Here they come.'

We heard the steady drone of engines over the Manipur Hills. These must be the gliders. A free Dakota would not make that noise. Then we saw them, high up in the night sky, out of the clouds into a clear patch, disappearing in pairs over the Burma Hills, two gliders to each tug. We tried to imagine the feelings of the men cooped up in their frail craft. We were now standing out-side the mess, looking up, and we wondered how many Japs would be doing the same thing that night. The men too were gazing up, wondering and counting as the planes went by. Then there was silence and we went into the mess.

A short while later we heard another drone and rather sur-prised we walked outside again into the night. They were gliders but they were coming back. Something must have gone wrong. We thought hard over the possible explanations. This could not be failure, the end of all our schemes, the defeat of Wingate's idea. Perhaps some had gone astray. We returned to the mess once more a little dubious.

An orderly arrived at the mess to tell me that the phone in the cipher office was ringing. I hurried over and picked up the receiver. There was a very agitated voice at the other end.

'We have just sent you a most important message. Have you received it?'

'No, sir.'

'Well, it's on its way. Very important. The Brigadier must be fetched at once.'

I rang off and sent an orderly to summon the Brigadier, who was then having a last party with his old regiment, the 4th Gurkhas. He would not like this.

A little while later the message arrived and I started to decipher: 'Most secret – Most immediate – Owing to a change in plan, your first flight must be at starting —— by evening of 7th.' A word was missing and I checked back with the originator. 'Starting point', the airstrip from which we were to fly, 30 miles away. 'Change in plan', something wrong. I remembered those returning gliders.

The Brigadier arrived rather disgruntled, took one look at the message and exploded. His entire plan was thrown out, the plan which he had worked out to the last detail, and I think he was under the impression that it had been done to fit in with 77 Brigade; we always had a sort of feeling that we were playing second fiddle to Wingate's old brigade. He stormed up and down the tiny office saying things which would have ended his army career had he committed them to paper. Jack Masters collected the less libellous of his remarks and put them into a message, 'Cannot comply unless sufficient transport for whole brigade supplied.' The Brigadier then rang up General Scoones, the corps commander, told him the sad story and asked for all the transport available. Scoones assured him that it would be forthcoming. The Brigadier rang off and walked away, perplexed about the reason for the wrecking of his plans.

The rest of the night was spent in feverish conferences, startled COs hurrying up from their battalions. Jack Masters made lightning calculations, long division sums involving men and mules, miles and minutes. The first flight was to be ready to move off to the airfield the following morning, while elements of the second flight were to start marching with the mules. The troops were as yet quite oblivious of the 'flap', though I think some of the more observant of them must have wondered why some of the gliders had been flying from east to west. We ourselves were still in the dark as to this sudden change in the plans. I had little, if any, sleep that night, enciphering a long series of messages, and I think I had as much knowledge of what was going on in the brigade as anyone else. Just before dawn we stopped and stumbled off to our *bashas*, a little dazed at the events of the last few hours and wondering what fresh troubles the new day would bring.

Next morning the troops were gathered and pushed into lorries. The transport was waiting for us dead on time. Some of the mules were put on also and the trucks set off towards Imphal, raising a thick cloud of dust on the unmetalled road. Brigade headquarters lined up on the small airstrip and took a last look at itself. We certainly looked a warlike collection of office wallahs, weighed down under mountains of kit, priming our grenades rather delicately and packing them away in our pouches. I also had the cipher books, which could not be jettisoned, unless in a grave emergency – which arose – they had to be destroyed. I was allotted in my plane two mules, one pony and twelve Gurkhas including Birbal, just under the maximum permissible weight of 6,000 lb.

We reached the airstrip that evening. It was situated three miles south of Imphal at the small village of Tulihal, from which it took its name. The strip was remarkable in that it was 4,000 yards long. Apparently the engineers had been instructed to build 4,000 feet of runway but had misunderstood their instructions, so that there it was stretching for over two miles across the paddy fields. So vast was it that planes used to operate from the centre, taking off in both directions; the wind must have been a hazard but that was how they operated. It was unmetalled and in consequence was exceedingly dusty, a miniature sandstorm being set in motion every time a plane warmed up its engines. We marched across it with a quick look at the Dakotas parked over the area and made camp just beyond the village of Tuliyam.

We brewed up to the sound of aeroplane engines and bedded down in the paddy waiting rather anxiously for news of the gliders. Next morning we heard rumours, and they were rather disturbing. There were tales of crashed gliders, trapped men, mounting casualties. The Public Relations Officer had plunged straight into the ground. The strip was filled with stretcher cases waiting to be evacuated. Frankie Baines, who was possessed of a very vivid imagination, conjured up scenes of fearful carnage, and, I am afraid, with his usual frankness he transmitted his fear to the rest of us.

By midday we had found out the truth and it ran something like this. A last-minute reconnaissance of the two sites chosen west of the Irrawaddy had revealed that one of them, Piccadilly, was blocked by large tree trunks through its entire length. When this was discovered the gliders were loaded ready to take the air. A very hard decision had then to be made. Should the operation go on or had the Japs spotted our intentions? If they had, we would be in a very sticky position. It is said that in his decision to continue the operation Wingate was influenced largely by Cochran. Having met Cochran I think this is not unlikely, though I doubt if Wingate would do anything unless he himself was completely convinced of it. But he certainly had moments of anguish and hesitation.

The entire fleet of gliders was then switched to Broadway, and set off shortly afterwards. From the beginning things went wrong. The Dakotas found great difficulty in getting over the Chin Hills with their double tow, some returning to base (the ones we had seen), others casting off in various parts of Burma. The gliders that managed to reach the strip found tree stumps under the long grass. The first landings were successful, but the undercarriages were carried away and it was not possible to haul them out of the path of the following flight. This resulted in a series of fatal collisions and a number of casualties. There were sixty stretcher cases on the strip awaiting evacuation.

Our brigade took no part in this nerve-racking business and I describe it merely as the reports came through to us as we camped by the airstrip. I heard later the experience of one of the officers who had been in the first flight and I was very thankful that I was elsewhere. He said that he and the troops with him were scared as they had never been before, the two gliders on the tow lurching towards each other, the tow-rope whipping back with a crack against the fuselage in the air pockets over the Chin Hills. His story had rather an anticlimax: he landed safely but a short while later sprained his ankle.

The official reports had confirmed the less wildly pessimistic of our rumours and a gloom descended on us that day. I remember going over and over again the reasons why those lives should have been sacrificed without meeting a single Jap. There should never have been a double tow. The gliders were overloaded. The landing site had been badly chosen and hastily reconnoitred. A padre who did not know the full news said, 'I believe there were some people killed.' 'Yes,' I replied, 'quite a few.' 'Japs?' 'No, just gliders.' The troops had got wind of the events of 5 March and found it hard to hide their apprehension.

Late on that day, 7 March, better news reached us. The strip at Broadway had been successfully constructed and on the night of the 6th the first flight of Dakotas carrying elements of 77 Brigade had touched down without incident. The reason for our more sudden move to the airstrip was that Wingate feared that the build-up would not be quick enough on one strip and intended to send in our brigade to Chowringhee across the Irrawaddy, where originally only one battalion had been planned to land. This battalion had already landed its gliders on the night of 6 March and the operation, carried out on single tows, had been successful, the only casualties being the American glider pilots who overshot the strip with a bulldozer behind them. This was the best news we had yet received and it restored to some degree our diminishing faith in gliders.

The first flight of our brigade, half the 3/4 Gurkhas and elements of brigade headquarters, were due to leave that night, 7 March, from Tulihal strip. Plane commanders were given long sheets to fill in, stating the personnel, animals and weight to be carried. As almost every Gurkha's name sounds like the next man's, we had a little difficulty picking out the Rambahadurs, Ranbahadurs, Danbahadurs and Tamangbahadurs who made up our complement. There were scratchings out on my sheet. Personnel were reallocated. I found myself with Mules, Large in place of my Mules, Small. This brought my party above the maximum permissible weight and I had to dump a load of grain. K-rations were issued to us, seven days to the first flight and six days to the second. The weight was appalling and the more sensible stripped away the two outer wrappings, tucking away the little tins and cellophane packets in odd corners of equipment. We always made sure that tea, milk and sugar were in accessible positions.

All sorties that night were cancelled. Planes taking off earlier from another strip had discovered on arriving at Chowringhee that the runway was not long enough. A few planes had managed to land, but all flights from Tulihal had been washed out. The men climbed out of the Dakotas and returned to the camp with the prospect of having to go through all this again. We naturally felt that the sooner we were in Burma the better. The Japs had not yet reacted to our moves, but they would not be slow to hit back, and Chowringhee was especially vulnerable to attack. The time of waiting was spent in idle and rather hesitant discussion. We coached the troops in the passwords, which in our case were songs. The challenge was the tune, 'The animals came in two by two', and the answer was 'One more river to cross'. Wingate, of course, had devised these strange passwords, but I am afraid he left the Gurkhas out of his calculations. It has never yet been discovered how to teach a Gurkha to whistle an English tune, and my efforts by the airstrip were no more successful than those of my predecessors; they achieved merely a tuneless monotone.

All through the long day of 8 March we waited, and in the evening the first flight were ordered to stand by. They marched off to the long dusty strip, while the rest of us prepared another meal of bully and tinned vegetables. Later that night we heard the roar of the engines as they gathered speed along the runway and saw their wingtip lights coming low over us as they turned and circled for height. We did not yet know how many sorties we could fly in one night, and I remember lying awake under a bush hoping very much that we could get our full quota away.

News next morning was good. All the landings had been successful and no Japs had been contacted. The only trouble was water, which was in very short supply in the arid Chowringhee area. We would have to take in water by plane. One incident occurred that night which kept alive our feeling of apprehension. In the blinding dust of the strip two planes had in error started to take off together, the one behind the other. The rear plane started gaining on the one in front, but saw it just in time, swerving off the runway. The two wingtips met but the planes were pulled up safely and the occupants got out unharmed. As our confidence in the outcome of the operation was not yet wholly established it was rather unnerving.

That evening, 9 March, a date that I will always remember, the last of brigade headquarters and the Gurkhas were called forward to await further orders. The unfortunate people who had marched all the way from our old camp had only just arrived and were commenting rather slanderously on the arrangements. We lined up and inspected our men. I went down the line and checked – 12 Gurkhas, 2 Mules, Large, 1 pony. Some of the recent arrivals were still filling in manifests under some pressure from staff officers who did not seem to realise that these men had only just come in from a thirty-mile march.

Shortly before 7.00 p.m. we moved down to the strip to the cheers – or maybe jeers – of the battalions that were to follow us, the Cameronians and the King's Own. We handed in our manifests at the Control Office, checking up loads and weights. 'You're 100 lb light. Take five petrol tins of water. Sergeant, plane 25.'

The tins of water were produced and we marched off to the planes which were standing in a long row down the side of the strip. By the side of each plane was a large mounting ramp for the mules, which we dragged up to the wide open door of the Dakota. The mules were remarkably amenable. I have always believed that if mules are decently treated they will never give trouble. The three animals were led right forward, until their heads were touching the back of the radio operator's cabin. Bamboo poles were fastened between each of them and then behind them stretching across the plane. The pilot came to have a look and was not very impressed. The previous night a pony in his plane had had to be shot, and would we please fasten the animals a bit more securely. We did.

We were loaded by 7.00 p.m., but not due to leave until 9.30, so I got out and strolled around the strip. The moon had risen and was lighting up the entire runway, shining through a thick haze of dust as the planes warmed up. The first sorties were taking off now, following the jeep with the green light into the middle of the runway. Then a roar fading into a drone, lights low over the trees and circling up. I went to the front of the plane to talk to the crew, who were RAF. They were naturally inquisitive about our business. I told them and, aware that none of my fellow-officers were monitoring the conversation, indulged in words of harmless bravado, strengthening my uncertain resolve by articulating the greatness of our adventure. For their part they attempted to reassure me about the flight. The Control Tower officer had said that we were being escorted by a mass of fighter aircraft. I was ready to believe what of course was nonsense.

At 9.15 we climbed aboard, the ramp was pulled away and the doors shut. We stacked our kit in the middle of the hard steel floor. The engines opened with a roar and the animals began shuffling uneasily, stamping their hooves against the floor. I looked at them rather apprehensively, my imagination conjuring visions of plunging, panic-stricken beasts. But the engines settled to a steady beat and the stamping ceased. We watched for the green light, followed the jeep into the middle of the runway and turned into wind. Throttles wide open the plane surged forward. My chief worry at that moment was whether there was another plane just in front. I felt the tail lift and the pitch of the engine change. The little men were clustering round the windows gazing curiously at the ground which was now disappearing below us. We circled up and saw the long flarepath growing smaller as we reached for height.

At 10,000 feet we levelled off over the Chin Hills, then across the Chindwin, which was, I suppose, a sort of Rubicon for us. I was looking out for it, but I missed it, and we flew on into Burma. Forty minutes had elapsed and we were now over the precipitous ridge of hills known as the Zibiyu Taungdan. This was the part-ing of the ways. It had been agreed beforehand that in the event of a forced landing west of this ridge we would march west to India; if we were forced down east of it we would strike east and attempt to reach one of the strips. As we passed over we were committed to Burma. We had been going just over an hour when we passed over the Irrawaddy near its junction with the Shweli. It was unmistakable, the broad stretch of water glistening in the moonlight, then fading into darkness as the moon went into a cloud. Almost immediately after crossing the Irrawaddy we sighted Chowringhee and I roused the Gurkhas, who were by then fast asleep.

I will always remember that first sight of Chowringhee. I do not know what we were expecting to see; perhaps some rather subdued, cloak-and-dagger stuff. What we actually saw was a brilliantly lit flarepath cutting a long, narrow path through the jungle clearing. A shaft of light was sweeping down the runway as a plane came in to land, while round the area several planes cir-cled waiting their turn. We joined in the procession. It was 11.15. The lights were put on and we fumbled for our kit. For half an hour we continued to circle waiting for the green light and I watched with fascination as each of the planes came in, forgetting our nakedness to the enemy. The approach was perfect with a wide flying gap between the trees and the strip, so that the planes were ready to touch down as they passed the first flare. Then a slight wavering of the landing light as a bump was negotiated, a gradual slowing down, a brief pause at the end of the strip and a quick turn-round. At last after half an hour's circling it was our turn. We banked, flaps down, landing light on, pull back, brakes. We felt the bump as we rode over it and also the continuous pres-sure of the brakes. The turning area I had been warned about. It was like a ploughed field, and as the engines tore us round the plane pitched as in a heavy sea.

The engines stopped and I tried rather unsuccessfully to open the door. After several attempts it flew open and I was confronted by an irate Chesty Jennings. 'What the devil do you mean by hanging around all this time?' The remarks were meant for the pilot, who apologised for keeping me up so long. Considering how skilfully he had deposited me behind the Japanese lines his apology seemed a little out of place. The animals jumped off, sank on their knees and staggered up. We unloaded the water, then loaded it up again as no more was needed. I thanked the pilot; he had another trip that night. He got in, closed the door and roared off into the night.

A guide met us and when we had collected ourselves together he led us to the side of the clearing and into the jungle. The night was much quieter – we were one of the last to land – and it was very hot. I knew the next day would be a scorcher. The warm air was filled with the buzz of insects and underneath was the crackle of dry leaves as we waded through the parched jungle. I stumbled on sleeping forms and petrol tins of water scattered about the undergrowth, looking for a place to bed down.

Then the voice of Jack Masters. 'Is that you, R. J? Had a good trip?'

'Grand, thanks.'

It was a conventional exchange in a wholly unusual situation. Thus do the English greet each other.

It was some time before I could realise where I was, though I had been training for this for eight months. It was Burma, and the Japs were around us in every direction, and yet there was a feeling of complete security in that remote spot. Whatever the future should bring, and it brought quite a lot, it could not cheat me of that moment of enchantment as I lay in the parched jungle at the start of the great adventure. Our dreams, hopes and prayers through the long months of training had become a reality. We had not been cheated at the last moment of the chance to prove ourselves, and they could not take us back now. We would have to march, as we had marched over the hills and scrub of central India, and we would have to fight, to prove the ideas of a strange man whom we did not wholly understand but who had cast his own special spell over us.

I fell asleep.

CHAPTER FOUR

ACROSS THE IRRAWADDY

The sun rose very hot next morning and the dry deciduous jungle was breathless. We sorted ourselves out and collected our kit. No more sorties were to fly into Chowringhee as Wingate was nervous about its vulnerability and Broadway was taking 110 sorties a night. Our other two battalions, the Cameronians and the King's Own, were flying into Broadway and joining us later. Meanwhile our first objective was the Irrawaddy, which lay between us and our operational area.

We set off and halted at midday near a filthy pool. This, we were told, was the only water in the area. We accepted it and after elaborate precautions drank it, aware of a steadily growing thirst. We joined the 4/9 Gurkhas, who had landed before us and who were now leaving us to cross the Shweli to the northeast. The Brigadier came up and said it was the worst bivouac he had ever seen. We agreed and stayed where we were. Messages coming in from India were very cheering. The two battalions were flying in faster than we had hoped and another night would see them all safely in Burma. Meanwhile, the plans for our crossing of the Irrawaddy were worked out.

Wingate was obviously determined to do things in a big way. He had tremendous resources and in these first weeks used them lavishly, like a child enjoying a new toy, though with a deep sense of his responsibility. Our crossing of the Irrawaddy was to be accomplished with the aid of supply drops and gliders. A plan to land a bridgehead force on the west bank was abandoned as the country was entirely unsuitable, and instead the landings were to be made on a large sandbank on the east bank between Katha and Tigyaing just south of the small village of Inywa. The gliders would bring the boats and engines necessary for a swift crossing, and the entire force of one battalion and brigade headquarters would be over in a few hours.

That night we moved into our first bivouac several miles nearer the river. It was rather an important occasion, as we were trying out a new drill, evolved because of its great simplicity, and designed to get us into position with the minimum of fuss. It was a complete shambles, men and animals straying all over the jungle until eventually recalled by some rather loud shouting. Mac went around muttering, 'This is hopeless. If we meet the Japs in bivouac, we're done for.' He had been on the previous Wingate expedition and had bitter experience of imperfectly organised bivouacs. As a first tactical manoeuvre it was not, I am afraid, very impressive and we felt somewhat humiliated.

That night final details for the crossing were fixed up and we set off rather late the following morning, aiming to march due west until a mile from the river and then strike south to the crossing place. At this juncture Briggo and a wireless set disappeared. The thick jungle had apparently swallowed them up and, what was more disturbing, Briggo had on him an emergency message which had not yet been deciphered; I had the ciphers. For all we knew this message might contain a complete change of plan and we marched towards the river with the feeling that we were not quite 'in the picture'. All attempts to contact Briggo failed, and getting into our stride we raced through the belt of open scrub down to the east bank of the Irrawaddy. Briggo rejoined us twelve hours later, guided by the flarepath. The message was giving the OK to the crossing.

By this time we were suffering rather badly from thirst, and Doc Whyte, fully aware of this, said we could drink the Irrawaddy water without bothering to sterilise it. We were surprised but grateful. We filled our canvas *chaguls* and water bottles and in the manner of Gideon's men lay down on the sand drinking the river water in great gulps. The sandbank stretched nearly a mile down the river with a width of about 300 yards, closing the gap between the two shores so that there remained only 600 yards of water to cross. The opposite bank rose steeply up into the jungle-covered hills, and the river wound in a great curve downstream towards Tigyaing.

We retired to a small patch of scrub, sat down feeling much refreshed and made our plans to cross. Jack Masters had worked out every little detail and was telling off parties. A platoon was to enter the village of Inywa to the north and secure river craft. Two parties were ordered onto the sandbank, one to light the flarepath and the other to retrieve the parachutes, while a third party was to stand by to work the boats. They filed off into the night and I settled down to some messages.

News came in shortly from Inywa, 'Rafts south of village', and the village itself was reported free of enemy; our north flank was secure and we were not unduly worried about the south. Brushwood was stacked in small bundles along the sandbank, a man at each stack ready to set a match to it. Then at nine o'clock we heard the Dakotas. They made their run-up from the north and dropped the chutes fairly and squarely down the flarepath. It was a good start and we dragged the loads off the strip: rubber boats, marine gear and a host of sundry items. The gliders were due in half an hour.

There were three of them on single tows and the first one appeared exactly on time. It cast off at about 500 feet flying north. As we sat in the *bashas* we heard the whistle and hum of its fabric and saw it bank steeply at the north end of the strip, slipping to lose height and touching down with a bump on the sand. It seemed to have overshot rather. The second one followed, also overshooting, and I was down by the flarepath as the third one came in. I was at once struck, as I think everyone was, by what appeared to be a big defect in these American gliders. They came in at a very shallow gliding angle so that any slight overshoot would mean landing a long way from the strip. It also meant that a low approach was essential and this was not always possible in Burma. This particular glider was coming in very low, so much so that I thought it would hit some Gurkhas who were standing about a hundred yards in front of the first flare. Yet it touched down some distance from the strip. Fortunately, the landing area was lenient to errors of judgement and all three gliders pulled up safely on the sandbank about half a mile beyond the strip. Two of them had bumped badly and only one was fit for snatching up. We were thankful that at least there had been no crashes, but our faith in gliders was not very much strengthened. On looking back, I feel we were asking far too much of these gliders and operating them under conditions which had never been tried out before or, as far as I know, experienced since. Expecting much we were annoyed at less than the best.

Carrying parties marched off up the sandbank and started unloading the gliders. There were large Ranger boats and outboard engines, small boats, rope, petrol, oil. Somebody had thought carefully about this and we were grateful, but it all had to be carried half a mile to the place chosen for assembly. This was the beginning of our troubles. The massive engines were hauled, pushed, carried and rolled over the uneven sand. Even under the full moon the men sweated freely, and to the fatigue of the march was added the fatigue of aching arms and strained backs. The boat parties were ready to operate and the first flight of troops was standing by ready to cross. Still away in the distance the men were dragging the boats across the sand. Time was slipping by rather fast and the night was not as young as we would have liked. There were no reports yet of any Japs, but we did not feel secure. The little body of troops by the water's edge was growing and we were compelled to hold up the fresh arrivals and send them back.

As we waited there came the sound of an aeroplane engine. A Dakota appeared out of the night to snatch up the surviving glider. It made its run from the south passing to the side of the glider, which could be distinguished by the lights on the posts of the pick-up apparatus. The glider engaged and was lifted straight up, following the Dakota over the hills to India. It was a remarkable feat of airmanship. Inside the glider with the pilots was a strange cargo of passengers, some Burma Traitor Police we had caught a short while before, and who had been drugged to keep them quiet in the glider.

The first few boats reached the assembly point and were hastily put together. Smithy and a small party of Burma Rifles pushed off to the other bank. We saw them reach the bank, clamber out and disappear into the jungle. We waited for an answer and soon over the walkie-talkie radio came the all-clear. There was no enemy and it only remained for us to cross. It was getting late now, but we reckoned we would be just over before dawn broke to reveal our movements. A spearhead of Gurkhas was due over first to hold and expand the bridgehead in case the Japs got wind of our activities. Then the first flight of brigade headquarters, followed in no particular order by the rest of the troops and animals. Troops and men were now being detailed off and the boats assembled in the bright moonlight.

The first boatload of Gurkhas scrambled aboard, or rather

tumbled, for the Gurkha has an inborn fear of water and is not seen at his best when confronted with a river crossing. The boat coxswain had great difficulty in preventing the boat from capsizing as the little men leapt in. There was a wrench at the starting rope and the boat went chugging off into midstream. There was a splutter, the engine failed but soon picked up again and the men tumbled ashore on the west bank. More boats had now been assembled and soon we had a fleet of them serviceable. I took over one myself and started off, my glasses flying off my nose into the river as I pulled the rope. Halfway across the engine died and the Gurkhas peered uneasily over the side. The engine spluttered into life again and once more faded. We reached the west bank in a series of short hops and the journey back with the empty boat was even worse. I eventually rowed myself in.

What I had taken to be my bad watermanship was now apparently general practice. Very few of us had ever handled these boats before, and soon there were only two serviceable boats left. There were dark mutterings about sheer-pins. Our troubles were beginning and the Brigadier, when he came to the beach to inspect the progress, was far from satisfied. He saw several boats floating downstream out of control and most of the others beached for overhaul, their engines obstinately inactive. He returned to the Command Post and sent a message to Force headquarters reporting slow progress.

The next, and final, calamity was the animals. We could use every resource known to science, but having led the mule to the water we could not make him cross. The animals were too fresh and the slope of the bank too gradual. Also we had not in our training faced them with a river anything approaching the size of this one. The first method was to lead a horse down to the water – the horses were more amenable than the mules – and then drive the other animals after it. They went in up to their knees and then turned back onto the beach. We tried catapulting them into the water, but they were far too strong for us. We tried swimming them across. I got onto the back of one mule and swam him halfway across. As he was swimming strongly for the opposite bank I let him go and came back. The mule covered three-quarters of the distance and then he, too, turned back.

Dawn was now breaking over the river and the situation was becoming critical. We had not reckoned on having to cross in daylight and the Brigadier asked for continuous air cover. Shortly after daybreak the first flight of Mustangs arrived and roared low over the beaches. They were a most heartening sight, singularly beautiful planes and to my mind one of the finest aeroplanes the Americans have produced. They were Cochran's boys, No. 1 Air Commando. We must have looked rather like a crowd of trippers on holiday dotted over the sand with fires rising as meals were prepared.

The men on the beach were completely exhausted. They had been working now for twelve hours at a stretch and had little to show for their work. The transport officer of the Gurkha battalion was working with a kind of frenzy, realising, I suppose, how much this was his show. We knocked off for a short time to brew up and regain some of our strength; the planes were still overhead and we felt reasonably secure. Then we started in again. This time we tried towing the mules behind the boats and achieved our greatest success so far. But often the mules would pull the boat round until it became hopelessly out of control and as a final indignity haul it back to the shore. Then the engines started giving trouble again. We had got about twenty animals over, but that was only a small fraction of our total complement.

The Brigadier was very worried. The west bank was dominated by the hills behind, and should the Japs catch us in the middle of the crossing we would be in serious trouble. He then wrote out a message, 'Unless sufficient progress made by three o'clock will leave one column [a half] of 3/4 Gurkhas on east bank to operate with 4/9 Gurkhas and will proceed with the other column towards objective.' It was a very hard decision, and the Brigadier came down to the beach almost pleading with us to get the animals over. We procured a large raft, put two outboard engines on the sides and loaded it up with twelve mules. The weird craft pushed slowly out into midstream and the engines cut dead. We were faced with the prospect of losing twelve mules and their leaders. The raft began floating downstream with the Brigadier shouting instructions at us. All attempts to start the motors failed and the raft finally came to rest on the west bank about three-quarters of a mile downstream. We tried a smaller raft and got this safely across on two trips. It looked as if we had at last achieved success.

But the time was now past three and the Brigadier gave the order to cut our losses. The balance of brigade headquarters and 30 column were to cross as quickly as possible; 40 column (the other half of the battalion) and all the mules that had failed to cross were to remain behind. This last was our greatest blow, for without mules we could not carry heavy weapons and we were losing some of our best animals that had been with us all through training. Maggie, of course, had swum straight over and must have had a very low opinion of the others. One other of our stalwarts was drowned in the crossing.

It was evening when the last boatloads of men pushed off. I saw a native canoe and persuaded the Shan* to take me across. I was gratified to discover that I could make myself understood. There were no Japs nearer than Katha and Tigyaing. British troops had come here last year; he remembered the first Wingate expedition. We grounded on the far shore and I paid him two rupees for his trouble, a sum I afterwards discovered was shamefully low. We assembled in gloom on the west bank and counted our mules.

---

* A native of the Shan states that lie to the south-east of Mandalay.

There were about thirty. The total complement of one column and brigade headquarters was 100. Then came the dismal task of gathering equipment. We kept two wireless sets, but the rest had to go overboard for lack of mules. We had to choose between Vickers machine-guns and 3-inch mortars and decided to keep the mortars. Flamethrowers were out, following the other equipment into the Irrawaddy. Some sank but others floated downstream disappearing slowly in the direction of Tigyaing.

We moved into bivouac, this time quite successfully, a short distance from the river. We were dead tired and bitterly disappointed, each feeling in some way responsible for the debacle, yet conscious that we had been defeated by something outside our control. The operation had started with a fiasco. The world was waiting for news of us. Wingate, who had given us such lavish equipment, would be anxious about our progress. We had failed him and he judged failure harshly. A savage message arrived asking us to make urgent inquiries into the reasons for the failure of the crossing, with special reference to the outboard motors. We brewed up and sat late into the night filling in our demands for the first supply drop.

CHAPTER FIVE

FEELING OUR WAY

We started off very early next morning. Briggo was back with us having rejoined us on the sandbank after twelve hectic and anxious hours. This was our only consolation. We were dispirited and the going was very hard. The Brigadier decided that we must cross the mountain range on the west of the Irrawaddy, and cross it in one day, so as to escape being bottlenecked between the mountains and the river. We had still about three days' rations in our packs and were carrying full water *chaguls*. The country in front of us was not plentifully supplied with water and we were taking no chances. We felt very heavy and singularly unprepared to fight.

After proceeding north for a short distance we turned west up the mountain. We entered a waterless *chaung*, the loose pebbly sand pulling at our boots and dragging us back. The mules, what few we had left of them, were making heavy weather of it; they did not object to a steep slope, but in soft going they were helpless. The sun had risen overhead and reached down to the open *chaung* bed. The *chagul* started slipping in the sweat of the hand and every few minutes we would have to hitch it up, stopping at the same time to readjust a particularly abrasive piece of equipment. The first halt was at the head of the *chaung* and we sank down into the sand, very conscious of our weakness and wondering why on earth we were not in better training. The Irrawaddy crossing had taken more out of us than we cared to admit.

We turned left off the *chaung* up a very steep slope so as to get a footing on the lower slopes of the mountain, and the pace increased. I find steep slopes exhilarating; your goal is clear and you can usually assume that a steep slope will be a short one. The dry vegetation of the Irrawaddy valley gave way to green shoots of bamboo and the air became clearer. In fact we were going very well when John Hedley decided, or rather the Brigadier decided for him, that we had taken the wrong route. We sat down on the path, which was rather a feat in itself, and waited for the head of the column to come down, the troops cursing between their gasps for breath. Down to the *chaung* again for a few hundred yards and then sharp right up an even steeper slope. After a few hundred yards of hectic scramble we reached a path and started up the long trail. The track was very narrow, just sufficient for one man, and the surrounding jungle sometimes caught on his equipment and dragged him back. The corners were sharp and sudden, rising steeply to gain height. Big gaps started appearing in the column, breaking one of our golden rules. If a man fell back it was often impossible for those behind to overtake him and beyond some rather blasphemous encouragement there was little that the troops could do. I remember one unfortunate man who was making particularly heavy going. He was a small Anglo-Burmese gunner who was with us on account of his knowledge of the language. Physically he was quite unsuitable, being small and podgy. The only way to keep him going was to let fly at him with everything from sarcasm to sheer terror. Sympathy would have stopped him in his tracks. One has to assume the role of a slave driver.

Shortly after midday we reached the top of the pass, 2,000 feet up. It was a good effort and as we started down the other side we reckoned on an early bivouac. We were due for a disappointment.

The trouble arose because the track along which we were proceeding was not marked on the map, and we were therefore aware
only of the general direction of our march. We followed the track
in a north-easterly direction dropping very slowly with darkness
coming on and finally dropped into a bivouac at about eight
o'clock after more than twelve hours' marching. There was no
water and tempers were very short. Somebody thought they
heard a Jap and rifles were cocked; one of our own men appeared
from the bush. Briggo was going round in circles trying to locate
his wireless sets and cursing the arrangements. The troops sat
down and drank not too wisely. The signallers rose from their stupor and put up their sets. I sat down to a message and gradually
routine grew out of weary chaos. Later on we received a message
from Force headquarters picking us out for special mention. We
were more than mildly surprised after the fiasco at the Irrawaddy,
but Wingate had been quick to note our long march over the hills
and to dispense praise as forcefully as he did blame. We also
received a message asking us for the reasons of the failure of the
Irrawaddy crossing.

Our first need next morning was for water, which we found
close by, enjoying one of the finest brews of tea I can remember.
The highlights of those days were reckoned in drinks of tea and
running streams, and the memory of that unknown little stream
is with me still. The gruelling day that followed made it even
more of a landmark. We marched over the parched sandy soil and
over riverbeds that had been wrung dry. The hills were much
smaller now, but our fatigue was growing. As the day advanced
and the country yielded no moisture we began to be worried.
Finally, we turned back into a maze of dried-up streams and in
the late afternoon, after digging several feet down, found a dark,
smelly liquid. That was enough and we stopped after a futile,
exhausting day's march. We sent off a message, 'Owing to lack of
water have been forced to return to . . .' We had not actually gone

back on our tracks of the previous day, but we had made very little ground. There was a feeling that Wingate's 'Well done!' had been a trifle premature.

News came of the enemy. They had bombed Chowringhee and were advancing on it in strength. The bombing had been carried out the day after we had left the strip. We were pleased at our good fortune; we were even more pleased that we had not been attacked as we sat on the sandbank waiting for the outboard motors to function.

Food was our next problem, and our first job was to find a suitable place for a supply drop. Next morning we came down into a little valley by a running stream and were just settling down waiting for darkness when John Hedley conceived a brilliant idea. It would be good practice for us if we had our drop in thick jungle. We would thus get used to working under difficult conditions, and could we not afford to improve our technique? To most of us the idea seemed mad, and we said so. But the Brigadier was struck by it and we marched discontented to the jungle beyond.

This was an event, our first operational supply drop, and by it we could judge our hopes of successful mobility in the future. Chesty Jennings laid out the L-shaped line of brushwood in jungle so thick that we wondered if the flares would be seen from the air. Collecting parties were detailed off and we heard the drone of engines overhead. The fires were lit and the parachutes came tumbling down through the trees, some catching in branches, some disappearing into the thick undergrowth or rolling into the bottom of *nullahs*. The Gurkha collecting parties had an almost impossible task, as the moon was on the wane and the parachute loads were scattered over a wide area. At about three o'clock in the morning I was woken by Mac, who was in a very bad temper; only about half the loads had been collected in and the Gurkhas could not do any work. I hurried off rather surprised by this last remark. The little men were asleep on their feet, hauling sixty-pound loads up steep jungle-covered slopes, wandering off into the jungle in search of more. I picked up a container and staggered a few yards. A Gurkha, horrified at the sight of a sahib doing manual labour, relieved me of my burden. The loads were stacked on the track and then taken down on mules to a dump near the bivouac area. We planned to move off at first light, but this was obviously going to be impossible. Dawn was breaking and only about two-thirds of the drop had been collected.

The rations were distributed, three days instead of five, and an extra 'luxury' meal of bread, bully and tinned fruit, which we found hard to stomach in the heat. We searched frantically for the mail and John Hedley rampaged round the jungle shouting regretfully, 'Where are my intelligence summaries?' We were not in the least bit interested, stuffing the rations into our packs and scooping bully out of tins. Our schedule of march was hopelessly upset and we learnt our lesson, that if a supply drop was to be properly collected at least half of the following day would have to be wasted. At about ten o'clock in the morning we set off again.

We had now been in Burma five days, groping after a clue to our strange new life and finding only bewilderment. In our training in central India we had not envisaged the scenes of confusion on the Irrawaddy sandbank. The sweltering heat of central Burma was more than we had experienced before. And we were in enemy territory. We had met no enemy, but they were around us. Our operations were furtive and secrecy has its own special apprehensions. We were avoiding the enemy in pursuance of a tactical plan, but the ordinary soldier, sweating through the jungle, might wonder with reason where he was supposed to be going. There was a sense of frailty. We had come into Burma backed by the promises of Wingate and all the resources he had been able to wrest for us from the higher command, but in the end it was our capacity to march, to fight and to sustain our morale that would bring success. After the drama of the fly-in this was a rather weary anticlimax. We awaited our first tasks and hoped they would be good ones.

We soon had evidence of our state of nervousness. We had an easy day's march after the supply drop, for which we were thankful; after having a complete clean-up in a nearby stream we moved into an excellent little bivouac area. We dined well and our strength revived. We lay down well content. Then in the middle of the night we were roused and told to assemble at once in the *chaung*. We fumbled into our equipment and made our way uncertainly to the dry riverbed, our tempers at breaking point. We were told that there were a few Japs around. So what? We had earned our sleep and wanted to continue it. There was just enough light in which to reorganise and we moved off west, our eyes half shut, cursing and stumbling in the growing light. For three or four miles we marched, utterly depressed at that early hour. At six o'clock we stopped and the order was given to start working the wireless sets. It was a cruel order and the signallers were not slow to show their resentment. I let my sergeant and corporal sleep and took up the ciphers.

Our action had been entirely wrong, and the later news that the 'Japs' were only four Burmese villagers did not improve the matter. The feeling of the troops was correct. We must avoid the enemy, but why shamefacedly flit in the night at the slightest whisper of a Jap? This could not be easily distinguished from running away. The Brigadier was feeling the physical strain of the first few gruelling and rather bitter days. He was, in fact, too old for an operation of this kind, and his exhaustion brought on a nervousness that was both obvious and acutely embarrassing.

News came through from our other two battalions. They were having a far harder time than us on the long march from Broadway. They had a big distance to cover and a formidable range of hills to cross near Katha. Messages from them were not encouraging. The going was very bad and the King's Own had even to resort to blowing trees. Our first Jap was shot in an encounter near Indaw, at which we were duly satisfied, but our schedule was days behind. We were due to concentrate in a few days west of the Mandalay railway and north of the station of Nankan preparatory to large-scale operations against the road and the railway, and at the present rate we would never do it. What would Wingate say? We sent him our explanation of the Irrawaddy debacle: 'Crossing place suitable for supply drop, boats but unsuitable for mules.' Two weaknesses were pointed out: faulty sheer-pins on the outboard motors and of course the mules. We never heard any more about it from Wingate, though I gather that the man responsible for overhauling the outboard engines heard quite a lot.

All that day we 'lay up', a curious military expression for lying down. We switched over to the BBC and heard the news of the Airborne Invasion of Burma interspersed with eyewitness accounts designed to stir the blood of the outside world. There was one particularly lurid account by a man who had flown in with us and whose sole exploit '200 miles inside enemy territory' was to drink us almost out of water. Wingate's name was not yet mentioned, but we felt flattered and pretended to be amused. His first expedition was shrouded in secrecy; his second was being trumpeted from the start.

We were given a new job, not an especially exciting one but interesting enough. A special patrol was to be landed by glider led by one of Wingate's almost mythological veterans, Major Blain. This patrol, known as 'Bladet', was going to operate south-west in the area of Wuntho, blowing up bridges and generally creating confusion. It was one of Wingate's ideas; they did not all come off, but no one could complain that they lacked interest. We were to provide the glider strip in the valley of the River Meza that we were just entering. Minimum length 400 yards and a good approach. Our experience of gliders had not been happy, and we immediately decided to increase the minimum length to 500 yards. It was a wise move and saved some lives.

We reconnoitred an area and approved a site. Wingate was duly informed and arrangements were made for the gliders to arrive on the following night. Then it was decided that the site was not suitable, and conscious of our mistake we sent off another message. Back came wrath, black wrath, at an error that had caused a lot of trouble at our base in India. Would we ensure in future that we sent accurate information? We would.

At about this time we received another message from the General. It was one of his famous Orders of the Day, written in a flamboyant, rhetorical style, holding aloft the torch of adventure. These Orders of the Day always presented rather a problem. The officers, with the contempt of sentimentality that they always affected, were apt to laugh at these stirring little pieces, and they were apt to convey some of this cynicism to the men. This was dangerous as the men for the most part worshipped Wingate and it was a direct blow at their idol. I think that secretly we were rather ashamed of our scorn. This particular message told us that we had placed a dagger in the guts of the enemy and that 'in days to come every man will be proud to say, "I was there"'. This concluding sentence, curiously reminiscent of Henry V at Agincourt, we could not afford to laugh at unless we cared to laugh at ourselves. Since that day we have not ceased to say, 'I was there.'

The site for the gliders was finally chosen. It was not very impressive, a small strip of paddy about half a mile from the Meza Valley with a good enough approach but thick jungle at the other end. At the Irrawaddy the gliders had all overshot; if they overshot this time, we would have some bodies to dispose of. That evening, as the light was fading, the Gurkhas started preparing the strip. We did not want to be observed, so it was almost dark when we started work. The Gurkhas were learning some of the ways of strip building and Chesty Jennings coaxed, encouraged and rewarded them into a high state of efficiency. The Gurkha learns slowly, but once he understands a job, he will do it with total thoroughness and as many times as he is required to.

Levelling paddy fields with entrenching tools is a long and wearisome business and the work continued until well into the night. The Brigadier was anxious to provide a smooth touchdown for the gliders and he ordered out an extra shift of troops to add a final polish. Headquarters went into a huddle and Jack Masters, fluent as ever, explained the details of that night's work. It was going to be a busy night. First in the programme was a supply drop, which we hoped would be more successful than the last one. Then the gliders, six of them, bringing in the patrols, and finally at dawn some light planes to carry off our first load of sick. Chesty asked for a burial party to be detailed for the glider landings. He was always very much to the point, and although we tried to laugh this off we were not wholly convincing.

As we were waiting for the supply drop a message came in giving us first news of 77 Brigade. They had established a block of the railway north of us and in a very fierce encounter had inflicted many casualties on the enemy. This was first blood and we were very pleased. I read the message over and over again, noting the rather conscious way in which Wingate had framed it in a tone of exaltation and triumph. 'The enemy fleeing in all directions and in disorder.' I confess that we were envious of their success. While we were messing about building strips they were killing Japs.

Shortly afterwards the Dakotas arrived and dropped their loads. They were far easier to collect than on the first occasion – we had had enough of John Hedley's brainwaves – though a parachute load is never easy to carry. It was not until next morning that we found out how many items were missing and we started to curse our suppliers.

The first glider appeared and gave its recognition signal. The flames which had been doused were lit again, and we waited. We saw the wingtips circle down, turn abruptly at the north end and approach the strip. It looked like an overshoot. The pilot, apparently aware of this, pulled back the stick and brought the glider down with a crack that carried away its undercarriage. The troops climbed out, a little shaken, and marched off into the jungle. The gliders followed one by one and each landing was a moment of awful suspense. Only one glider made what might be called a good landing, all the others thumping down and skidding off the strip. One landed at the far end of the strip and crashed into the jungle, but by some miracle the passengers were unhurt though badly shaken. When the fifth glider landed the pilot rather lost his head. With memories of Broadway he was afraid that the last glider would land before his was pulled off the strip, and he fired a red Very light into the air. The remaining tug, not unnaturally taking this to be a danger signal, banked away and returned to India with his glider. The glider pilots who had landed took a poor view of this as the last tug was to have snatched them up, and they were now faced with the prospect of marching with the columns. Amazingly none of the glider crews or passengers sustained any injuries. The patrol collected and, accompanied by some of the glider pilots, made off into the night.

Finally came the light planes as the dawn was breaking. The strip was rough, but it was ample, and the pilots had many worse ones in the future. It was indeed fortunate that the first air evacuation was such a success, as it meant a lot to the attitude of the troops. For the last few days we had been marching with some very sick men including one signalman with pleurisy, and they were a weight on our minds. The sight of the planes setting off with them in the early morning light was very heartening. These planes were to become the linchpin of the whole operation and were a bigger factor in sustaining morale than anything else.

Many were the days we waited anxiously by a jungle strip with our wounded, straining our ears for the magic sound of the light plane engine. Then we would see it coming low over the hills and answering our recognition signal. There were taut moments as the planes came in to land on a strip they had never seen before and a great welcome for the pilots as they pulled up by our stretchers.

We did not start off again until late in the morning. We had examined the parachute loads and found much wanting. There were only three and a half days' rations instead of five, there was no mail, and worst of all we had been sent oil instead of petrol for the engines that charged our batteries. This was very bad. We sent a sharp reprimand to base. We were the ones to demand and they to supply, and I don't think we ever really understood the difficulties that they worked under. How could we? They were hundreds of miles away.

We continued our march, very tired. The River Meza was crossed without incident, though one of our other battalions had a spot of bother crossing it further up, and we started up the hill on the west side of the valley. That day was our weariest yet. Perhaps it was the continuous work of the night before, or the late start. We had come to learn, what I suppose is fairly obvious, that hot weather marching must be done in the early hours of the morning, when the temperature is reasonable and the body has time to acclimatise itself to the gradually increasing heat. Perhaps we had fed too well; that luxury meal of bully and tinned fruit. The track swung steeply up the side of the hill. It was not a big hill but it required all our effort.

The bivouac for the night was to be at an old forest rest house, a name enchanting enough to keep us going. We had about another two miles to go when it was discovered that the Burmese guide had taken us on the wrong track. When we halted to reconsider, I did what I had never done before: drained my waterbottle,

drinking the tepid water in great weary gulps. The Brigadier realised how tired we were and smiled his apologies as he doubled
back past us with three miles still to go. We arrived at the forest
rest house late in the evening. Needless to say there was no rest
house, just a wreckage of wood and a bare concrete foundation,
but there was a stream and a shady bivouac. That night we
decided to change the duty officer hourly on account of our
fatigue, and the Brigadier promised a late start on the following
morning. Considering that we had not yet met the enemy, we had
expended a vast amount of energy.

The following day we were due to arrive at our operational
area. We were to cross the road, then the railway, and blow the
railway bridge near Nankan Station. When the other two battalions arrived we were to operate together against the road and
railway, blocking the Jap supplies to the north. It was all delightfully vague and left the commander in the field with a great deal
of scope, of which he was not slow to take advantage. There was
a touch of 'guerrilla' about all this, and we looked forward to it
with relish. Elaborate precautions were taken for the crossing of
the road so that we could continue on our way unobserved.
Troops were sent out on either side of the crossing place to act as
blocks and we advanced cautiously. Coming out of the thick jungle we were confronted with a small overgrown track which had
not been used for some time. We crossed it and on questioning an
officer I discovered that this was The Road. It struck us as farci-
cal. We had marched all this way and arriving at our destination
we found that there was nothing to do. I found this an intensely
disappointing moment. The efforts of the past two weeks
appeared to have led us nowhere.

It was clear that our plan had been based on inaccurate information. It was easy for the planners to say, 'Block that road.
Strangle the enemy's supply line.' On the map it looked a neat
vein to cut. On the ground it was an artery that had long since

ceased to play a part in the enemy's circulation system. It seemed to us that we were in the wrong place at the wrong time. It was a discovery designed to discourage.

The Brigadier was not feeling well and got onto a horse. The speed of the marching began to increase, and soon we were almost running down the dusty track that led towards the railway. We continued for some time and were beginning to get despondent when we suddenly came on the railway, a single-metre-gauge line cutting its way through the dense surrounding jungle. We crossed over it into the jungle-covered slopes of the Tatlwin Reserved Forest. We had a short delicious halt for a brew of tea and then went into night bivouac. It was another hard and rather disquieting day.

Our next job was to blow the Nankan Railway Bridge, but before we could do that the Brigadier decided first to have a supply drop in order to have a full five days' mobility in case of eventualities. Here we struck trouble, which might well have had serious consequences. As I have mentioned, on the last supply drop we had received oil instead of petrol for our battery-charging engines. The result was that we found all our batteries flat and our wireless almost useless. Unless we sent off our supply demand message our batteries would cease, we would be out of communication with India and no more supplies could be demanded. We would disappear and unless we joined up with another battalion we would starve. I remember Briggo leaning anxiously over the set as his best operator, a determined Yorkshireman, tapped away on the key. Before long we were all clustered round realising that our future depended on that operator. At last after tremendous efforts we got the message off and waited for the answer. It came shortly afterwards and it read, 'Your demand too late. Submit fresh demand for another date.' We tore our hair and heaped curses on our suppliers.

I enciphered another message and we started off again. This

time a fresh difficulty arose. Unknown to us, our base had moved
from Imphal back to Sylhet in Assam, as the Jap threat to Imphal
was growing. The move had upset wireless conditions and on our
flat battery it seemed hopeless. Then an answering signal came
back from a strange station. It was the rear headquarters of 16
Brigade, who were coming to our rescue. First they put us through
a recognition test.

'What is the first letter in our CO's name?'

'Major S.'

'Correct. Pass your message.'

Falteringly and with agonising slowness we passed the message and sat back very relieved, thankful for the quick wits of the
base operator. Our curses died and we got our supplies. We were
in business again.

News from the other battalions continued to come in, but it
was not very encouraging. Progress continued to be painfully
slow and we sent a sharp message to one of the battalions, 'Do
not engage in unnecessary battles, advance to your objective.'
This referred to a little battle near Indaw. The other battalion,
the Cameronians, had also had a little battle when crossing the
Meza and emerged successfully from a very awkward position.
Many Japs had fallen and we were pleased, though the Brigadier
was still very impatient.

The demolition party with protective troops moved off
towards the Nankan Bridge. There had been an air strike on the
village earlier and we reckoned that the Japs would have moved
from the locality. Brigade headquarters stayed behind in the jungle and waited for the explosion. Shortly after midday we heard
the bang and prepared to move. This was guerrilla activity but it
was not always easy to stifle the feeling that we were running
from the enemy. The demolition party returned to report that
the entire central span had collapsed into the riverbed sixty feet
below. There were no Japs to guard it.

So after two weeks in Burma we had blown a bridge, which was repaired in a few days. Papers were already publishing reports about 'ghost columns spreading their tentacles around the Jap rear'. The troops regarded this as rather comic. They were uncertain about how much confusion they had spread amongst the enemy. They knew their own confusion at the Irrawaddy, their own weary struggles to conquer the jungle, their arrival at an area where there did not seem to be any enemy to confuse. It is a peculiar discipline of Long Range Penetration that the design of the whole is often obscured by the frustrations of the parts. 77 Brigade were doing great things and killing many Japs. We were still fumbling in the hot jungle and seeking a role. It seemed to me an expensive way to use all these troops.

The Brigadier sent a message reporting on the absence of Japs and suggesting a move up north where more might be found. The troops must be given a job, and quickly. We prepared to move to a more fruitful area.

CHAPTER SIX

ORDE WINGATE

Permission was given to move and we set off north in rather leisurely fashion as the two battalions due to meet us were still a long way off. Next day we sat down and built an airstrip to take out our second batch of sick; no wounded yet. We were quite pleased with the strip though perhaps its approach off the hills was not perfect, and we settled down to wait for the planes. I went over to the strip with the Brigadier and a few other members of brigade headquarters. We waited some time and there were no planes.

Towards the airstrip from the camp came John Hedley with his devouring stride and a look of even fiercer determination than usual. 'A very important message has just come through, sir. It starts, "Much regret to report General Wingate killed in air crash." I did not see the end of the message, but I thought I had better let you know at once. They are deciphering the rest of the message now.' This terrible information was met with a blank silence. It was too much to absorb, and in the silence we tried to adjust ourselves to what had happened. The complete message was brought over and read: 'Much regret to report General Wingate killed in air crash. All ranks will agree that the best memorial is a speedy fulfilment of his objective.' Then a further message,

'Personal – Tulloch to Lentaigne. Have suggested you as commander of Special Force. Signal if you are willing to accept.'

The Brigadier turned sharply away and started pacing up and down the side of the strip. I tried to picture his thoughts and as I did so I realised what a lot of thinking there was to be done; Special Force had been conceived by Wingate as a great dream and had been created by him as a potent instrument of war. 'The form of warfare that I have perfected.' It was his own creation and almost, one might say, his toy, though he played with it seriously enough. To the outside world our operation gained its significance by association with the name of Wingate, and the two – man and force – were indivisible. Now this force was to be taken over by another man of whom the world knew nothing. He was a commander with a fine military record but no personal legend of the kind we had been sheltering under. This was the problem of the 'one-man show'. There was another more personal problem. I had served on Joe Lentaigne's headquarters long enough to realise that between him and Wingate there was a deep antipathy. Their temperaments were wholly dissimilar. They viewed warfare in two totally different ways. Lentaigne was not short of ideas, but they were within the framework of an enterprising regular soldier and not a wayward genius. To me it appeared that he always regarded Wingate as something of an upstart. He did not resent his rapid rise, but he thought his ideas were dangerously unsound and totally unproven. This, added to the fact that physically he was not up to the rigours of the campaign, had made those first few weeks a very testing time for him, and for the officers in his headquarters an embarrassing glimpse of senior officers at loggerheads. That such a man should take over Wingate's job posed problems of its own.

To the officers as a whole Wingate's death came as a shock and a sudden revelation of how much it was a one-man show. To them he had always been an enigma. *Personal contact with Wingate was a bewildering experience. The untidy, wispy beard, the atrocious hat and the hard, ungracious voice that sounded like the grating of stone against stone, this was our first impression. I remember considering seriously with my fellow officers the question Is he mad? He would approach you staring straight at you with his piercing eyes and in a hard monotone fire off a string of questions. He seemed to want to wring everything out of you and you were conscious that your answers, however prompt, would always be inadequate, for his standards were unattainable. He was living in the clouds and inattentive to the ways in which he clothed his spiritual self. As you looked at him – it was difficult to stare back into those eyes – you saw at first a Bohemian who did not mind how he looked. You felt: 'He doesn't look much like a soldier.' His appearance compared oddly with other great men of arms.*

To the officers of his staff Wingate was a perpetual headache. He seemed seldom to consider their feelings or admit the existence of the impossible. He acted as if an order from him was sufficient, if necessary, to end the world. It appeared to be a lack of contact with reality, an inability to clothe his dreams in terms of practical life, and to his staff devolved the task of trying to find the covering. His schemes contained the germs of brilliant strategy, but the problem was to bring the schemes to birth. You can plan, said his staff, but when you have planned please let us alone to work out the details, and accept our advice. This Wingate could not do. He could not let alone. So fiercely eager was he to realise his idea that he must himself watch over every part of the growth of that idea. This would give rise to a lot of subsidiary ideas, thrown off by his mind and flung on the tables of his bewildered staff. These ideas were constantly developing as his mind turned over fresh problems and came to new decisions.

Personal contact was bewildering. To get through to Wingate you had somehow to penetrate that most unpromising exterior. First, you must get him talking. Wingate had no drawing room conversation; I don't think he had much use for drawing rooms, but he had a mind which, if stimulated, could scintillate. Here the mind of the dreamer would be unfettered, and the thoughts that he so often concealed from the world would come tumbling out, not trite generalities but ideas polished into little gems of argument. Like his eyes his thoughts pierced. At our camp on the Imphal Plain he had advanced the astonishing proposition: 'Ball games are not only unnecessary, they are harmful.' We, a gathering of dedicated athletes, had argued furiously. He made an impossible proposition wholly plausible. We did not give in, but we learnt a lot.

Wingate as a speaker was no good with small crowds. He was brilliant in argument with a few officers in the mess, he was deeply impressive before a large gathering, but with small crowds he was either too brilliant or too oratorical. It was at the Jhansi conference that we saw him in action before a large audience. As he began in his small, rasping voice the immediate impression was one of disappointment. You had expected a rich baritone, not the sound of sandpaper. But the unimpressive quality of his voice was more than compensated for by the quality of his words. The grating, which at first jarred, came to add emphasis to the ruthless precision of his speech. Wingate did not suppose, he knew, and this conviction he transmitted to his audience however odd his theories seemed. There was no hesitation. He seemed hardly to look at his audience, and one felt he was speaking as much for himself as for the people listening, thinking aloud and showing how clear his ideas were. The hard monotone should have developed into a drone, but it did not. His ideas developed as he spoke and each development was a challenge to his listeners. They were too busy following him to fall asleep.

He was a great man, but his greatness was elusive. He was aloof, and in his attempts to come down to earth he clashed with his fellow men until many of them gave him up in desperation and spread abroad that he was a menace. He was tolerated for his greatness and this toleration was sustained only by a great deal of patience. I often wonder if Wingate knew just how much he cost in patience and exasperation to the men who had to work with him, men who had made a lifetime study of the art and science of war and who were compelled to obey a man whose ideas were very odd and whose manner was odder. And there were the senior commanders, the

Slims and Mountbattens, who suffered the whims of his character and yet at the same time protected him from those who sought to frustrate his plans; they also protected him from himself when he did and said things that he should never have done or said.

If you want something badly enough you will get it. That was the secret of Wingate's life. It accounted for his disregard of personal feelings, the apparent unconcern for anyone but himself and any ideas but his own. That he survived at all in his career is a tribute both to the quality of his ideas and to the greatness of other men who saw the man he was and deemed him worthy of special protection and encouragement. Those men were few, but they were big enough to do the job: Churchill, Wavell, Mountbatten, Slim. What a bodyguard!

And what of the troops, the men who had ultimately to carry out his plans? They did not have the same personal contact with him as the officers, and therefore their conception of him was more idealised. Wingate was more of the great legend and less of the enigma, though he was puzzling enough. That first glimpse of him at the final training exercise had been sudden and, I think, a bit unfortunate. He appeared too close and was ill at ease. He had no chance to speak to them and his manner was nervous and almost uncouth. The troops went away puzzled. But gradually as the final day drew near they began to recover some of the legend. Wingate, when he came to speak to them, said the most extraordinary things and was quite unlike anyone they had seen before. His final address to the Cameronians before they moved from the training area was a remarkable performance. Quoting large chunks from the poets and the prophets, he said, 'Gentlemen, life is fleeting. There are many of you who will never come back from this.' What a message of hope and good cheer! The officers were alarmed and annoyed, the troops themselves were a bit put out. Yet how different he was. There was perplexity and there was awe.

This perplexity and awe gave way to admiration. What was evident to the troops was Wingate's intense concern for them, which had in it far more than the ritual concern of a well-trained army officer. He advised them, if they were to remain good soldiers, to take great care of their arms;

they must be provided with ample supplies of rifle oil so that their weapons were always ready for action. They must take advantage of the weapons which he had provided for them. He had fought red tape and argued with great men in order to get them the best, and they must use well what he had given them. Gathering his thoughts quickly together he started on his final peroration. He had done with the details and now he would lay before the troops the whole issue, the Cause which he had undertaken for them. There would be blood, sweat and tears, but he would see to it that there was no unnecessary blood and that the sweat and tears were not in vain. There was a hard task ahead, harder than they really knew. If they came through they would be proud men, proud to have served with such a force. The troops understood this and approved it. Some of this enthusiasm waned in the fatigue and danger of Burma, but it never died, and when they heard Wingate had been killed they realised they had lost someone quite unusual.

Then there were the hill peoples of Burma – the Kachins, Chins and Karens who inhabited the area over which Wingate had operated and who formed the backbone of the Burma Rifles. I mention this as another example of the Wingate legend, the spiritual hold of a man over a people. Mac, our Burma Rifles officer, said, 'It's all up. We might as well pack up. He's gone and there isn't anyone else who understands Burma.' His Karen under-officer said, 'He is dead. We are lost.' We told Mac to cheer up and not to be so infernally defeatist. But he knew the hill peoples too well to alter his opinion and he was, in fact, echoing their opinion. In north Burma the name of Wingate was a name which meant protection and deliverance. Did he not adopt the Chinthe, *the protector of the pagodas, as his emblem? He was the Lord Protector of the Pagodas, risking his life for them and trying through untold hardship to bring them succour. I asked a Kachin lieutenant what he thought of Wingate. 'He was such a man,' he replied. 'When he came to a river he stripped and swam across, he the brigadier, and he did not ask for anything but to share the dangers and discomforts of his men.' This was the appeal of a man to a race of men, a hardy folk who lived precariously in their little bamboo villages scratching a living from the soil. They only understood men who did things, and above all who did things for them in the poverty and danger of occupied territory. On Wingate's first campaign the village headmen said pathetically, 'We will pay for the help we have given you. Are you coming back?' 'Yes,' replied Wingate, 'I am coming back soon, and with me there will be a mighty army to bring you deliverance.' Wingate had fulfilled his promises and the mighty army was on its way. Then as deliverance approached, the Lord Protector was killed. News like this spread swiftly through Burma, and soon all would know of the great loss. Only Wingate understood. A great people was losing heart.*

Joe Lentaigne accepted the mantle of this extraordinary man, perhaps an unwilling Elisha. We asked for planes to take him and others out. They did not arrive and we sent off another message, emphasising that it was now essential they should arrive to take the Brigadier back to India. As we waited, a message came giving us our plans for the future. It read, 'Situation at Imphal critical. 14 Army requests you to block enemy L of C to Chindwin by operations north of Pinlebu. Utmost speed essential.' We groaned. Mac said, 'Just what I had expected. We are going to be used in any old stupid scheme to help out the Imphal show. What will the hill people say? We are breaking our promises to them.'

That short message confirmed our fears and changed our whole attitude to the future. We had been devised as a special force with a special mission and an independence of operation. The idea, conceived by Wingate, had been fostered by Churchill. We would subordinate ourselves to no other commander; only one man knew how to use us. Now that man was dead we were to be at the beck and call of anyone who felt in need of help and our strategic plan would be discarded. Already we heard that 23 Brigade, one of the reserve brigades, had been taken over by the 14th Army for the Kohima operations in the Naga Hills. Were we to become a plaything of the 14th Army? It was a lousy plan, we all agreed.

What was the use of blocking supplies north-west to the Chindwin when they had been taken there long ago? There would be another deserted road to watch and this time not even a railway with which to play tricks. We would mess around the countryside worrying over suitable supply drop areas and light plane strips from which to fly out our sick – there would be no wounded as there would be no Japs; only a lot of weary and aimless marching, waterless bivouacs and possibly a few more midnight flits. When we flew back to India, what would we say that we had done? What we did not take note of, perhaps because we were not fully aware of it, was the extreme crisis round Imphal and Kohima. This crisis had changed our position in the scale of priorities. With the 14th Army *in extremis* and India almost at the mercy of the Japanese we had in some ways become suddenly redundant, a wasted force. It is interesting to speculate how Wingate would have reacted; people have been speculating about it ever since.

CHAPTER SEVEN

ACTION

However there were tasks to be done. The soldier is entitled to bellyache; but he is obliged to obey orders. The question now arose as to who should take command of our brigade. 'Suggest Morris,' signalled Lentaigne, but Morris, CO of the 4/9 Gurkhas, was over the Irrawaddy. 'Masters able to carry on,' and so it came about that Jack Masters, the Brigade Major, took over command. He still retained his rank of major, which was distinctly odd, as he had two lieutenant-colonels under him and was later to have two more. Still, Jack was quite amenable and carried on without any apparent qualms. The less charitable murmured, 'That's a gong for him,' while others said, 'I wonder if he'll be able to make it.' It was certainly a tall order.

We waited for the plane to arrive, and we waited a long time. Finally, after several hours, two L-1s came into sight and made their run-up. They were coming in at the wrong end against the slope of the paddy and Chesty gave them a red Aldis lamp to warn them. The planes not unnaturally took this to be a signal to clear off and did so, disappearing over the horizon to India.

The Brigadier was annoyed. 'Why did you give him the red?'

'He was coming in at the wrong end. He would have piled up.'

'But couldn't you tell him to wait?'

'I did. The Americans seem to have different signals. My "clear-off" sign is a red Very light.'

This was serious. We were due to start our march over the hills west to the Pinlebu area and we could not get going until the Brigadier had been flown out. A message had been sent to the other two battalions ordering them to march at full speed to the new operational area. 'Moonlight and tracks if necessary.' And here we were stuck with the Force Commander on our hands. It was decided after a perusal of the map to march ten miles to the north on the first leg of our journey and on the following morning to fly out the Brigadier from what looked a likely area.

We marched until late in the evening and bedded down. At five next morning work started on the strip, the Gurkhas hacking at the *bunds* between the rice fields with their kukris. The site was a 200-yard strip of paddy with at one end a clear run-in of about 400 yards. The difficulty lay in a line of trees which stood between the approach and the strip itself. The planes were due at seven, but owing to slow progress they were put back to eight. The strip was completed and a charge was set to the last tree as the planes were approaching. The charge was blown, but the tree remained obstinately upright.

I will describe the landing in detail, as it is an example of some of the amazing things accomplished by the light plane pilots. Sometimes planes were crashed unnecessarily by pilots inexperienced at the game, but at other times we were treated to some truly great piloting. The planes came up the approach and were about to slip between the trees when they realised that the gap was not big enough, and they pulled back just in time. We sat there wondering what would happen next. The planes then tried approaching from the other end. We held our breath, for at this end the only possible means of approach was through a very narrow jungle clearing set at an angle to the strip, and on the end of the strip itself was a small tree which prevented a straight touchdown; in fact the thing looked impossible. The first plane shut off its engine and glided down into the clearing, flying below the level of the trees and actually having to dodge round some of them. The tree at the end of the strip had to be negotiated and to do this the plane had to be banked. It arrived for the touchdown in a banking attitude across the strip. It looked as if he had had it. Then, just as he appeared to be settling down on one wing, the pilot gave a sharp kick to his rudder and the plane settled gently on the narrow runway. The second plane followed and we let out a tremendous cheer as it pulled up. The pilot wiped his hand across his brow and turned the plane round. It was a wonderful performance and cheered us up a lot.

The Brigadier climbed in and with him the two glider pilots who had been marching with us for the last two weeks and who had had quite enough. One of them was our old friend from Imphal and he wished us luck as he climbed in. The offending tree was then blown down and the two planes took off. That was that. We carried on, as there was a long way to go. A fearsome schedule of marching was proposed involving half the night. 'We'll never do that,' said my gloomy sergeant, 'I know we won't, I certainly won't.' I could not decide if this was mutiny or an admission of weakness. We set off on the long trail, and before we had gone very far it started to rain.

The operation, which as yet had been so uneventful, was entering on a new phase. With the death of Wingate our great hopes of the future disappeared. The sense of intoxication we had experienced when waiting to fly in was gone, and in its place was a resignation to do some rather ordinary and pointless soldiering. We readjusted our minds to think smaller and hope less, and in doing so prepared ourselves for the disappointments we felt sure would come to us. We had no doubt in our minds as to what we had lost and no illusions about the future, though we hoped desperately for something more interesting than the last few weeks;

that was perhaps our only consolation. I think even in those early days of training some of us suspected that perhaps all our plans and ambitions of glory would somehow be frustrated. Everything had gone so well, it must end somewhere; though when we had been deposited safely in Burma our fears seemed to have been confounded. The first two weeks of what appeared to be rather aimless wandering had taken the edge off our enthusiasm, and now with the death of our leader we became, if not unwilling, at least somewhat less zestful soldiers. We would march and fight, but where it would land us we were not quite sure.

This sudden upset revealed a weakness which had existed potentially in the Force since its inception. It was the danger of anticlimax. And the danger was centred in Wingate himself. If he were removed there was a danger that the Force might collapse, having lost its reason for existing. It did not do that, as we were already committed to the operation, but it was the start of a new frame of mind in the brigade; if in future things went wrong they would say, 'Wingate would not have done that.' We became in a sense a brigade looking at the past and criticising the present.

Anyway, we had a job to do. Midday halt was at the foot of the Mangin Range. It was drizzling, but we were allowed to brew up, something of a concession at midday. Little tins of meat and cellophane packets, sweaty feet and a steaming mug of tea. The drizzle stirred our appetites, which had rather gone off in the heat, and we ate with more relish than hitherto the chopped pork and Egg Yolk and Ham and Eggs supplied by courtesy of the USA. The Corned Pork Loaf was still uneatable unless well camouflaged in a stew; its ingredients were exciting but the general effect nauseating. A little conference round Jack Masters' fire and the promise of a hard march. 'But,' he said, 'there will be as few restrictions as possible on fires.' Sweet words. We would do anything if at the end of it we saw a warm fire and a hot meal.

The track climbed up the hill, muddy slopes and awkward corners curving round the hillsides, slipping mules and cursing men, halts and starts. The rain turned from a drizzle to a steady downpour and the way grew muddier. We were now starting to climb the final slope, which outdid all the others. False crests and false hopes, final efforts that had to be repeated a dozen times and the sting of the rain across a sweaty face. The final gradient reached a point at which it was necessary to claw the ground to retain one's balance and the fatigue of the legs was transmitted to the stomach in aching breathlessness. The jungle slipped below, and through the trees the rainswept valley; behind it the hills of the Irrawaddy. But even in that aching weariness there was exhilaration. 'Grand marching weather,' said John Hedley. And in a peculiar way he was right. We had had enough of parched watercourses and shadeless trees and thirst. The stinging rain was a stimulus rather than a hindrance except for the muddy track, and the depressing monotony of the morning wore off into an afternoon of delicious struggle.

We topped the final crest and sagged down the reverse slope. It was still raining and Jack Masters, aware of our condition, ordered bonfires to be lit off the track. This was highly unconventional and I think would have shocked us a few months before as we crept round central India on tiptoe. Now, far from being shocked, we were delighted and piled damp wood onto the fires, stripping and basking luxuriously in front of the darting flames. Again the little round tins of meat, the mug of tea and a glow of physical well-being. We were learning many things, and one of them was that the troops must be given every opportunity to rest. Goodness knows, they were stripped of every luxury, their entire possessions being on their back. We did not go through all this because we enjoyed it, and so it stood to reason that we should use every opportunity to relax the restrictions. We had overcome the heroic humbug of the early days when we thought we were giants. Finding ourselves very ordinary people who disliked fatigue and discomfort, we looked to chances of comfort. We found them in the blazing log fires and deep contentment of that night.

Next day was an easy march down a narrow valley which cut through the Mangin Range. The rain had stopped and it grew hotter, but our pace was a very fast one and we seemed to have found new strength from somewhere. Dotted over the map were strange signs marked 'Salt Spring'. A queer place for a hydro, I thought. The village of Taungmaw, the centre of the springs and a crudely elaborate apparatus of bamboo for extracting the salt. The recce platoon had surprised a few Japs, who had hurried off into the jungle leaving behind them some uniforms. A Burma Rifleman swaggered around in a Jap hat, first spoils of war. A good bivouac, but no brew-up. Jack Masters had disapproved of our march discipline and was 'getting tough'. Briggo came over to me and swore for a long time as he picked the cold meat out of its tin.

My sergeant had been right. There was no midnight marching, as we were making good progress and so, we gathered, were the other two battalions. We struck north off the valley up into the hills again 'to put the Japs off our tracks'. As we went off in line into the jungle we felt rather pleased with our tactical sense, though I do not think there were any Japs for miles around. This part of the range was much lower, but the slopes were rather sudden and steep. We halted for the night on a very precarious spur jutting out between two almost dry *chaungs*, not a comfortable night as we slept on jagged rocks. Next day we reached our concentration area east of the road which ran north from Pinlebu.

The two battalions arrived shortly afterwards, and we met for the first time since we had left India. Tales of great hardship, hunger and thirst. The King's Own had been without food for four days owing to a supply drop that had gone astray in the mountains and had been saved by food dropped from light planes. The hills round Indaw had been terrible and had taken it out of the men, who were clearly feeling the strain. I'm afraid hard words were said about the supply pilots, rash and rather ill-considered words. The Cameronians recounted their little battle at the Meza crossing, when the Japs had merely to fire on them in the water. But the Japs were bad shots and had been kicked out. It was generally voted that the light planes were 'the goods' and we could not have enough of them. Wingate's death was discussed in a rather faltering silence, and the prospects for the future. The men were very tired, but they were anxious to get on to a job after all this marching, and they felt they had the measure of the enemy.

I went round to visit my cipher NCOs, two in each battalion. They were grand lads with a very tedious job, sitting into the early hours of the morning after the long marches. One corporal had been sick since the day he landed, jaundice and malarial sores round his mouth. But he was game and had just begun to march. And there was a sergeant who was killed later in the campaign, a very likeable and quiet Scot, who was always talking about his mother. He was still on his feet and I never knew him to complain.

Food. We must have food before we started on our next job. The Cameronians and the King's Own had been very unlucky in this respect and chided headquarters for their luxurious life. They had never had more than three days' rations for each five-day period. We felt this must be due to something else besides bad luck, but we did not say so. Each battalion was allotted a different night for its supply drop and for several nights we heard the crackle of parachutes falling through the trees. 'Free drops' of boots and socks came crashing to the ground and we were scared, standing up against the tree trunks unwilling to be put out of action and possibly killed by a sackload of boots. Mail, if I remember rightly, reached us then; my bank balance and a final demand for my income tax form from an office in Meerut. It was a good joke and a new experience being able to leave this sort of letter unanswered. The sum was ten rupees.

A plan was evolved and was roughly as follows. The column of the 3/4 Gurkhas and the King's Own were to operate on the road south of our present position, while the Cameronians were to operate further north, ambushing the road within a specified area as they saw fit. We regarded the Cameronians as our 'crack' battalion and always gave them as independent a role as possible. Jack Masters worked out time and space allotting roughly a week for the first phase, after which he would think again and probably move north. It was dangerous to hang around the same area and we would lose the element of surprise which we valued so much. As far as we knew our movements had not been followed and we were in a position to cause a certain amount of alarm and despondency. There was still a doubt at the back of our minds as to how much traffic there would be to block and whether this was going to end in a fiasco. Still, we had our hopes, as we were on a recognised line of communication.

Later in the afternoon the column of the 3/4 Gurkhas set off south-west to attack a village. It was April now and was getting hotter than ever. Smithy, who knew the country, said gloomily that we could never fight through the hot weather, and as for the rains . . . As we had already gone through a good slice of hot weather successfully his forebodings seemed to lose some of their force. But as for the rains . . . We tried not to think of that and lay down among the crackling leaves awaiting news of the Gurkhas.

The news, when it came, was bad, and like all bad news it became contorted into a minor disaster. The Gurkhas were about to attack the village when their presence was given away and the Japs opened up a sharp fusillade. Still in the assembly position the Gurkhas were at a disadvantage, and as all surprise had been lost it was decided to move off, bivouac and attack from another side.

The Japs apparently followed their movements and their night bivouac was mortared, causing considerable confusion but not many casualties. These casualties, however, had to be carried over several miles and when they reached us the stretcher-bearers were all in. As the hopes of a co-ordinated attack had now disappeared the column was withdrawn.

We received the news with gloom. Here was our first chance to prove ourselves and we had come off very badly. After our weeks of marching and hopes of battle, this was all we could do. There was another reason for our despondency and this concerned the Gurkhas. Here I am aware that I will be treading on several toes, but I must tread. The Gurkha is one of the world's finest soldiers. He is smart, superbly disciplined, brave and if well led cannot be stopped. His weakness lies in his mental capacity. His reactions are slower than the European's and he is apt to rely on his immediate superior to give him all his orders. In a set attack this is highly desirable and as assault troops the Gurkhas are unrivalled, but we were not doing set attacks. We were fighting a war in which every man must think for himself, and quickly, a game of hide-and-seek, far removed from the pattern warfare of the Training Centre or field exercise. The Gurkhas were thus caught at a disadvantage and this first period was for them a period of training in new ideas. They learnt their lesson with their usual thoroughness but the interim period was one in which they became the target for some rather uncharitable criticism. It was, I think, a reflection of our own mood of disappointment and our failure to live up to the high hopes of the past.

The King's Own set out on the following evening to operate in roughly the same area as the Gurkhas. Again we waited for them and again the news, when it came, was bad. During the night march a large gap had appeared in one of the columns, the breaking of one of our golden rules. Unfortunately, the gap appeared between the fighting group and what was known rather anatomically as the 'soft belly'. The Japs, who were lying up off the track, were quick to spot this and engaged the soft belly, which was now almost half a mile behind the head of the column. There was confusion and a Jap officer rushing down the track severed the head of a King's Own officer; the Jap was killed immediately afterwards by a burst of Sten. Somehow out of all this confusion the King's Own managed not only to extricate themselves but also to inflict more casualties than they received, which in the circumstances was a remarkable effort.

But we were not in a position or in a mood to consider the circumstances and thought it had been a complete shambles. This was our first and last night operation. Wingate had conceived ambitious plans on night attacks. 'The British Army,' he would say, 'has always neglected night training, and in doing so has lost a great opportunity.' He pictured night attacks with flame-throwers, requiring, he admitted, very good training and a steady nerve. It seemed to us to require a lot of luck as well, and after this rather disastrous essay in night operations we reserved the night hours for sleeping.

Fresh plans were formed for moving north. The Cameronians had already gone off on their first task and the rest of the brigade was to follow. There were wounded, our first wounded, and they must be got away. The stretcher carry to the nearest flat ground was several miles, along a narrow path crossing over a small ridge. The path was so narrow that one of the stretcher-bearers was usually walking with one foot over the edge, and if he slipped the stretcher would come down with a jolt. We soon found that it was better to have two per stretcher for short periods in preference to a team of four. There was one badly wounded officer, Mulachy-Morgan, who had been shot in both thighs. He was jolted badly in that rough journey, but he never murmured except to give a word of thanks to the stretcher-bearers. This was our first experience of stretcher-bearing, and we did not like it.

The Cameronians were ahead and built a strip for us. But they had not acquired much skill in this business, so that when the pilots landed they said freely what they thought of it, and at the same time, 'Are there any Japs around?' We assured them and loaded the wounded into the planes. With another dirty look at the strip they took off and climbed out of the narrow valley, leaving us with a great load off our minds as well as our shoulders. The Gurkhas were just returning and we heard their whole story. It was not in the least discreditable, and Mike McGillicuddy, the Animal Transport Officer, had done wonders. A message from the General criticising Jack Masters' plan: 'Successive areas of operation too widely spaced out. Suggest the following . . .' But our commander was up to this and replied, 'Have taken everything into consideration. Urgent you read my appreciation sent out by light plane.' He thought of everything and, besides thinking, invariably committed himself to paper, so that the General would soon be in possession of a detailed analysis of our plan.

We crossed the north–south road against which we were to operate, finding it agreeably wide with signs of recent use. Some shots rang out at the rear of brigade headquarters and there was a moment of very ungallant confusion. Despite our long and strenuous training we had not yet evolved a drill for this sort of situation and felt very foolish as well as a little frightened. Frankie Baines' rear section engaged what turned out to be six Japs and killed three of them. I heard a British soldier remark gloomily, 'That means no brews for a week,' remembering our first furtive days in Burma; but he was wrong and we settled down to our usual hot meal that night a mile or so west of the road to await another supply drop.

There followed what I have always considered the perfect supply drop. The site chosen was a narrow strip of paddy lying between two belts of jungle and by a small stream. I took the mules to the watering place, which happened to be in the middle of the dropping zone, and the first plane arrived. There was a moon, but the plane was taking no chances and switched on its landing lights to make more sure of an accurate drop. It came in very low and the chutes bounced neatly onto the paddy. The mules were now watering and we had a merry time dodging the chutes in the rather confined space of the paddy. They dropped all around us in a succession of soft bumps, until the mule leaders became rather bewildered and led the mules back to their standings. When the last plane had left, we looked and saw that it was very good, a mass of white shrouds on the paddy. The speed of collection was an all-time record, four of the five days' rations being collected in the first hour. Stacks of mail; one officer in the Gurkhas received sixty-five letters and I often wonder how long it took to get through them. We sent a special message of thanks to the RAF for their great effort and continued next morning, feeling rather pleased with ourselves.

North across the east–west road at a point a few miles east of the village of Naungkan. Another well-used road and some telephone lines which we cut with a sense of satisfaction at a job very easily done. An ancient car came up the road with two Jap officers inside. Everything opened up on them from Vickers to .38 pistols, but the car continued on its way unmolested. A few hundred yards down the road it drew up, the two officers climbed slowly out and wandered off into the jungle. Rather an amazing show, but not a very creditable one, and Jack Masters was furious.

News from the King's Own and this time good news. Two trucks had been engaged and completely destroyed together with a complement of about twenty Japs. The PIAT, our anti-tank weapon, had exceeded all expectations, and the first truck had just disintegrated. It was a pity, they said, that no Japs had attacked them as they had a beautiful position. This was our first success after a month in Burma and we felt we had started at last.

The Cameronians, too, had had some very good hunting. A

block of theirs had been attacked and they had engaged in some very one-sided slaughter. The Jap troops were of a distinctly inferior quality and debussing from their trucks had charged wildly up the slope in the full moonlight. The Jocks took the pins from their grenades and rolled them down the hill, adding a touch of Vickers. At least fifty Japs were disposed of; we had one casualty. At last we were in our stride and had shaken off the earlier feeling of frustration. We were killing Japs and blocking roads – we were not entirely wasting our time.

This went on for some days and daily we notched up the score. The battalions were then ordered further north and we joined up with the King's Own north of the east–west road from Thayetkon through Naungkan to the Chindwin. Another supply drop and this time rather an unfortunate accident. The transport officer of the King's Own was knocked on the head by a 'free drop', severely concussed and unconscious. We had several other seriously ill men with us and as the battalions moved off for further operations against the road we moved northwards to a new location with a rather grim cargo of casualties. The first problem was how to carry the unconscious officer. He could not be sat on a mule and we tried building a bamboo stretcher on top of the mule. The mule of course was Maggie; we could trust no other for this delicate task. The first improvisation was not a success and a stretcher was then built to drag along the ground, the front end attached to the animal's rearquarters. This was rough treatment for a mule, but Maggie could take anything and plodded patiently through the jungle with the awkward burden dragging in the leaves behind. We always remembered Maggie for this.

We made a strip and waited, but we could not wait long and moved on leaving the medical party at the strip. When Doc Whyte returned to headquarters that night he returned with a dead man and a light plane pilot. The plane had landed successfully but on taking off it had run off into the paddy. A dysentery case had been killed and the still-unconscious transport officer hauled from the wreckage. 'I guess I've a lot to answer for,' said the pilot grimly. 'I've come straight off B25s.' When the party was on its way back to headquarters we received a message to say that more planes were due to arrive at the strip. But it was too late to warn Doc Whyte and when the planes arrived there was no one on the strip. They flew off again. Rather a tragic day, and we still had some very sick men with us.

A direct attack was planned on the village of Naunglon. 'Don't attack prepared defences,' said the General, 'but call in air support.' 'What's all this talk about not attacking?' asked my sergeant. 'They're yellow.' Jack Masters must have sensed the feeling of the troops and, deciding that there were no prepared defences in Naunglon, planned to attack. There would be air support, but the King's Own would follow up. Tactical headquarters moved off and set up at the edge of the jungle near the village. The King's Own got into position and waited. No planes. We continued to wait, still no planes; something must have gone wrong. The King's Own now decided that the planes were a wash-out and prepared to attack. They were already moving in when the planes arrived, Mustangs with 500-pound bombs. They came in for the run and then Briggo, who was on the ground-to-air wireless set, saw our troops dead on the target. He yelled a warning to the pilots, who deposited their bombs beyond the target line. One King's Own man was killed, but a disaster was averted, and we were pleased with what we considered was a very prompt action. The troops entered the village. There were precious few Japs but booty in large quantities. Rice stuffed into the troops' packs, swords, shells, piles of documents, postcards, military pamphlets, notebooks and, we hoped, some operation orders. There were also bicycles, but the troops had reluctantly to leave them, contenting themselves with rice and the choicer postcards. The documents we bundled and we called for light planes, three planes being barely sufficient to carry them away. If anyone complained now of a lack of documents . . . We left the village watching the petrol and stores blaze up. A good day.

The following week was a gay succession of incidents. The Cameronians continued on the road and found plenty to destroy. A large motor transport park had been dealt with and convoys suitably mauled. The King's Own operated on the east–west road, sniffing out supply dumps and calling for air support. 'Don't attack prepared positions,' said the General. 'They're yellow,' said my sergeant. But we did not attack, contenting ourselves with locating the dumps and calling on our private air force. They seldom failed. Jack Masters compiled elaborate target maps and dispatched them to India, providing work for the air force for several weeks to come. B25 Mitchells added to the fun when the target was away from the troops and their 75-mm guns used to echo up and down the valley. The villagers were invaluable in the work of sniffing out dumps and one evening when we reached night bivouac our guide informed us that through the town was a village and in the village a temple, and in the temple a store of ammunition. Frankie Baines and a platoon of Gurkhas went off, Frankie getting a big cheer from us, a camouflage officer going into action. One Jap was found, who scuttled away. The gallant Frankie fired after him, but he escaped. The ammunition was there, and there were some documents. These were carried back to the bivouac and we perused them. One was a lecture notebook compiled by a very conscientious officer. Probably recently commissioned, I thought, but perhaps in the Jap army conscientious enthusiasm survives the early stages.

More plans. Operations to commence on the road leading east from Thayetkon to Banmauk and Indaw. Also operating on this road was 14 Brigade, one of our reserve brigades recently flown in. We were to pinch this road out of action, and to do this Jack Masters dispatched the Gurkhas and Cameronians. They went off on their various tasks and brigade headquarters was left in the parched jungle, sitting, sleeping and eating, finding life a little tiresome but not too unpleasant, with the King's Own as protection and reserve. Smithy continued to make gloomy observations on the Burmese climate, which received little attention. Jack Masters totted up the score and was pleased. At last we had done something.

We were now nearing the end of the traditionally Wingatian phase of the operation, that is to say, the 'guerrilla' activities of the last month. We had fought as in theory Wingate should have fought in his first campaign had he been properly supplied. We had engaged successfully in that rather nebulous form of operation called 'raiding the enemy's L of C', and though we sometimes had a feeling of going round in aimless circles we felt we had achieved something. Nothing as spectacular, perhaps, as 77 Brigade in their ferocious battles at Henu, but quite a solid contribution.

In the future we were to switch to the new Wingatian idea – which was rather a concession to regular soldiering – the block or, as Wingate had more imaginatively called it, the stronghold. Whether we were prepared or trained for this type of warfare was a moot point, but our days of hide-and-seek were finished. And with them, I think, the whole of the original theory of Long Range Penetration passed away. Perhaps we had been living in a dream and were dazzled by our Robin Hood existence. We were living in a tactical world which had died with Wingate, and yet we were going to try to carry out the last of Wingate's ideas, not moving elusively through the jungle but setting up a strong position and defying the enemy to dislodge us. We must now face the Japs in the open and kill them, a task which could have been better performed by regular troops. I felt a bit sad at this end of an age; a sweaty strenuous game it had been, but one of which only we knew the rules.

CHAPTER EIGHT

LAKE IN THE NORTH

The new plan was to take us far to the north and back to a job of our own. General Stilwell was now advancing with his force of one American brigade and two Chinese divisions south towards the monsoon objective of the line Mogaung–Myitkyina. For the past month 77 Brigade had been holding a road and rail block near Mawlu on the railway south of Mogaung and had inflicted severe casualties on the Japs, materially assisting Stilwell's advance. But they would have to lift the block. To prevent the opening up of the Jap supply lines north we were to establish a road and rail block further north between Mawlu and Mogaung in the area of Hopin and Pinbaw until the Chinese reached Mogaung, when the campaign could be declared over. To assist us in our operation 77 Brigade and 14 Brigade were to act as 'floaters' round the block.

The 'floater' system was the last of Wingate's many ideas. The floater force would operate in the country surrounding the block, engaging the enemy as he assembled for an attack on the block. Thus, if everything went well, no major attack could be mounted against the block. Should a small enemy force manage to slip through they would be engaged by an inner and smaller floater detached from the garrison of the block and acting as local protection. In this manner it was hoped that the Jap superiority in heavy weapons could not be exploited by them. 'The block,' said Wingate, 'will fight to the end, and should have no difficulty in beating off the enemy.' 77 Brigade had already done this with great success and the future for us looked bright, if rather strenuous.

Just before we set off John Hedley was sent off on an independent mission with a handful of troops. His object was to scale the precipitous Zibiyu Taungdan to the west, reach the road on the far side and verify a claim made by the air force that the road had been blocked. It was an unenviable job involving some very strenuous marching and no fun at the other end. John called up his troops – there were four of them, I think – and briefed them. He would never do anything by halves and went into the minutest details, instructing the men to carry toggle ropes and gym shoes for the climb, also a plentiful supply of salt. There was something rather scout-masterish about him in his brimming enthusiasm and we chided him, but he was quite impervious to ridicule, answering back with one of his rich, throaty laughs. He disappeared into the jungle with his long raking strides so that his men found some difficulty in keeping up.

American carbines dropped from the sky – another of Wingate's promises fulfilled. We unpacked them from their crates and appraised them, light and rather flimsy weapons but delightfully handy. We retired into a corner of the jungle and practised with them. They were apt to jam on the first few rounds but soon cleared and were refreshingly free from recoil. They looked as if they would be rather difficult to clean in the rains, but we had hardly started to think about the rains. The carbines were slung and we prepared for the first stage of our eighty-mile march.

As we were setting off John Hedley rejoined us, looking very tired but with a glow of satisfaction on his face. The road was not blocked, contrary to reports, but he, John Hedley, had killed a Jap. He regaled us with details and his fierceness was a bit frightening. The victim had been in a parked lorry, sitting at the wheel; John Hedley lobbed in a grenade and followed up with the bayonet. Lo! the spoils. John, ever the good intelligence officer, laid before us a badge of rank and an identity disc.

Jack Masters issued an Order of the Day to the troops to thank them for the great work of the last two weeks and to prepare them for the future. After Wingate's clarion calls it seemed a sober document, setting out how many men we had killed, how many trucks destroyed and at what small cost to ourselves. I think this Order was as much addressed to higher command as to the brigade, as if to assure them that all our circuitous wanderings had been to some effect and that we could put something against the spectacular achievements of 77 Brigade. The troops could note the list of destruction and assure themselves that their efforts had not been in vain. Some of the officers looked at the list and said with spite and envy, 'That's a DSO for a cert.'

The troops assembled and Jack Masters addressed them. 'There are some of you,' he said, 'who think you are nearing the end of your strength. You are wrong. In the past months you have consumed the surplus energy you built up before coming into Burma. Now you are down to scratch and from now on you will be drawing on your strength. You have not reached your reserves and will not do so for some time. There is a big task still to do.'

That was plain enough, and I mention it because it was meant as a counterblast to a dangerous tendency of thought among the troops, a tendency that was to shadow us for the rest of the campaign. This was what might be called the contract complex. Wingate had promised us that we would not be in Burma for more than three months and would certainly be out before the rains. We were fit to operate only for a limited period, after which our 'contract expired'. A lot of the high morale of the troops was based on this; the idea of a short, sharp campaign followed by a period of rest was one to appeal to a soldier used to limitless horizons of toil. The thought that it was going to be a cut-and-dried show and no mucking about was always there to encourage them in their moments of extreme depression; this discomfort and fatigue would not go on for ever. Whether this is a gallant frame of mind is rather doubtful, but the British soldier has long since ceased to be consciously gallant and his sacrifice consists of involuntary acts in battle, not a state of mind.

As the weeks rolled by the troops, and if truth be told the officers also, started to count the time and speculate on the 'contract date'. Some wishful thinkers considered we should have had enough at eight weeks, others ventured twelve as an absolute maximum. As rations became less and less palatable, there was always the consolation that in a short time . . . I supposed it was a variation of the demob complex, living our lives in the future and finding the present unbearably long with us. But planning ahead is a dangerous game if the plans of the future do not lie in one's own hands. There was a grave danger that the men were not prepared for disappointments, blissfully accepting their own plans and transmitting them into the reality of the future. They must be told that their contract was by no means yet expired; nor were they so frantically tired out as the heat of the Burmese summer had led them to suppose. I have no doubt that many of us, especially the Cameronians and the King's Own, were very tired men. But to admit this would have been to accentuate the contract complex and to set up a prejudice against their commanders, who, as they supposed, kept them in the field beyond their physical limits. There must be a firm denial of any rumours of a return to India, and in its place a promise of blood, sweat and tears. Shame the men of their physical misgivings and in the place of sympathy put sharp rebuke. Curse them out of their complex, if necessary, but at all costs do not pamper them. But I am afraid we never overcame this problem.

The first leg of the march took us due east, skirting the village of Mansi and then up into the hills; after that south-east through the hills to Manhton. This was a village on the River Meza and had been set up as a safe base for the bringing in of supplies and the evacuation of casualties. Moving out of the dry, parched jungle we crossed the road again without incident and set off into the hills. The going was good, it was a firm track, for we had abandoned the attitude that good tracks should be avoided. Brigade headquarters had had a comparatively restful time in the recent operations against the road. The heat still clung around and after a fresh supply drop we were heavily weighed down, but the track soon left the valley and struck up into the hills, which are a northern extension of the Mangin Range.

At the midday halt we heard news of Bladet, the glider-borne party whom we had helped onto the ground. For ten days they had been lost after the breakdown of their wireless and it could only be supposed that they were in a bad condition. We could pity them but could in no way assist them, until they suddenly contacted the Cameronians. It was pure chance, and they were almost at the end of their powers, having had to carry their wounded over a long distance through some foul country. Receiving a message of congratulation from the General for their fine work they were instructed to proceed to 'Aberdeen' – this was the code-name assigned to our base at Manhton – and fly out.

Afternoon found us at the top and marching across a small plateau of paddy. We halted for the night in a small belt of jungle. Jack Masters decided that to ease us a bit we should have a gala night. There were no Japs around and it would do the troops good to show this. We had kept our 'luxury' rations from the last drop and were thus able to accumulate quite a store of food – bully, tinned fruit, tinned peas and even some tins of meat and veg. Vast bonfires were lit and we wondered if a stray aeroplane would drop anything on us. We relaxed in a way that we had not done before and we felt very good. With the fires blazing we fell on the tins, tearing them open and depositing their contents into our mess tins. We had rice as well, and tinned tomatoes, unheard-of luxuries. They sizzled in the mess tins and we poked them critically. Rum, which followed us all over Burma, was produced and distributed to the troops. Only the Gurkhas would touch it, but to them it is the elixir of life. Onions came from the bottoms of our packs and popped into the stew, which in my case was a novel recipe of rice, meat and veg, tomato, bully and onions. The effect perhaps was not quite as much as the sum of the ingredients, but after K-rations it was a royal meal.

I wandered off to the Gurkhas with Frankie Baines. The rum was flowing freely and the little men were beginning their peculiar chants. Frankie and I decided it was our turn to amuse them and started on a few traditional English melodies. They were received coldly and we decided that perhaps something a bit hotter was called for. The jazz idiom was well exploited that night and the Gurkhas, whose own songs contain a large element of swing, applauded vociferously. We found a primitive delight dancing and singing by the light of the blazing fire, losing for a moment our fears and forebodings for the future. The Gurkhas were beginning to react to the rum and their applause became rather blurred. Their little faces gleamed and sweated in the firelight and their little eyes twinkled. I knew them all, these men who guarded our headquarters and led our mules, knew their bewildering names and their moods, their unquenchable cheerfulness and their resignation to any task that came their way. They lived and in living fully did not inquire why. Frank Turner joined in our gathering and his rich Gloucestershire Urdu echoed through the night. The mule leaders cheered wildly; he was their sahib and they must show it. Maybe Maggie was looking on from the darkness. As the singing died down and the Gurkhas fell down to sleep I crept back to my bed. We sat for some time by the glowing embers and Jack Masters talked quietly and excitedly about everything and nothing. John Hedley, exhausted by his long march over the Zibiyu Taungdan, was sleeping soundly a few yards away. Doc Whyte whistled tunelessly. He was always whistling something sentimental and was always out of tune. Finally, with the prospect of a long day ahead, we went to our beds and lay quietly down. It had been a delicious interlude.

Next morning we were met by some beaming villagers who were delighted at our contempt of the Japs. We should have said that it was they who were making Burma safe for us, but we did not and continued on our way. The track led downhill now along a narrow valley towards Aberdeen, an easy route that we travelled very fast. Aberdeen was the base established by 16 Brigade at the end of their epic march south from Ledo. Our packs were a little lighter after our midnight celebrations; but we felt our gala supper. Frank Turner went ahead on a horse to Aberdeen to fix us up and on the last stretch of the march we passed a patrol of West Africans operating from the base.

Aberdeen meant to our troops, the British troops, a way back to India, and as the battalions converged on it, there was the unsaid question, 'When will we finally return here for evacuation?' There was the strip, 1,200 yards of it, and there were the Dakotas. But our way lay north and we must turn away from the thought.

We stayed a whole day at Aberdeen and found it very pleasant; the village lay sprawled along the banks of the Meza, a slow, peaceful river winding down the narrow valley. Behind was the strip running along the bottom of the steep hills with a long approach from the south over the trees. It was not an easy strip, and as we marched up we saw the wreckage of three Dakotas heaped against the paddy. Early every morning the Japs were in the habit of strafing the strip, but otherwise they never came near, and Aberdeen remained a quiet retreat in enemy territory, our own little kingdom and a peaceful life.

We tore off our clothes and sank into the river, dirty and tired. We started to itch furiously and after the bathe found it hard to sit still. It was rather an anticlimax. Doc Whyte diagnosed and asked me to send a message about the infection that we had caught. The long, weird name and Doc's strange scrawl made it hard work for the ciphers. That night the 'base wallahs' arrived from India, our Administrative Officer and base signals and cipher officers. For one brief period in the campaign we were able to meet and discuss our difficulties. 'Grand seeing you again,' and all our complaints harboured against the day of meeting disappeared. If only we could have met more often, how many problems we could have settled! We sat talking into the night and felt rather conscious of our 'toughness' as we met these 'office boys'. We asked cautiously what impression we had made at Force headquarters. Had we done anything good, or did they think we had been fooling about? We were glad to clear up this suspicion but waited anxiously for the reply. The Administrative Officer replied, 'You are the only people who have been doing proper Long Range Penetration.' We felt he was not saying all, and that we had not perhaps been quite in the limelight, but we did not press the matter further. The base wallahs for their part expounded their difficulties and we listened sympathetically. 'Why no torch batteries or watches?' we asked. 'Supplies very sorry they won't release them.' The matter of the rifles without slings, oil instead of petrol, missing rations and many other complaints. We began to see why we could not get everything we asked for, and in the future we were less ambitious and less imperious in our demands. We were beginning to admit that the imperative and the impossible were not always reconcilable.

A few 'luxuries' flown in from Base and a quiet day's rest. Jack Masters started writing again, this time a Treatise on Defence to be issued to battalion commanders before going into the block. His pen was prolific and his writing crystal clear. Base was asked for more details about the block. We said, 'If block is to remain effective, must have 25-pounders and anti-tank guns.' They replied, 'Artillery will be flown in. Air photos of area being dispatched.' A glance at the map showed that in the area there was no ground suitable for a defensive position which was near enough to the road and railway to be able to block it. Base suggested a site in the bottom of the valley alongside the road. We laughed that one off and started looking along the contours at the side of the valley for a sufficient height on which to perch ourselves. We could hardly have been given a less promising area for the block. That was our opinion, but we were in the hands of the mighty and would have to make the best of it.

Off again north up the Meza. The first day was the wettest we ever had, crossing and re-crossing the river until we wondered if it would not be better to walk straight up the middle of it. The more statistically minded counted each time we crossed the river and the answer was, I believe, thirty-two. We were now coming into a country which we knew was free of Japs and that night we dried ourselves very ostentatiously by the side of the river; a bit of a picnic. But the next day's march was no picnic at all. After continuing a short way up the Meza we turned east up the steep hills which overlooked the river. I say steep, but perhaps I should say precipitous. And it was endless. Up and up along a narrow, muddy track. A mule with a wireless set on its back stepped over the edge and rolled down the hillside. Coming to a stop in a *nullah* bed it picked itself up and looked around for help. Another mule had somehow got into a reverse position on the track facing downhill, and so narrow was the track that it was only turned round with the greatest difficulty. A long gap now appeared in the column and we at the back started to close it up. Behind me was a mule which, realising that it was left behind, started to charge up the hill at a great pace. With the alternative of being butted in the back I was forced to increase my pace, and in the next few minutes I came nearer to vomiting my heart out than I had ever been before. After a short while I gave up the unequal struggle and sank down on the side of the path watching the mule dash past in a shower of churning mud.

Midday halt just under the crest. Briggo fuming. 'There's Jack Masters. He's been sitting there for the last half-hour and never told us it was the halting place. *He's* all right.' Frankie Baines cheerfully breathless and John Hedley so tired that the glint had gone out of his eyes. Frank Turner picking up the mules in the rear arrived late and for the first time in the whole campaign admitted that he was done. 'I'm too old for this game,' he said and went off to inspect the animals. Tea drunk in silence and a view east over the Meza valley.

Night harbour at last and a very good one, just beyond a Kachin village. We asked the villagers if there were any Japs around. No. Fires until late and not too much fuss about noise.

We trusted those villagers absolutely and never found our trust misplaced. The whole country was covered by an intelligence system which guaranteed our safety. A lot of ill-informed nonsense has been talked about the Burmese with little attempt to differentiate between tribes. Let no man give the Kachins anything but unstinted praise. Day by day they looked over us, guiding, warning, advising. Their food had been pillaged by the Japs but they gave us generously of their scarcity. Should we require a guide for the day's march, the village headman would detail his best man and warn the next village of our approach. What had these men to gain? We gave them money and parachute cloth, but from the Japs they got death. As we passed through the villages they implored us to stop. 'Stay with us, or if you can't do that come back soon. The Japs will kill us for this.' And they did. We heard tales of death in our wake, villages being made to answer for their generosity to us with slaughter and pillage. Mac begged Jack Masters to do something about it. 'We can't let them down a second time.' But do what? Our commander sent a message to Base explaining the situation and suggesting a holding force to garrison the area during the rains. The answer, of course, was 'No.' We left the villagers and we left one by one pathetic disappointment; a crowd of villagers watching us disappear down the track, then turning back to their village to await the wrath to come. Loyalty like this is unmistakable and pathetic. We felt it deeply and felt too a sense of base ingratitude.

A long and very dry day's march followed as we dropped down the north face of the hills and finally fetched up at the side of a river. Jack Masters was standing at the head of the harbour area asking us how we felt. We told him a lot of lies, but our feet and aching backs told us the truth.

We lived a strange life and by now had built up for ourselves a world of our own, whose limits were the limits of our minds and bodies and whose rules were the rules of necessity. We did not like it, but we had to put up with it and this enforced toleration created our mood. Nothing mattered except sleep and food. From the moment we shouldered our packs in the early morning our thoughts were constantly being invaded by a craving for rest. Arranging one's thoughts on the march became an art and our success in this matter could be judged by our ability to push out or suppress the two dominant urges. In the first cool hour of the morning it was possible to take pride in a sense of physical wellbeing, but this could not be relied on to last beyond the second halt. I tried to create a sense of wonderment in our adventure and imagine what my friends would think could they be transported to this spot and watch us trudge by. I could compose stories I would tell when I got back. 'I've hardly fired a shot,' said Frankie one day, 'but by gosh! I'll shoot a pretty line when I get back.' The future was always shadowed by the thought, 'How much longer?' Thoughts of England and the beauty of Burma. Was there any comparison? These hills would always bear our sweat and, until the next rains, our tired footprints. No, we could not like them for all their beauty. Only the streams we liked, the moments of comfort and refreshment.

Fatigue brings irritation and there were constant flare-ups. An order shouted to a Gurkha in imperfect Urdu might not bring immediate response and would be followed by a string of oaths. 'These —— Gurkhas. They don't understand their own language.' The Gurkhas for their part bore all patiently, puzzling their heads over the exact requirements of their rather choleric sahibs. Over difficult country there would be frequent halts and starts as animals picked their way over fallen trees or sudden streams and from the back would come a moan of protest. Anything that upset the rhythm of the march was an excuse for a torrent of oaths passed on until it stopped rather abruptly at the column commander, who turned round with a disapproving eye. Only Frank Turner managed to keep a grip on himself, rolling out his Gloucestershire Urdu in slow measured tones, repeating it until the Gurkhas were in no doubt as to what was required of them. *'Mere sab adme daine baine hath* fall out *karo,'* and the little men would slip quietly off the path to left and right for a halt. For the rest of us there was a constant effort to control ourselves at a waterless midday halt or a late bivouac. I understood now why we had transferred Mad M and some other warriors. Brilliance was not such a desirable asset as patience and a quiet mind. There would be times when dash and gallantry came into play but most of the time was the monotony of the march. The continual plod through dust or mud, the back of the man in front, up, down, up, down, eyes fixed on his boots inspecting each scrap of dust as it was shaken off his heel, the periodical shifting of his pack or changing of his arms, waiting for him to negotiate a difficult part of the track. Watching him impersonally, unconsciously, but cursing him for what he was, the maddening rhythm in our eyes. Mad? No, just very weary and inexpressibly bored, when each unusual move or faltering step becomes a major event. What the commander sees in the operations room at headquarters is a line drawn across the map and a line that seems to be moving very slowly. We measure it not in miles but in checks, halts and starts, the presence of a midday stream and the quiet shade of a night harbour. We knew our bodies, every inch of them, recognised every ache as it appeared, learning that it would eventually ease itself away until a fresh strain appeared elsewhere.

But the physical strain and mental chaos of the column was redeemed by the men themselves. A British signalman used to march in front of me. He was the worst marcher I have ever seen, scarcely able to put one foot in front of another. I spent a lot of time cursing him and pushing him on, but at a halt we used to discuss memories of the past and prospects for the future. In civilian life he had been in the show business, travelling through England in a caravan, and he used continually to bemoan the fact that he now had to use his feet. 'You miss your caravan a bit, I suppose?' I used to say to him when he was in difficulties and he would smile a groaning affirmative. Sergeant Wilkinson, commander of the signal detachment, a rather cynical North Countryman, found it hard to hold his tongue and used to have brisk exchanges with Briggo. He was our best operator and looked on his men as his very own. Corporal Durant, quiet but very efficient and a terrific, great-hearted worker, another signalman. Signalman Atherton, another from the North, always shockingly dirty with long, wild hair falling off his head. He worshipped his wireless set and would think it an utter disgrace if he had to admit failure to establish contact. Mad keen on his job, he would shout out his difficulties as he struggled at the set and give a running commentary on the man at the other end to satisfy himself and to show us that there was no funny stuff going on. We invariably had to shut him up and tell him not to broadcast his presence to the whole of Burma, but he was irrepressible. Corporal Jock

Yuille from Glasgow, he was my man. He joked his way round pretty well everything. I knew him under fire drawing roars of laughter from some very nervous soldiers. The Gurkhas loved him, and he would send them into convulsions with his Glasgow Urdu, gathering them round him as he responded with an amazing flair for their particular brand of humour. He worked with me to the end when the others had become casualties and became for me an anchor of sanity in a world that was rapidly sinking into confusion. In the enforced intimacy of the column men became neighbours and bedfellows, sharing fires and pooling rations. Every man was found out for what he was and those who stood the test, like the ones I have described, had good reason to be proud. We were certainly proud of them.

The Gurkhas, who guarded us and led our mules, had fewer personal idiosyncrasies, but as I learnt to know them better their characters became distinct. In brigade headquarters with the exception of Jack Masters I was the only one who spoke the language and in moments of stress when assailed by orders and wild oaths they would come to me for elucidation. Ananda Bahadur was the strongest of them. His physique was remarkable and he would stride down the track as if he was out to stretch his legs. Budi Bahadur, a handsome and exceptionally cheery little farrier who knew his job thoroughly and could shoe a mule at night. Prem Lal, the dresser, a rather cheeky little chap, who was ready with his box of physic for the animals' minor injuries, and he sometimes had to be suppressed. And poor little Kalu, who was not a true Gurkha and shunned by the others, a pathetic little figure who mended the saddlery and kept himself to himself. The Jeeves of this little band was Didi Ram, Frank Turner's orderly, the envy of us all. Didi carried a pack almost as big as himself, and it always included extra comforts for Frank, who in night harbour lived like a king, covered with a bower of bamboo and fed with delicious stews. Nothing was forgotten and as a reward Didi was content with the approval of his sahib, answering with his shy smile. He could reasonably be called a mighty atom.

And so, sweating, aching and living full days we crossed the hills north to the Indawgyi Lake. Jack Masters studied air photographs which were dropped to us on the march and decided on the area of the block. It would be near the village of Namkwin, just south of Pinbaw. The country round there looked suitable for a Dakota strip and there was sufficient high ground on which to build defences. There was a final supply drop on the edge of the hills – I don't think the pilots liked this much – and then into open country at the southern end of the lake. This was the first time we had been in the open and we felt very naked. A light plane appeared and dropped further orders for the block. To the north stretched the lake, hemmed in by the high mountains, a fifteen-mile stretch of water. During the remaining three months of the operation – it was the end of April now – our whole lives revolved round this lake. It was to be a lifeline.

We marched up the east side of the lake hoping to arrive at Mokso Sakan by nightfall and eventually came to a halt in an involuntary bivouac long after darkness; a shambles. On the following morning we reached Mokso Sakan, a deserted village by a stream, lying at the foot of a pass which led east over the mountains to Pinbaw and the railway valley.

CHAPTER NINE

BLACKPOOL

Plans were cleared up and troops allocated. There was a general preparation for the task ahead. The column of Gurkhas was to remain behind at Mokso to provide a safe base for us in case we had to retreat. 'The trouble with ⸺ Brigade,' said Jack Masters, 'was that they didn't have a foot on the ground.' This 'foot on the ground' was a bit of an obsession with our commander, but also a very wise precaution. I suppose that in Long Range Penetration the tendency is to thrust ahead in lightning raids with an emphasis on speed and mobility. This may easily result, and in some cases did, in a disregard of security, so that the striking force on meeting difficulty and suffering casualties had no safe base at which to reform. 'You must have a foot on the ground,' said Jack Masters. 'Unless you do you are like a boxer trying to hit out with one foot in the air. The result is that you lose your balance and are at the mercy of your opponent.' The column of the 3/4 Gurkhas was allotted the role of 'firm base' and ordered to remain at Mokso Sakan.

The Gurkha officers took rather a dim view of this plan, as they were denied the opportunity of a scrap. Mike Dibben, the column commander, accepted it all in his blasé, rather matter-of-fact manner. He never seemed to care about anybody or anything, a good companion but a very frank one. Mike McGillicuddy (of the Reeks), their transport officer, must have felt a bit sore. A member of the Irish gentry, impetuous and quite indefatigable, he used to charge up and down with a riding crop inspecting each mule and horse for badly placed loads or leg injuries. He was the officer who had distinguished himself so much in the scrap near Pinlebu.

With the Gurkhas stayed the majority of the brigade animals, another very wise precaution. In the 77 Brigade block at Mawlu dozens of mules had been killed by shellfire, as it was impossible to dig them in. They stood there patiently in the open and fell one by one. Frank Turner remained behind with the animals and at last had a chance to look them over and rest them, feeling their backs and bellies and giving them a thorough grooming. Frankie Baines also stayed behind with one of his defence platoons. He was very annoyed at this and said so emphatically, until Jack Masters had to ask him to desist. Poor Frankie. He was longing for this opportunity to fight and make good. Perhaps later he was not so very sorry at what he had missed.

We marched over the pass. Frankie went on ahead with his platoon to guard the pass until we were through. We heard noises of firing and wondered if we would have a safe passage over the top. The track had been patched up in preparation for our march, but it was still in very bad condition and some recent rain had turned the dust into putty. At the top of the first rise we had a wonderful view of the Indawgyi Lake lying in a huge cluster of mountains, stretching north and south in a great green gash. The climb up was a series of small hills, up and down until we wondered exactly how much height we had gained. With every hill came a vista and the sight of the next climb. The pass came into sight suddenly round a corner and we were in a clearing with a few scattered *bashas* perched on the high ground with a magnificent prospect. There was delightful air and we sat down to cool off. Frankie was roaring about after suspected Japs and disappeared south along the ridge; there was sound of much firing and news came of a fierce little engagement.

Confident that we would reach the valley by nightfall we struck along the ridge and then down through thick jungle, which grew steadily thicker. There had been some argument about the track we were following, and for good reason. The track became less and less distinct until we found ourselves confronted with almost impenetrable jungle. There was nothing to do but to slash through it with kukris, which slowed us down to a crawl. A night harbour in a thicket and an anxious glance at our schedule. Next day after some more furious hacking we reached the Namkwin Chaung and a delightful bivouac. We bathed and Doc Whyte whistled, 'Moonlight becomes you'. 'Why are you so incurably optimistic, Doc?' I asked him. 'Well,' he replied, 'we must keep our spirits up.' John Hedley was still very tired, but was trying to persuade himself that he was not, washing in the stream with tremendous vigour and his gurgling laugh. Jack Masters had informed Base that owing to the delay the block could not be put into position until 7 May, the following day. Chesty Jennings was to go forward dressed as a Kachin and reconnoitre a site for a Dakota strip, as this had to be done in the open in broad daylight a mile from the main Jap lines of communication. I think that Jack Masters with that inventive mind of his was rather proud of this little ruse. He himself was to go forward and recce the block position.

7 May. Faltering progress down the Namkwin Chaung towards the valley, stops and starts and a lot of rude words. Briggo set up a wireless on the steep bank of the *chaung* and cursed it into life with Jack Masters hovering round with a message and an itching pencil. Finally arrangements were made with Base; a supply drop on the day we moved into position; picks, shovels and wire. 'Essential dig in immediately. Maximum picks, shovels, wire

required.' A lot would depend on our ability to prepare our position quickly. 77 Brigade had had a nasty scrap when half dug in and we were not keen to repeat the experience. Wire, wire and more wire. We must fence ourselves in and impale the enemy, shooting them as they struggled to break through. These were not pleasant thoughts, but we thought them. The General signalled urgently. The Dakota strip must be prepared with the minimum delay to fly in heavy weapons. Those first few days would be a gamble, and we knew it. A large force of enemy, and we were finished. Bad weather and no Dakota sorties, and we would have to clear out. We were working to a fine and rather anxious schedule.

Jack Masters went forward to make his recce, accompanied by Chesty in full Burmese garb. We sat down on the damp pebbles of the *chaung* and waited. There was an explosion somewhere in front. The pin had dropped out of an officer's grenade and there were several wounded men. We continued to sit, rather vague as to what was going on. Rations were opened and eaten cold; no fires. Dead minds and rather weary bodies; patience transformed into a sort of mental vacuum. Late in the afternoon our commander returned and we started on our way, off the *chaung* and up into a maze of ridges and sudden steep paths. It was further than we thought. Night fell and there was some confusion. I passed some troops already in position and hastily dug in by a little stream. Then up a steep, muddy path. Jack Masters in the darkness making frantic signals and asking the mortars where the —— they thought they were going. I do not think they really knew. Left, up the final pull onto the ridge, steep as a cliff. Orders to dig in immediately. Briggo cursed, said he would do no such thing and lay down under a bush. I followed suit after a few scratches at the surface and found it difficult to prevent myself falling down the hill. On the flat ground to the east parachutes were falling. Picks, shovels, wire. Everything had worked out very well. Parties went off into the darkness to collect the loads while I lay back and felt a vague sympathy for everyone. I had only a slight idea where I was, but there were no Japs around, yet. The last Dakota droned away into the distance and there was silence, punctuated by the tramp of feet and the clink of picks and shovels.

As dawn came we could look round and take note. The position lay on a series of ridge features jutting out from the lower slopes of the hills we had just crossed. They were small ridges, but very sharp; what might, I suppose, be described as razor-edged. Brigade headquarters was sited in the middle at the top of the highest feature, Command Post on the east facing the valley, Signals and Intelligence on the west and the dressing station a little way down the path. To the west the position eased down into a small valley by a stream, facing the slopes of the mountains in all directions. This the King's Own defended through some very desperate days along the ridge that ran north-west by this little valley. East were two prong ridges thrust out into the valley held by the Cameronians. Below that was the valley, or rather The Valley, it was our target, the reason for all the battles of the next two weeks. Now it looked peaceful enough. A long narrow stretch of open country directly below, a river, and the railway a mile away. Namkwin village, with its little railway station, a prime target. The road, disappearing north to Mogaung and south to Indaw. On the far side of the valley were more hills and in these hills 77 Brigade was resting after its weeks of fighting at Mawlu; 14 Brigade was away to the south moving up from Banmauk to protect us and moving, as we thought, very slowly.

It was strange to sit down after all our wanderings without the thoughts of an early rise and march. Packs were flung down and we felt free men. We were no longer furtive. We were blatant, daring the Japs to come and crack us. We could look for the first time across open country and feel the open sky above us. We could light fires at any time instead of that brief hour in the evening, and we could walk about easily without the perpetual anxiety of the long, winding column and the jungle closing in on us. We knew what we were about and the issue was much clearer than in the hide-and-seek of yesterday. The valley lay below as a constant reminder of our task. Road and railway, block, no supplies north, Japs fall back, Stilwell advances south, we hand over and clear out. The sequence was logical and obvious to the simplest soldier. Rations, we were told, would be something better than K, which for all its ingenuity still left an aching void and an increasing distaste. The heat could be endured in a foxhole as it never could on the march.

But there was work. Dig and wire, dig and wire. Picks, shovels. More supply drops. Hauling the loads up the steep path. Mortars dug in uncomfortably near the headquarters. Jack Masters named the positions as on the cricket field – 'Wicket', 'Point', 'The Deep'. He drew diagrams, fire plans, expounded to commanding officers. Briggo demanded miles of wire and laid lines to every small outpost, wondering whether to lay them on the ground or above the undergrowth. The scene was peaceful enough, but we had a feeling that our days were numbered; there would be a time when little yellow men would be scrambling to get a footing on those slopes. If only we could dig in in time and face them with a jungle fortress instead of a few mud holes. Briggo and I marked out a site and got some Gurkha orderlies to dig. It was a palatial little place with ample room and a solid roof of mud and timber but not much protection from artillery. The cipher office my NCOs constructed was an even flimsier device and would not have withstood a shell within twenty yards; the nearest was about twenty-five. We opened our packs and laid our equipment in neat rows along the shelf of the dugout: tins, packets, ammunition, notebooks, water bottles and a large tin of adhesive plaster that I always carried around. It was all very good and we were going to enjoy ourselves.

Next night there was a burst of fire from the northern edge. We had not heard fire for a long time and raking through the night it was uncomfortable. Long, sustained bursts of Vickers and answering fire, the peculiar whippy cracks of Jap rifles. The firing continued for some time and it sounded like a big scrap. Maybe it was a company attack or a recce in force. Jack Masters phoned up the position, which was having no difficulty. There were lots of Japs, but mostly dead ones. They were wild and without a plan. Next morning we heard the full report and did not feel terribly pleased with ourselves. The attack had been launched by one platoon which had suffered many casualties, but the man on the Vickers had fired enough rounds to kill a battalion. It was an attack of jitters, an uneasy finger on the trigger, long bursts into the bushes which were moving. Perhaps we were not in for such a good time after all. The column was desperately tiring and monotonous, but perhaps weariness was better than fear. There was no sudden fire in the night and anxious inquiries on the telephone. There was only sleep, deep and unrestrained, against the rigours of the morrow. Here we could sleep all day, if we were not hauling loads or digging positions or doing guard or watering mules. But with the night came fear and our sleep would be broken by noise, and we would sit up in our foxholes waiting for the next burst, to place the fire, and then turn over in an attempt to knit up our fears in sleep. That first night brought us a foretaste of the future.

Our most urgent task after the initial defences was the construction of a glider strip. The gliders would bring in bulldozers and graders for a Dakota strip, the Dakotas would bring in guns and troops. It was all so easy, but we must hurry. It was a race with the Japs, who were well aware of our presence. The General sent messages continuously on the need for speed. He was worrying about the guns the Japs would bring up and realised our comparative helplessness against them as we stood. If we were to block the railway from our present position, only guns would do it. Chesty took gangs down the hill and dug and scraped in the paddy. Working at night they dodged parachutes, and by day they worked in full view of the Japs without any protection. Why did the Japs not attack them? But the Japs despite their habits were at times quite unpredictable. Perhaps they had received no orders.

Five hundred yards were cleared leaving a good approach from the north, and a message was sent off to Base, who replied that four gliders would arrive that night. But no gliders came; it was the weather. Next night we waited again. A message came at midnight saying that the sorties would be postponed until 0600 hours next day. At 0600 hours there was nothing, but about an hour later in broad daylight the first glider appeared, flying north up the valley at 500 feet. The tug circled, taking a good look at the strip, while below, the Japs opened up with light anti-aircraft fire. Then the glider was released north. The Jap machine-guns were now firing continuously. The glider came down until it was about a hundred yards from the boundary, and then suddenly it banked round vertically when about fifty feet off the ground and plunged straight in with a great shudder and a crack which echoed up the valley. I was watching from the top of the hill and stood bewildered. One by one the gliders came in and one by one they crashed, until we had four wrecks on the paddy. Why, in broad daylight and with a perfect approach? I swore that gliders were doomed. Of the four pilots, two were killed and the remaining two, badly cut about the face, walked up to brigade headquarters. They said they could not see the strip distinctly. One of them said he must go back immediately and fly in another glider with the machinery. He did, a very brave effort. For the moment we were left with a bulldozer and a smashed grader. We could not build the strip until we had a new grader, and until we built the strip we could get no heavy weapons. If the Japs caught us now we would have little to say for ourselves.

Next morning came the shells. I was woken up at about 5.30 by a whistle and a bang. But they were far away and did not concern us. I turned over and dozed. But the bangs continued nearer, until fear could not be kept back. We were in range and we were being destroyed. A distant thud, then we would get lower in our foxholes, a whine and then a deathly pause. Explosion, a shower of tree and mud. Silence. Then again the distant thud. There was no escaping this. It was steady and relentless. John Hedley sat in his trench counting the shells, their bearing and estimated calibre. He was lucky to have something to engage him. My NCOs sat in their flimsy shelter enciphering messages, working with awkward breaks and pauses and a great inward tension. Jock Yuille cracked jokes and raised a few nervous laughs.

We knew fear that morning in a new way. We had no guns to answer back and our planes would have great difficulty in spotting theirs. We would be destroyed. 'There will be no retreat from the block,' said Wingate. Instead of retreat were we to sit here and be consumed?

At last the noise ceased and men crept from their holes. Briggo learnt from Jack Masters that there were plenty of bodies about. When one of my NCOs later reported for duty, he was white and shaking like a leaf. He had just been digging out his pals who lay buried round him. A message was sent to Base reporting 300 shells and moderate casualties: 24 killed, 20 wounded. The General replied, 'Well done.' 'Why well done?' asked my gloomy sergeant, who always knew far too much about what was going on. 'The sooner we get a few guns the better.' I think many of us prayed for guns, and though the day was peaceful we felt very ill at ease.

Work on the Dakota strip continued all day and into the night. The scraper was working intermittently and progress was very slow. Still the Japs did not intervene, but continued to watch the troops as they scraped at the paddy. The American engineers were in charge and Chesty stood by. The scene was a very peaceful one and the chug of the bulldozer sounded like the noise of a tractor and binder in an English summer. It was summer all right, but just over there were the Japs. There was a difficulty over the strip; a large bump at the north end which was the approach end. A second day, and all day they scraped at that bump. The General was getting anxious, but no more so than us. At last the strip was considered fit to take Dakotas and the code-word 'Texas' was flashed to Base.

The first Dakota was overhead when it was discovered that the strip was only 750 yards long and not the required 1,200. The pilot was told and asked if he wanted to have a try. He switched on his landing lights and came up to the boundary. There was a bump as he pulled back too soon, a bounce and then with full throttle he was off again – he landed in India on his belly. The second one, carrying some engineer equipment, approached next, dropped over the hedge and pulled up. Magnificent. The plane was unloaded and roared off again into the night. No one else tried their luck. Jack Masters sent a message to Base, 'Regret Texas muddle due error estimation, co-ordination.'

Next day we scraped and levelled, and reported that although there was still a big bump the strip was the required length and had a perfect approach. 'Texas' was signalled again and the flare path lit. The planes came in one by one and I watched from the hill. There was always a moment of agony as they throttled down, whether they had come too low, too high, too fast. One plane burst a tyre, shot off into the paddy and burst into flames. A gunner major standing next to me turned away, saying, 'I hope to goodness none of my men were in that.' He was dead twenty-four hours later. The crew got out of the blazing plane – there were no passengers – and walked off; Chesty dived gallantly into the plane to rescue the mail. I walked down the strip to collect personnel. It was an amazing scene, a continuous roar of engines, huge flashing lights and an organised chaos of men deplaning, stores being offloaded and jeeps rushing about with trailers behind them. These jeeps were the first wheeled vehicles we had seen. Our column RAF officers were controlling, and with every pilot wanting to get down and get off it was not an easy task. A plane came careering madly down the runway and we ran for it. After some very irregular manoeuvres it came to rest facing across the strip. The American pilot leaned out of the cockpit and shouted, 'Gee, I guess I must have had my fingers crossed.' A jeep hauled him round again and he was soon off. As each pilot got out he would look at the blazing plane and ask nervously, 'Who is that?' A damaged Dakota, which would not be repaired, stood by the side of the strip. A Yank approached me and said, 'Is that going free? I'd like the radio. I'm kinda mad on radio.' I assured him it was going and he climbed in complete with screwdriver, followed by a lot of other Americans. I followed them in and seeing that the clock had gone took the first-aid kit.

Then Luke came up out of the darkness. He had left us just before we flew into Burma and was now on Dakotas. 'Hello, I didn't recognise you, R. J. How are the others?' Very well, I said, and how did he like our strip? A bit of a bump at one end. 'Bump!' he shouted, 'it's a mount'n. We were doing a hundred on the clock when I last looked and let her down nicely. Then wow! up we went. Pretty rugged. Well, so long.' He strode off.

The two gliders bringing the chassis and body of a scout car were overhead. All Dakotas were given red and we waited anxiously. They cast off, then up north. A steep bank and a perfect touchdown. Whew! The glider was pushed off the strip and we looked for the other one. The crew of the first glider could hardly bear to look, and we realised at once the terrific tension these pilots had to face. 'He's gone too far away,' he yelled and turned his back. But he was wrong. The glider came in very nicely; it did not attempt to brake until it was almost on top of a Dakota, when it pulled up sharply. Two complete gliders, a record. A British soldier rushed up to the glider pilot and asked him if he would swop uniforms.

There was another pile-up. An RAF plane came in very fast and showed no inclination to slow up. It careered past the dispersal bay and piled up on the paddy. Some rather bewildered and shaken REME personnel scrambled out followed by the crew, who thought it was all rather a joke. We were just preparing to unload it when there was a bang and a whistle of bullets. I did not realise immediately what had happened until I saw the others run madly across the strip. I followed them and thought that if there was a more naked place than an airstrip I would like to hear of it. We crouched behind the bales of supply containers feeling rather foolish. An officer exhorted us gallantly to charge the enemy. But I swore that if ever I did that I must first know where the enemy was. The last Dakota roared off down the strip, did a ground loop and hobbled slowly back. The men were now dead tired and dawn was breaking. I went up to Jack Masters to explain the situation and to ask for relief to be sent down. This he did promptly. When day broke the loads were still being hauled up the hill.

We had guns. We were able to answer back to that early morning horror: 25-pounders; Oerlikons; Bofors. As they were hauled up the steep path men gathered round and cheered. We were helpless no longer.

But there was work, continuous wearing work hauling ammunition and supplies up the long track. And then the enemy came. He came in at The Deep and he came with a set purpose. There were not platoons this time, but companies. A continuous roar through the night and anxious voices over the telephone. During the day we would call up planes and Cochran's force (we called them the Young Ladies) would treat us to some fun. Mustangs dived down the narrow valley which separated us from the enemy, firing a few yards from the noses of our troops. Then came the Mitchells with their parachute bombs, which on the first occasion gave us a bit of a surprise. The Japs were given no respite except at night, when they would emerge and renew their attack on the King's Own, rushing wildly at the wire and getting no further. We were holding and killing, but we were also tiring. The firing used to start at dusk. First the 105 mm, then the 75 mm, which gave us little chance to go to ground, the mortars, the grenades and finally the machine-guns. There was an expectancy with each dusk, waiting for the distant thud and the whine, the sharp bang and explosion of the 'whizz-bang', the more open crash of mortars and grenades. Men charged the wire and died as they tried to get over, men blown up on our mines or maimed by our booby traps. In head-quarters we heard merely the noise and chatter of the weapons and could only wait for news. With the morning came relief but also an overriding weariness, fatigues on the airstrip, digging and guarding. The King's Own were being steadily worn down and they knew it.

Then one night the Japs decided to finish it all off. That dusk was a noisier dusk than usual and the shells were more persistent. As darkness fell the smaller weapons opened up and the Japs massed. Late at night came distressing news from The Deep. A platoon had been heavily shelled and in its present state was not in a position to offer much resistance. The Japs might break through here, and if they broke through we would have little chance of ejecting them. Briggo went off to take some more ammunition to The Deep and Jack Masters rang up the Cameronians telling them to bring up a platoon. Tim Brennan, their second-in-command, came hurrying up and they went into a hud-dle. Better stand by until the situation cleared a bit. Our commander rang up the King's Own. The platoon which had been so badly mauled had reorganised and was in a position to fight again; the casualties were less than had been at first feared. The fighting died away and the dawn came very beautiful.

The Japs beat a retreat. The constant hammering of the last few days, if it had tried us, had cruelly hurt the enemy. A patrol was sent out into the Jap position and found carnage and desolation; a bloodstained dressing station and bloody equipment scattered about. There were no bodies of course – the Japs had taken care of that – but evidence enough of a mighty slaughter. We sent a message to Base giving the situation, not quite sure of the enemy's intentions but knowing that we had given him a nasty battering.

CHAPTER TEN

CRISIS

There followed days of peace in which we tried to regain some of
our strength. But it was not possible. We were the slaves of our
supply system. Every night, to keep up our supply of food and
ammunition, planes would land and men would work through the
night, unloading, stacking, dragging bundles of shells, mortar
bombs, small arms and rations. Great coils of wire up a muddy
path at midnight. Sometimes I used to go down to the strip and
see the troops at their work, wondering how much longer they
could stand it. Jack Masters was wondering this, too, and sent off
a message asking Base to cut down sorties to a minimum to enable
the men to regain their strength. They tried but it was impossible. One night's let-up and battalions would be crying out for
more bombs or rations. Give wire a priority and our stacks of
ammunition would drop until we became anxious. We were working a supply system which was only just enough to keep us going.
It was different in the column with 400 troops and no heavy
weapons to feed. Here we were 1,500 and encumbered with guns
that fired heavy ammunition, mortars that ate greedily everything that was fed to them. We would maintain ourselves, but at
a cost. Our men could not go into reserve, there were no 'back
areas' here, unless they were the enemy's, and there were no fresh

troops to relieve us. We could only shift round and we removed the King's Own from the Deep position, putting the Cameronians in their place. The King's Own were utterly tired out and their wild eyes told the story of those nights of fear that had just passed.

If we were not in a position to hit back at the Japs, our planes were. Every day they came over and at our command they strafed and bombed. We had evolved a system of close support which even today has not been surpassed, a precision of communication which made every strike a joint effort by ground and air. 'Annihilate the village of Namkwin,' said Jack Masters one day, probably tired of looking at it every day across the valley, and our request was carried out. These planes were our long-range artillery and though they were not as readily available their accuracy was amazing. It was very good for the men to watch such spectacular destruction of the enemy, watching as it were from a grandstand and applauding loudly.

At the ground-to-air wireless set sat 'Robbie', Flight-Lieutenant Robinson. I should really have introduced him before. He had been with headquarters in the early training before going over to the King's Own and had made a big contribution to our communal life. Robbie was what you might call rough and ready. In 1940 he had been flying Blenheims in daylight raids over Cologne, which was as near to suicide as was possible without putting a pistol to your head. Robbie was proud of the fact that he had got his commission in the teeth of public school prejudice and had been married in his flying clothes. His speech was not butter, but it was gay, fearless and zestful. In the manner of a lot of the RAF, rank meant little to him and his superb assurance always carried him through. One day he rang up Jack Masters and told him there was a good jazz programme on the wireless, putting the telephone mouthpiece against the receiver. Jack Masters growled that perhaps Robbie might have something better to do, but Robbie was unmoved. But he did make one mistake, mentioning our codeword 'Clydeside' over the blower. The name was changed to 'Blackpool', by which name it will always be remembered. I welcomed the change; it was easier to encipher.

There were new faces in the night; officers climbing from Dakotas and reporting for duty. There was 'The Baron', who took over the job of Brigade Major and who always looked like a veteran deerstalker, issuing orders continuously, quite impervious to the complaints of those who received them, for his orders were sometimes very peculiar. He had a habit of shouting for officers as if they were office boys, but he could be excused for his calm in battle; not a quiet calm, because he could never be quiet, but an unawareness of danger and an unquenchable enthusiasm.

An American turned up one day and said he had come from over the hills. I asked him which hills and he pointed down the valley. 'These,' he said. 'I look after the Kachin boys.' The boys, apparently without knowing a word of English, operated the wireless sets and the ciphers of the American intelligence detachments. 'But how do they work the ciphers?' I asked, feeling a professional interest. 'That's easy,' he replied, 'they just transpose the letters in a certain order without knowing what the letters are.' He sat down and talked about the Kachins with whom he lived in the isolation of the hills. I thought it was a strange job for an American; they are meant for great companionship and a life lived quickly, not a lonely outpost in the hills with the native folk. We received information from these outposts, and I was glad to see the men who did it all. We fixed up a mutual cipher and he wandered off to his hills.

There was another detachment wandering the hills and combing the villages for information. This was Mac, who had been sent out to organise the locals for news gathering. The villagers were willing enough to give us the information; it was merely a question of organising them. News came into the block of movements through the hills, strong parties of Japs passing through for food, and even the intentions of the enemy. The Japs always told the villagers what they were going to do, but we did not have the opportunity of finding out exactly how much of it was false. Occasionally Mac would come in, looking more tired than ever, and give a verbal report, then wander off again with his beloved Karens.

One day John Hedley, fretting at inaction, bethought himself of an idea. He would reconnoitre the road in the valley and he would do it by himself. In fact I believe he took a sergeant and slipped off into the night. He returned only with great difficulty with grenade splinters in his knee; a Jap section had spotted him. That was that. He had to be evacuated. To John this was a bitter pill and for once his reckless enthusiasm was somewhat dimmed. He said he had never felt fitter and would soon be back. Doc Whyte thought otherwise and packed him off one night in a Dakota. We never really found anyone to replace him.

News came to us that 16 Brigade had been evacuated to India, and we felt they were very lucky. But where was 14 Brigade, who had been ordered to 'float' round us? They were still a long way off and we said some rather hard things about them. For the next few days we were to watch their progress with anxiety and exasperation. What did they think they were doing? It was not at all clear to us and we said it rather bluntly. 77 Brigade we did not count on. They had done a terrific job and we felt they could afford to rest, which in fact they were doing.

The Chinese were beginning to hold our attention. Their two divisions, 22 and 38, were advancing down the Hukawng Valley towards Kamaing, which was the last obstacle before Mogaung. When Mogaung was taken our task would be at an end. But things seemed to be going rather slowly now, or not as fast as we could have wished. We were in a critical mood, and as the duration of our campaign was conditioned by the speed of the Chinese advance we could never excuse delay of any kind. Our fate became linked with the Chinese from now on and the link was at times almost broken by criticism and misunderstanding. They appeared in our Situation Reports for the first time and we chalked up their progress on our big operational maps. The Chinese . . . 14 Brigade . . . why were they so slow? Would we be forced to sit here for months to come, soaking and sickening? This was at the moment only a hidden thought. It was soon to become an obsession.

Then we received a message saying that we were coming under the direct command of General Stilwell. This had, I suppose, been fairly obvious for some time, as we were coming into his sphere of operations, but the effect on us was disastrous. It had at this stage nothing to do with the man, who probably knew more about Burma than any other soldier. We did not object to Stilwell as a man; we objected to him as we would have objected to anyone, as a symbol of the loss of our independence. Up to now, although we had been used for a job by the 14th Army, we had always been an independent force under our own commander. We had, since the beginning of the campaign, been helping Stilwell in his advance south, but our operations had been carried out by our own methods and with complete independence. We were willing to help, but we would do it on our own terms in our own particular, shall I say, peculiar way. Only as an independent force under a commander who knew our potentialities and limitations would we be used effectively. We would then be understood and not asked to undertake tasks for which we were not suitable. Our official title was Special Force, and that was how we saw ourselves. Of course troops were scarce in Burma and we must make ourselves available, but we thought they might be even scarcer if we were misused. We could not see the broader issues that faced the higher command. We could see only ourselves, stuck out in the middle of enemy territory, where we had been for over two months, and we remembered again Wingate's promise that we would not be in Burma for longer than three months. It was the old business of the 'contract'.

Jack Masters flew to Stilwell's headquarters in the Hukawng Valley and came back looking rather gloomy. We would be at the disposal of Stilwell for any job he might want us to do, and there were as yet no signs of the end of our campaign. It was obvious that Stilwell would give this answer to our commander's queries, but it only served to confirm our fears. Briggo came back to our trench and gave us the news, gloomier and more bitter than ever. We sat down that night to a silent, savage meal and saw the future as a hopeless eternity of toil and danger. Doc Whyte saw it as a grave threat to the men's health. He had plenty of experience of 'combat fatigue' and the illnesses it brings in its train. He was very worried and talked for hours with Jack Masters, who sent off a message stating that he would not vouch for the health of the brigade after the end of May. Perhaps not, but necessity might force us to fight on as sick men. We could only state our case, and we did this with considerable emphasis. On their heads be it, the heads of those who decreed our future. On Stilwell.

Then one day we had our first shower. This was the end. The rains. The steep sides of the ridge became a bog and a treacherous foothold. The water seeped into our foxholes and ran in great gushes down the slope, carrying the mud with it. The track from the airstrip was an adventure, but for those who carried the stretchers down to the strip it was a nightmare. The strip itself was soggy. The shower soon passed off, but it left a feeling that we could not get rid of. Rains, misery and sickness, vistas of mud stretching into the endless future, tearing at our boots, covering our bodies, filling our bivouacs and folding over us as we slept. These were our visions and to them was added another and very real danger. How would we get our food? It had never been shown that supply-dropping aeroplanes could operate in the rains and why should they now? How would we be able to build strips to evacuate our casualties? Already the one below was losing its firm surface. We might tolerate dirt and discomfort – we had no option – but we could not exist without food and if we could not get our casualties out it would be criminal to expect us to carry on. We did not know that those whose duty it was to consider these things had weighed them up and taken careful decisions. We could see only the rain seeping through the mud and the low clouds scudding over the mountains. We could hear the dripping of the trees and the squelch of boots wrenched out of the mud, and seeing these things we could be filled only with a deep apprehension. Doc Whyte's whistling was not quite so frequent.

New troops arrived, not fresh in vigour but something to swell our strength and take some of the strain off our old battalions: the 3/9 Gurkhas, who had been organising the Broadway strip; a very businesslike lot officered by men who seemed quite sure what they were about. Their commanding officer, Alec Harper, who appeared at first to be completely careless and slapdash, yet a man who was never disturbed even in periods of greatest stress. And a company commander, Major Jim Blaker, whose gallantry was already something of a legend. The other battalion was the King's Liverpool, or part of it. One of the two columns had been ambushed when crossing the railway and had been split up. A man wandered up to the Command Post one day and asked for the Brigade Commander. 'Who are you?' I asked. He was wearing no badges of rank. 'I'm Colonel Scott.' Lieutenant-Colonel Scott, DSO, MC! There were no two opinions of 'Scotty'. He had a flair I have seen in few other men of attracting others to him. He was 'one of the lads' and his companionship with his troops was neither patronising nor forced. He had the same effect on officers. He was open, cheerful, matter-of-fact, the 'ordinary man' and at the same time one of the most exceptional men I have met. (Before the war he had, in fact, been a Liverpool tram-driver.) He could encourage his men with a glance and he became the natural object of their hero-worship. I heard a man who had lost his way and bumped into Scotty's column say afterwards, 'That CO's a grand fellow. Every night he gets the chaps round and tells them what is going on. That column is a very happy one.'

The King's Own recovered from their experience in The Deep and were sent as a 'floater' to the west on the 'parachute ridge' and the surrounding features, to sniff out the Japs and winkle them out of any positions which might threaten our security. It was a very tricky assignment especially in the rather involved topography of the area. It was something entirely new for us and the experiment was not an unqualified success. Even now we were still learning. But I am sure that the presence of that battalion altered the enemy's plans appreciably.

Then, after ten days of an uneasy peace, the guns started up again and pounded us daily. This time the shells did not come in large numbers but occasionally throughout the day, which was worse, as we could never feel sure of ourselves. Every now and then the familiar whine and crash, then the long silence while men repaired the breaches and carried off the wounded. Jack Masters signalled, 'Shelling not serious but causing steady casualties. Suggest continuous air cover instead of occasional strikes in force.' The trouble was that the planes could never locate the guns, which took good care to conceal themselves, and their only advantage lay in the fact that as long as there was a plane overhead the guns would not fire. We would watch for the Mustangs and as soon as we saw them we would get up from our foxholes and brew up. We knew that we would have a few minutes' respite, until the planes went and we crept back again to wait for the shells.

Of course the mules could not stand up against this. They stood there patiently in the open and one by one they fell. Of the four headquarters' mules two were killed outright and the other two I shot with a pistol, as they stood patiently with their great bleeding flanks. One of these was Maggie, the mule who had followed us from the very beginning and had not faltered. Maggie had been a great companion to us and with her we felt nothing could go wrong. She lay now on the steep slope while the Gurkhas heaped earth over her. Her mule leader was distraught and never really recovered from the separation, and when I say that Gurkhas do not normally show much affection for animals you will see what sort of animal Maggie was. We now had no mules to carry our wireless sets so that if we were compelled to move we would have to move without any communications with the outside world.

What of our guns of which we were so proud? What indeed! It was good to hear them pound away at the railway, but we knew it was a very ineffective way of blocking it. And above all we could not answer the guns of the enemy. We sent out raiding parties and took constant compass readings, but we could not locate them, so that our 25-pounders were helpless against them. Our position was as bad as it had ever been. We had anti-aircraft guns but only once did we meet enemy planes, Zeros flying at 100 feet, which put one of our Bofors guns out of action and got away without a shot being fired. The only time we did fire was when an Oerlikon gunner opened up on a Dakota flying at 1,000 feet. The simplest Gurkha could tell what plane it was, but not the gunner, whose fire was unpleasantly accurate. We screamed at him and he stopped firing, muttering that the Bofors had opened up and he had to follow suit.

14 Brigade was still a long way off, and we were beginning to get anxious when the storm broke. It started again at night and this time the attacks were launched against the whole perimeter. All round the wire the enemy probed, swamping a sector with fire and charging the defences. The Gurkhas stood firm and fired back until the wire was strewn with bodies. The stream from which we

drew our water was now in enemy hands, but we found it else-where within the perimeter. Night after night the bombardment continued and Jack Masters began to get anxious. How long could the troops hold out? They were in the last stages of exhaustion, and now the enemy was closing in against the wire on every side. Our guns were now useless, though they kept up a steady barrage against the railway. It was our mortars more than anything else that kept the enemy back. All night they fired until their barrels steamed, pouring a continuous stream of bombs into the enemy as he formed up. A ring on the phone and six bombs would go on to the target in as many seconds. The Japs loathed those mortars and suffered heavily from them.

One day two light planes ran into anti-aircraft fire. It was big stuff, and it became increasingly obvious to us that the enemy was coming up in great strength. The troops that hurled them-selves against the wire were now showing greater skill and were fresh men. The attacks were not as reckless as before; they were calculated and launched by troops who knew what they were about. Then the attack came which we had expected and feared, the attack from the valley across the airstrip. It was quite indefensible and we withdrew to the wire. The Japs advanced across the strip in close order and the Bofors guns had a field day. But they came on and overran the guns which were outside the perimeter, the crews getting away just in time. We were now without an airstrip, and this meant that if anyone was wounded his future was a fearful problem. That was our greatest blow, the nightmare that had always hovered in the backs of our minds and was now a reality.

The final and crowning disaster was the weather. All our sup-ply drops were carried out by night because of the proximity of the enemy, but one night no planes arrived, no food or ammuni-tion. The next night was the same, and the next. What we had dreaded had come true. The rains had beaten us, and maybe we would have to starve. But all day long the mortars continued to fire until the stock of bombs diminished to a bare minimum. And now the enemy was attacking by day, bombarding, probing and wearing us out twenty-four hours a day. Jack Masters reported the desperate supply situation and Base replied that they would carry out a daylight drop on the following morning. That morning no planes arrived but at about three in the afternoon we saw them. An escort of American Lightnings circled overhead. Then the Dakotas arrived and we were treated to as daring a display of flying as I have ever seen. The dropping zone had now shrunk to a very small area, which made a difficult target for the Dakotas. They started their run-in from the west, coming in off the hills down to about fifty feet. The Japs opened up with everything they had: small arms, anti-aircraft cannon and heavy stuff. The planes were a sitting target while they steadied for the drop and below we watched them anxiously. Some kept above the flak and we cursed them, but others came so low that we could feel the swish of their slipstream in the tree-tops. One pilot called over the wireless, 'I'm sorry if my dropping is a bit inaccurate, but my rudder controls have been shot away.' Another reported a burst petrol tank and Chesty directed them to Myitkyina, whose airfield had just been captured. But for all their reckless flying the parachutes were not falling within the perimeter. As each stick was released we watched the chutes drifting slowly but surely into the enemy's lines. Those that landed within the perimeter we cheered and collected greedily. The men were so delirious with joy at the sight of these planes that they did not realise what a failure it had been. They counted not the chutes which eluded our grasp but those that smashed through the trees around them, and they saw food and ammunition.

The supplies were gathered in and we started to count. Rations on a scale of one meal per man and ammunition to last another twenty-four hours. When they gave out there was no hope of getting any more. That day's supply drop had failed and further attempts would have no greater chance of success. Our casualties were mounting steadily and we had nowhere to take them. Where was 14 Brigade? Still struggling through appalling country to the south. Our feelings on the subject of this brigade became more and more outspoken. The fault was not the brigade's but the planners', who had allowed the block to be established without working out time and space. We heard news of the 6th Nigerian Regiment at the top of the pass from the Indawgyi Lake and they were approaching down the west side of the mountain. We hoped that somehow they would bring help in time, but they still had some rough country to go through before they reached us.

The most serious question of all was how we were to get out, as it became increasingly obvious that we must either get out or perish. The enemy were attacking on every side and would not be so negligent as to leave us a way of escape. Mokso Sakan, our haven of rest, lay over 3,000 feet of soaking jungle, and if the Japs should allow us to get out they would follow us up and clean us up as they wanted.

Jack Masters sent off messages explaining the desperateness of our situation and that night, the night of 24 May, the end came. Fighting had intensified for the last few days, but now it reached a climax of fury. Lieutenant Leck of the Cameronians gasped over the phone, 'Most of my men are wounded, I am wounded. And if I don't get help I've had it!' All round the perimeter the Jap pressure was mounting until our exhausted men could hardly hold them back.

I was woken early next morning by The Baron. He handed me a message and told me to encipher it personally. It read, 'Further retention of this block entails loss of brigade. Commander asks permission to withdraw.' No commander writes these words willingly. It must have cost Jack a lot. I sat down to encipher the message in the dawn. There was a mist hanging round the ridge and it was drizzling. The message was completed and I was about to hand it in to the Signal Office when an officer came rushing up the slope, shouting 'Stand to.' Brigade headquarters never stood to except in cases of grave emergency. We assembled at the top of the ridge. The enemy had crept up in the mist, penetrated our lines and captured a commanding feature, Pimple. Either they or we must be ejected. On the slope below there was confused fighting and little figures rushing about the undergrowth. It was impossible to tell if they were friend or foe. I took a party of signallers down to a position on the eastern slope. Grenades came over occasionally, exploding harmlessly on either side of us. A section of the King's Own who had lost themselves took up position to my right on a very exposed slope. A few minutes later a discharger shell landed among them, mortally wounding two of them, a fragment landing at my feet.

Meanwhile, an attempt was made to recapture Pimple from the Japs. Sergeant Donald of the Cameronians took a platoon and charged the slope. It was a magnificent effort. Sergeant Donald was wounded but carried on and the Japs were swept off the top. Sergeant Donald reported back to our commander trembling all over – 'I'm not a wee bit afraid, sir, I'm just shivering with excitement.' That effort earned him the DCM. But it was impossible to hold the position in the face of withering Jap fire and the gallant platoon was forced to withdraw.

Having failed to eject the Japs, without food and with sufficient ammunition only for another twelve hours' fighting and with no prospect of getting any more, with a large number of casualties and with no means of evacuating them, and with utterly exhausted troops, Jack Masters gave the order to withdraw.

CHAPTER ELEVEN

RETREAT

It was 25 May. I cannot remember a rougher day and I cannot say all that happened on it.

I received the order to withdraw from our engineer officer, Geoffrey Birt, who was in his trench and told me not to be such a bloody fool and get off the ridge. A platoon of Gurkhas came up the steep slope in front of me and for a moment I thought they were Japs, such was the confusion of the moment. The Subadar pleaded with me to spare him and I let him pass. Below, vague figures were running through the undergrowth and the morning mist was clearing away gradually. A sergeant-major passed me on his way back to report to headquarters. He said, 'Shell happy, that's what I am' and went on up the hill. Two mortally wounded men were being hauled away, screaming terribly. I wondered how they would end. There were no aeroplanes waiting for them and all around was the enemy. I got rid of my cipher books, burying them as deeply as I could. If I were taken with them on me I could expect especially harsh treatment and I would endanger the security of the whole force. We were now really out of touch.

Headquarters assembled on the west side of the main ridge on a little track that led down to the stream and so to the hills behind. How we were going to get out I did not know, but I followed, wondering. The track was completely blocked, orders shouted and confusion. Stretchers were brought up from the forward positions and lowered gently onto the muddy path. Their bandages were so red. A mortar bomb had landed by the track a short time before and my chief fear was that another one would follow, tearing the column into a red gash in the mud. On the left on the track lay some limbs. I turned round to a sergeant and for some reason smiled. He went very pale. The column started to move along the track and the stretcher-bearers slipped in the mud as we went down the hill. Down to the stream which gave us our water and where the heaviest fighting had taken place in the early days of the block. There was barbed wire across the stream and foxholes filled with empty grenade boxes. But there was no enemy. Why I could not understand.

There came a parting of the tracks, one leading through some tall grass to the left of a cluster of *bashas*, the other going across the paddy to the right of the *bashas*. Not knowing where I was going I turned left. This was the most fortunate decision of my life. Few of those who turned right survived that day. Coming out of the *nullah* bed we met the enemy, met them helpless and exhausted. The Japs had seen our move and were firing mortars and machine-guns from our right. In the shrubs above us was the continuous whine of bullets; then into a short stretch of open country by the *bashas*. Scotty was sitting there as if resting from the ardours of a country stroll, and was watching us go by. Another bomb burst just in front and we dropped. A man in front was hit in the thigh and ran down the path shouting for help. I passed him and felt like a murderer. Why not stop and help him? There were doctors for this job and the column must not be held up. We were going somewhere; we did not know where, but we must get out of this murderous fire, out of the trap in which we had placed ourselves. I prayed with unashamed helplessness and as I did so a stretcher exploded nearby, the wounded man and the stretcher-bearer disappearing into the air. The courage of the stretcher-bearers was magnificent to behold. They could not run across a nasty gap or drop suddenly to the ground. Some of them broke down and refused to carry their stretchers a step further, and I could not blame them. What chance had the badly wounded of surviving the 3,000-foot climb over the pass to safety? Others took up the stretchers and staggered on. As I watched I wondered if we officers had the right to command these men to carry stretchers unless we ourselves shared their danger.

We passed the row of *bashas* and to the right was the stretch of paddy along which lay the alternative route. It was a shambles. Men lay there helpless, crouching behind *bunds*, the dividing ridges in the paddy, while across from the right came the continuous fire of the enemy. One man had been wounded in the leg and was dragging himself across the paddy towards the path along which we were moving. On looking back at this moment afterwards I reflected how gallant it would have been to have rescued him. At the time I was conscious only of men pressing me from behind and the need to keep going.

And so we kept going. From the paddy the track went up a slope so steep that we had to crouch on our hands and knees. The peculiarly oppressive heat of that day, combined with the accumulated weariness of weeks of fighting, reduced us almost to helplessness, and that short slope cost us a lot. A horse was shot halfway up and rearing backwards plunged to the bottom. There was a check in the column and a growl rose up, 'Get a move on.' I said to the man beside me, 'They are just as keen to move on as we are,' and I looked back at the scene of suffering on the paddy. Finally, at the top of the slope the path levelled off into the jungle and there was silence. The noise of war floated away and we were at peace. We had escaped the inferno and it was now just a terrible dream.

Why did the Japs let us out? The question has taken up many of the half-conscious moments of my life since then, when in the stupor of an evening fireside or the quaint borderland of sleep I consider again the events of that day. By all the rules of war we were doomed, surrounded by an enemy 2,000 strong, who were fresh and determined. For two weeks we had beaten them off and could fight no more, defeated by our own system of war. When our fighters and bombers failed to turn up the enemy emerged and was free to roam at large. When the weather broke and the supply planes could only come by day, our days were numbered. Of all this the Japs must have been aware. We were faced with the alternatives, either to break out into the valley or escape into the hills and the peaceful seclusion of the Indawgyi Lake. To attempt the first would have been suicidal and the second could easily be countered. There was one main path out to the hills, which we took, a brigade in single file, and the enemy allowed us to escape along that track, albeit at a cost. The Cameronians fought a heroic rearguard action in the block along with the King's Liverpool, but their efforts could not of themselves have saved us.

Perhaps it was a miracle; these things do happen and it would be rash to assume that the hand of God was not with us that day. Perhaps the Japs committed a fearful tactical blunder somewhere along the line. Perhaps they were not as fresh as we imagined but were content to lick their wounds; they had just had enough. Perhaps, as we discovered earlier, they just did not like the jungle and preferred to keep down by the valley. It can hardly have been pity that made them let us go. But out we went, very tired but astonished.

Having escaped from the trap, the next task was to find our way through a maze of tracks down to our rendezvous on the Namkwin Chaung. Several lost their way and were not seen again, including a corporal of mine attached to the Cameronians who had become separated. I met Michael Bates of the Gurkhas in a thick belt of scrub, which seemed to be leading us nowhere. The entire brigade was at our heels, so that we had to decide quickly. After a wearing trudge across some paddy fields, this time far from the scene of fighting, we reached a broad *nullah* bed. Men were scattered along it, some resting for a further effort, others trudging slowly through the pebbly sand. Above there came the sound of planes and a Dakota appeared over the jungle followed by several others. These planes had been sent to drop more supplies on the block. Base had no knowledge of the events of the last twenty-four hours, having been out of communication, and could only assume that, though our position was grave, it was not hopeless. As a matter of fact when we moved off so hurriedly a message was on its way from the General giving us permission to withdraw. We produced our 'panic maps' (silk emergency maps of a bright orange colour) and started waving them. The first few planes did not see us and we watched the parachutes floating into the hands of the Japs. But one sharp-eyed pilot noticed the streaks of orange in the *nullah* and emptied his load beside us. We seized the packages: shells and mortar bombs, picks and shovels! There were a few containers of rations and we divided them up among ourselves, thankful for this little mercy but still very short of food.

I met my corporal, Jock Yuille, and asked him for news of the other men who had been split up. He was looking very white and I guessed that the news was bad. Three of them, he said, had started to cross the paddy (they had taken the 'death route') and only he had survived. The two sergeants with him had both been killed and his efforts to save Sergeant S, one of my finest men, had been of no avail.

The first night bivouac was a short distance off the *chaung*. Pain was there and exhaustion. Doc Whyte, whose efforts on that day were pure cold courage, assembled the wounded in a little clearing and from the poverty of his resources sought to allay the pain. The morphia was holding out, and the sulphonamide which saved so many. Darkness fell in groans, and the rain started. I lay down feeling almost ashamed to be whole and attempted to build a shelter. It was a failure and we lay in misery in a night of drenching rain. Rations were almost non-existent and a collection was taken to provide for the wounded. Meals had now to be reckoned, not in cartons, but in single biscuits and half tins.

Early next morning an officer was sent on ahead to our camp by the lake to inform the Gurkhas there of what had happened and to arrange for food supplies to be brought up to the top of the pass, also medical supplies and stretcher-bearers. The march was resumed of the first leg of the long ascent. We were a pathetic army. Many men had neither arms nor equipment, so narrow had been their escape; others for slightly less plausible reasons. One man had nothing but a Jap sword with which he helped himself up the slope. We could not march as we had done before and sat down at frequent intervals, hoping that when we next rose to our feet we would rise to meet the summit. But it was an idle hope. Three thousand feet could not be climbed by fervent thoughts, and we became reconciled to an endless ascent. The wounded who had escaped were with us, about two hundred of them. Some walked who should never have left a stretcher, bandaged and with expressions of terrible resignation on their faces. One RAF sergeant, I remember, who had been badly wounded in the head, tottered up the path with eyes that pierced you through with their pain. This man died walking halfway to deliverance on that rain-drenched mountainside. Another was riding on a horse, unable to sit up and sprawled across the horse's neck, jerking with each jerk of the horse, like a puppet with broken strings. Once his horse lost its footing on the slippery mud and fell down carrying the wounded man with it. He was set in the saddle again, too far gone to have suffered from the fall, and the horse continued on its way.

The smell of suffering is dreadful. The days that followed were permeated by it, in front of you, behind you, nudging you as it passed by. The wounded could not be segregated and dressed; they were with you all the time. And with the smell came the mud. In fact the two were inseparable, mingling in a devil's palette of red and brown.

The climb continued next day, slower than before, and the rain increased. Then just before reaching the night harbour, we saw steps formed with logs and cut out of the steep hillside. The West Africans were at work on the steps, huge black men on whom the mud and rain seemed to have made little impression. For us it was a moment of immense relief. We had been cut off and had felt that we were alone in the midst of the enemy. This was our first link with safety; somebody was helping us out of the mess and we could again see people from that outer world of which we had begun to despair. We ran forward to greet them and they must have seen some of the huge relief on our faces. They said they had had some frightful marching over the hills, often without food, and had been compelled to build steps down the mountainside in order to advance further. They themselves were short of rations and could not spare us any, but we thanked them for their staircase and moved into harbour, which was another patch of drenched jungle.

The state of the rations that night was worse than ever. We scraped round once more to provide for the wounded and remembering the previous night built ourselves substantial shelters, even contriving to keep dry. I emptied a packet of soup powder into a mess tin. Next to me was the commanding officer of the King's Own, Colonel Thompson, who had been wounded in a final desperate attack in the block. It was a nasty shoulder wound, but he had managed to walk all the way. I asked him how he felt. 'Pretty rotten,' he said, and he looked awful. The wounded were laid gently onto bamboo beds. Doc Whyte went round constantly inspecting dressings, but there was little he could do, as he had few medical supplies and he was confined to seeing that the men were comfortable.

Next day, the third since leaving Blackpool, we reached the top of the pass and met the other West African column. There, civilisation in the shape of half a dozen *bashas* which provided excellent accommodation for the wounded. There was no food yet, but the Gurkhas were sending some up that day from the lake. We sat down and lit a huge fire which seemed to me to have the accumulated warmth of all the fires that had ever been. Our drenched clothes hung precariously above the flames and we dozed off. The stretcher-bearers were still a long way down the mountainside on what was perhaps the most arduous stretcher carry ever made in the British Army.

That evening Mike McGillicuddy arrived from the lake with rations, dozens of mules loaded to capacity. We fell on him. The boxes were distributed carefully and anxiously; we had learnt what a little way these rations went when there were many mouths to feed. After allotting an ample supply for the wounded we were given two meals each, which was more than we had seen for many days. This was an excuse for a celebration, and carefully selecting our dishes we sat by the fire munching and chattering. This was luxury and security. Our trial was almost over and the way now lay downhill.

Why did the Japs not attempt to follow us up? Having let us escape they might yet have caught us on the long trail up the mountain. We were entirely defenceless having so many wounded to attend to that we had few men to fight, and those who were not on the stretchers were in no mood for anything except the steady plod to freedom. The enemy, if he had wished and so decided, could have wiped the brigade off the map. We heard later from escaped prisoners that the Japs had stopped directly they reached the block, contenting themselves with examining the booty and not even bothering to carry it off. A Jap diary captured later said we had repelled their attempts to follow us up. But we did not see them make any attempts. It is a mystery. Perhaps they had no stomach for any further fight.

We took our ease next day on the top of the pass, concerned chiefly with improving the lot of the wounded, who were now in *bashas* and feeding on local produce. A supply drop for the West Africans took place, but there was very little to go round and we chose our meals with increasing care, relying more and more heavily on tea and soup. Frankie Baines appeared with a platoon of Gurkhas and heartened us with his ceaseless flow of good wishes, feeling, I think, a little ashamed at not having been with us. A message was sent to Base over the West Africans' wireless informing them of our position. They had heard nothing from us for three days and an attempt to send a cryptic message 'Bailing out' was frustrated by an over-zealous signalman who started to dismantle the aerial prior to moving out of the block when the message was still being sent. So that for three days the General knew nothing except that we were very hard pressed. He must have worried fearfully.

Jack Masters, exhausted but still firmly in control, sent me ahead with a party of signalmen to set up communication at the lakeside for brigade headquarters. It was a very welcome order, but I felt a little uncomfortable going forward with all the sick and wounded still on the hilltop. The path down to the lake had been improved and after the weary slog up to the pass it was like a country walk. The men with me were in very good heart and we soon reached the stream at the foot of the pass, where we stopped to have our midday meal. They wanted to go right through without a stop, but I was getting rather used to the last mile which invariably turned into three, and insisted on a halt. Lines of mules passed us with more rations for the pass and for carrying down the casualties. The Gurkha mule leaders gave me a cheery welcome as we passed. I had a feeling that some of them thought we would never return.

After another hour's marching the camp came into sight. It was our Promised Land; no milk or honey but more than we could express. It was peace and safety after the din of battle and the cry of wounded men. Here you could sleep undisturbed by the crash of shells or the rattle of machine-guns. The camp was by the running stream and round it parachutes were falling. Here was food as well. The lines of chutes came tumbling down onto the *bashas* and dropped softly on the grass beside the stream as we crossed it. It seemed that we had come to the land of plenty, but we were wrong. I went round to the Gurkhas and looked up Frank Turner. Food here was very short, but as he said this his little men came thronging round offering me every kind of luxury. Always improvident, they were only half aware of what they were giving away; it was a sort of thanksgiving for our safe return. They must have gone hungry for several days.

We had returned safely and not without honour, but it had been a desperate failure and near to a complete disaster.

I have often reflected on the burning question Why? I talked to men at Base afterwards and they said that from the beginning there was a feeling that Blackpool was doomed. Fortunately we in the field did not share this opinion, being too busy carrying out our orders to question the soundness of them. But as the end came nearer we did feel a terrible sense of isolation and the thought that there was another brigade a few miles away that was meant to be helping us, a kind of Blücher who never arrived. 14 Brigade could have saved us. The second deciding factor was the weather, which all through the campaign we regarded as a threat hanging over us. Our system of war depended on a steady and continuous air supply which was only just able to maintain our brigade during prolonged engagements. Should bad weather intervene and prevent the planes from reaching us we would at once be placed in an extremely difficult position. It was a danger we all realised but one which did not really come home to us until it actually occurred and we were left foodless. The monsoon, or the preliminaries to it, caught us at the very worst moment when our strength was too far gone to resist this crowning misfortune, and when the tactical situation admitted of only two alternatives – fight in fine weather or retreat in the rain.

Had the new Wingatian idea been disproved? The block, conceived by Wingate and propagated by him so that we accepted it, had failed. But was the idea wrong? It may be not. The position was unsuited to the role and the weather would have made any large-scale operation of that kind hazardous. And so it is just another of Wingate's activities that continues to cause fierce controversy.

The long procession of stretchers and wounded men moved slowly down the path and pausing to look on the scene moved slowly into the camp. For the moment we could try to blot out the past while we bound ourselves up, and pay no heed to the future until we had to.

CHAPTER TWELVE

RECUPERATION

This might well have been the end of the story; we hoped and thought it would be. We were a spent force, not only in the drain on our manpower but also in the accumulated strain of the past months. For three months we had been operating with no more than an occasional day's rest. When the brigade entered Blackpool it was prepared to fight, but the continuous strain of long nights of battle and early morning shells had been more than we had expected. The marching had sapped our initial reserves of strength and the fighting at Blackpool completed the process. The struggle over the pass brought home to us very vividly our physical shortcomings, and to this was added the sudden reaction of a fevered body set at rest.

While we were fighting we could pitch our exertions as high as the emergency demanded, but when the emergency ceased the power to exert ourselves was no longer present and instead it failed to provide even for a state of rest. It is peculiar to find weakness in rest, to discover strength ebbing out in the quiet of a camp; it is also disconcerting. At Mokso Sakan we were for the first time able to assess our weakness and to admit what sorry men we were.

It was small wonder that our thoughts were now turned almost exclusively on India. We could not believe in our present state that we should be required for another task, and shutting this from our minds we turned mentally westwards. We had, of course, no proof that this was the end of our exertions, we could only feel in our bodies that it must be and that, unless we cleared out, the rain which had so nearly brought us disaster would wash us in muddy lumps off the mountain slopes into the lake below. The monsoons became a bogey so real that we found it hard to countenance any further operations. If the future did not mean India, it meant abject misery and sickness. It was a kind of blind optimism and it brought many and bitter disappointments, but for the present it buoyed us up. As cipher officer I was in a position to study this 'India outlook'. Every day I would be surrounded by officers of all ranks demanding the texts of the previous twelve hours' messages. I would recite them, omitting those marked 'Officer to decipher' and I would watch their faces as they listened for the magic order to march out. After each recital they would walk away with bitter words on their lips and sad thoughts. It was a daily ritual and though not a happy one it gave me a unique chance to study the breakdown of men.

From now on life became a tale of discomfort and disease, of hardships borne often not to further a military operation but merely to survive, in a sea of mud and rain. And behind the physical struggle there was the bigger and more decisive struggle of the mind to see it all clearly. We had passed a crisis of our campaign and henceforth we wandered we knew not where, however clearly we found ourselves on the map. Nothing mattered because nothing had an end to it. And in the acute discomfort of an operation which seemed to have no purpose men's minds failed to keep up the battle. It is true that an army marches on its stomach, but there were days when we had amply filled stomachs yet failed, because there is more to a man than his stomach. To us life meant more than battles, which were merely the more hectic moments of long days and thankful nights. Every minute was life, every step wrenched from the mud, until time became timeless and we were merely living hour by hour, hoping for release but being disappointed daily. Disappointment we at first fought against but later accepted though always it added to our fund of bitterness. We laughed at these things, but our jokes were cynical, critical and abusive. We flung commanders from their gilded chairs and rubbed their noses in the rich mud which oozed at our feet. We felt the better for it. We ceased to care, as we had cared, for our great cause and the glory of our name. We felt we had done enough to earn ourselves glory and anything we accomplished in this foul season was pure surplus. The old enthusiasms that had followed us into Burma had disappeared and in their place there came a sort of resignation, I was going to say dumb, but it was far from being that. When soldiers fail to see the purposes of those who direct their paths, they become surprisingly articulate.

Our first act when arriving at Mokso Sakan was to hold a thanksgiving service for our deliverance. The service was conducted by the padre of the Cameronians, who had performed valiantly at Blackpool. He turned our thoughts not only to ourselves in safety but also to our comrades in death and captivity and to the accompaniment of the thud of supply parachutes we gave thanks for ourselves. We sat down to consider the cost in meticulous detail, sending in casualty returns which ran into several sheets of paper. The enciphering was a very long business, but how short the telegrams that would spread the news around! Stragglers were still coming in and names were thankfully scratched off the lists. Captain Whitehead of the King's Liverpool arrived with the remnants of his troops after a hectic stand, and passing by our congratulations could only mutter, 'But I left them all there.' The men he left were desperately wounded and he had pulled his survivors from the very heart of the enemy.

The sick and the wounded occupied our constant attention; in fact our whole life was built round them. We constructed long lines of *bashas* and waited anxiously for the medical supplies. Doc Whyte worked all through the day, and most of the night still whistling to himself 'Moonlight Becomes You', and still hopelessly out of tune. He seemed to take delight in his complete indifference to his work. He used to go about clad only in the briefest of loincloths and carrying his carbine. I half expected him to take to the trees, until I saw him handle his patients and then realised where he belonged. His patients were not the only people he had to handle. There were his medical orderlies, who worked continuously and yet had to be coaxed to do more. Doc had an engaging knack of encouraging a man beyond his strength when occasion demanded it. Often towards the end of a tiring day's march that silly little whistle of his would restore to me a sense of values more real than the weariness within me, and I would persuade myself that perhaps I was not quite finished.

The wounded were carefully graded, and the more serious of these were carried down to the airstrip we had built by the lakeside. As each one went our burden felt lighter, but sometimes the stretchers would return and the men would wait another day until the ground was fit to land on. We sent continuous weather reports and evolved a complicated code system to indicate if the strip was 'sticky' or 'very sticky', treacle or just porridge. Then when the planes were about to start off from their base the weather would close in, the rain would fall and the stretchers would return once more to the camp. An irate message next day from Base — 'More frequent weather reports essential.' We became used to differentiating between two-tenths cloud and six-tenths, being almost tempted at times to lure the planes on with hopes of fine weather. It was a very dangerous thought, but with the wounded lying around us delay became unbearable. Every time the party returned from the strip we asked how many had been taken away that day and scratched them off our slowly diminishing list. The stretcher cases were, of course, given first priority, but stretchers are very uneconomical in plane space and to avoid wasting sorties a lot of sitting cases went in with them. We wondered why so few planes arrived each day and sent querulous messages. The answer was that no more were available, having either been written off earlier in the campaign on inadequate strips or being engaged on similar missions with other brigades. We were apt to forget that, though we were in a bad way, we were possibly not the only brigade sustaining casualties. Doc Whyte would announce periodically the passing away of another wounded man, but as the worst cases were taken off the announcements became mercifully infrequent.

The Baron flew off to Base to report on Blackpool. At Jack Masters' dictation he had composed a detailed account of the whole battle, assessing the causes of failure and above all praising the gallantry of the men. We wanted to assure the Commander and the outside world, if such assurance was needed, that the failure was not due to any weakness in the fighting quality of the troops. There was much speculation as to the causes of the debacle back at Force headquarters, but after receiving this report a lot of the ill-considered criticisms and 'I told you so' statements were silenced. The Baron took the place of a sick man, but he went on an urgent mission to reinstate us in the eyes of our critics in more comfortable places.

There followed days of brilliant sunshine and no food. Every day we searched the sky and at night we signalled in desperation, 'Why no sorties today?' The answer was always the same, 'Regret sorties abortive due to weather.' We looked across the placid surface of the lake and up at the blue sky and wondered, our wondering giving rise to some rather bitter comments. We could not know that the mountains between the Assam airbase and Imphal were continuously laden with storms, which if they did not turn back the Dakotas effectively stopped the fighter escorts. We had now changed from night to day dropping and the Dakotas required an escort. Sometimes this escort could not be found from existing resources, at other times it would be turned back over the mountains. Sometimes lone Dakotas fought their way through, but it was a chancy affair and a strain on the pilots that could not be repeated indefinitely. Our ace pilot was Squadron Leader Millington, who could probably do more things with a Dakota than anyone else in the air force. On occasions he battled through alone, but one planeload was of little help to a brigade. The story goes that once, caught up in the briefing of his pilots, he forgot to brief himself and was in the air followed by several other planes when he realised that he did not know where he was going. He was able to find a column and drop.

All this was hidden from us and we could only look up and be disappointed. There was not much else to do. No Japs were around and in any case we were without the means to fight them. We chose our meals with increasing care as the boxes dwindled. The Gurkhas with their usual improvidence ate all their rations directly they received them and for long periods went without. I used to remonstrate with them, but it was their business and they continued their system of feast-and-starve. One day we had no more and nothing remained but to kill some mules. Fortunately, we had plenty to spare, as they had not been at Blackpool and one mule goes a very long way. The carcasses were cooked for hours to soften them and we cut chunks off into our mess tins. The broth derived from the cooking was delicious, at least so it seemed to us, but the meat was very tough. The Gurkhas would not touch it and continued to starve.

We sent a final desperate message to Base on the state of affairs and received a very abrupt reply: 'Quite realise your position but famine not confined to your brigade.' It saved us from self-pity but did not improve our tempers. One day a fleet of Dakotas appeared over the mountains to the west of the lake and we made ready to receive them. The planes passed overhead and on east to 77 Brigade, which was now approaching the town of Mogaung. Somebody, we thought, was getting priority.

At about this time we were told to prepare recommendations for decorations, and we did so. Describing bravery is an odd business, an awkward marriage of truth and art, saying what you believe to be true in as compelling a way as you can. I put one of my corporals in for an MM, but nothing came of it as far as I know. Meanwhile, Jack Masters was writing his own word pictures. Frankie Baines, who seemed to know most of what was going on, let me know who was being put in for what. He even included me, which gave me something to think about. I cannot give details, because some gallant men who read these words might feel disappointment: certainly one Victoria Cross did not find its proper home.

The supply situation improved somewhat and we let the mules live. It was rather tricky to know just what items we should ask for. We were hungry enough, but we were also almost completely devoid of military equipment, all heavy equipment except that belonging to the 4th Gurkhas having been left in the block. Our natural desire was to ask only for food and hang the equipment, but militarily speaking that would not do at all, and we were forced to suffer the mortification of looking on with empty stomachs while sacks of boots fell from the sky. It was decided that we must send out some troops to justify our existence and the Gurkhas, being the fresher troops, were the ones chosen for the task. So we had to clothe them and equip them and ration them for a long period, while we sat in our *bashas* deciding whether to have soup and biscuits or tea and a bar of chocolate for supper.

The American planes came over for the first time; they had dropped previously to other columns but it was our first sight of them. They seemed less sure of flying by night, and some of their night dropping was not too good; but in the daytime they threw their planes about in a very encouraging way and were not afraid to come low. In fact they dropped lower than the RAF, dipping their nose just before releasing the chutes until we thought their propellers would catch in the tree-tops. A supply drop was always judged by the 'chucking out', and the criterion was how many chutes landed in the dropping zones in one run. The first American planes to arrive impressed us considerably in this respect, delivering some very 'tight sticks'. With precious little to do but watch these chutes we became quite adept at instructing these planes just when to drop. The free drops provided us with some excitement and not a little fear. Sacks of boots may not have the same lethal effect as bombs, but when they are released in a row directly above your head the chance of being hit is just about the same. We used to crouch under the eaves of *bashas* or flatten ourselves against tree-trunks. It was fun until we emerged from our shelters and found only boots and socks and webbing.

The Gurkhas were sent off on a patrol to the north end of the lake, the south end being secured by 14 Brigade and a column of West Africans. But we found a liability in the south when the Nigerians sent an SOS, 'No supply drop for eleven days.' This, we had to admit, was a worse case than our own, and we were obliged to try to meet their demands. The situation had eased sufficiently to allow a fairly substantial allotment for them and Frank Turner, who was now looking very ill, set off with a convoy of mules to carry rations to the starving column. We also sent off a very rude message to Base on the subject of supplies and felt satisfied. The Nigerians were saved from a very sticky position.

A message arrived from Base, 'Essential re-equipping is carried out with all possible speed.' Up to now we had merely been concerned with collecting enough equipment to call ourselves soldiers again and were not unduly worried by delays unless they meant short rations. Now we were being told to hurry up, as if there was a matter of urgency at hand. We certainly felt no urgency and wondered what all the hurry was about. It looked unpleasantly like another job just when we had resigned ourselves to an indefinite stay at the lakeside.

We moved a short distance from the village of Mokso for no particular reason except perhaps to get out of the rut of apathy into which the life of the camp and the quiet stream was forcing us. The move, like any move out of a comfortable billet, was not appreciated and involved the setting up of a new hospital. Brigade headquarters decided that it would build the *basha* to end all *bashas* and a section of the Burma Rifles was detailed to raise the edifice. It was to have a firm foundation on the muddy soil and bamboo cunningly arranged to divert the mud and rain, a couch of soft leaves and a roof to withstand the fiercest showers. Mac grumbled that his men might be better employed than building shelters for officers, but from the point of view of morale I doubt if they could have done a more useful job. It was an idle place to meet and gossip and to think longing thoughts of home and comfort. News of the steady evacuation of sick and wounded came up to us and we were pleased. Equipment was dealt out, and we hoped with a most impious hope that the stuff would not come in too quickly and compel us to get on our feet again.

One of the reasons for our move was that the RAF had made an objection. The dropping zone at Mokso was too near the hills for their comfort and when there was a mist against the mountainside the pilots felt very ill at ease. We told them we were unwilling to move, but we had no option. They had our supplies. Earlier in the campaign some columns had sited their dropping zones in the most ridiculous places right into the side of a mountain and the RAF taking a look at the map had laughed and told them to try again.

One day a bright idea occurred to us, and took definite shape. The long stretch of water below us, which was the Indawgyi

Lake, seemed to invite use, and what better than to land a flying boat? The thought first occurred to us when we debouched into the plain in our march from the south before Blackpool. There was now a good reason why we should use it, indeed an urgent necessity; for though the wounded were diminishing fast the number of sick was mounting daily and dangerously. The light planes could not possibly cope with the problem and anyway there was always the possibility that with the start of the monsoon the strip would be put out of action. The first task was to put the matter to those who were in a position to take action. Fortunately, Chesty was by way of being a flying boat expert and sent off a detailed report: depths, mooring facilities, underwater obstructions, suitable embarking sites. I heard later how the message was received at Base. They held their hands up in horror; the scheme was impossible. There were no flying boats, no bases, it was impossible to operate over the mountains. While the fit were sickening and the sick declining, the argument rose in fury. But the tale had one bright feature. One very senior officer on the staff was determined to see the thing through, mindful of our condition; and, I gather, went near to losing his job in his efforts to get us the flying boats. He succeeded.

'Gert' and 'Daisy' became household names to us, which meant health and strength. They were the names of the two flying boats allotted to us to evacuate, taken from the two music-hall performers, Elsie and Doris Waters, who acted out these two characters as cheery, blousy, comic charladies in the war years.* Based on the Brahmaputra, the flying boats used to operate alternately over the high mountain ranges and slip down into the lake. It was a hazardous operation, and we had to send weather reports with increasing frequency. For days clouds would gather over the

---

* By a strange coincidence I was to find myself with these sprightly ladies on my voyage home to England.

mountains and there would be no flying boats. The Japs did not come near and must have suffered some exasperation as they saw the planes take off with their load of men, though perhaps they thought we were evacuating.

Someone had a bright idea that with a few extra sorties the whole brigade could be flown out, and the same old train of thought came back: 'India'. We made calculations as to how many sorties would be required. It was a defeatist form of arithmetic and unrealistic. About forty sick cases were taken off on each sortie, but the sick-rate was also rising alarmingly until we could hardly keep pace.

Frank Turner returned from his errand of mercy to the Nigerians looking like death and we packed him off to India, where he succumbed to a long succession of illnesses. His mule leaders saw him go with a deep regret. They had always maintained that he was the strongest of the sahibs, chiefly I suppose because he so seldom lost his temper. His position was taken by Captain Ainscough of the King's Liverpool. 'Ossie' was a dealer in the Liverpool Corn Exchange and never called a spade anything but a spade. He was invariably cheerful and had none of the finesse that sometimes goes for polish. He was rough and ready but very effective. His Urdu was non-existent and he communicated his wishes to his mule leaders by a sort of sign language aided by personal demonstration. The Gurkhas thought much of him. He was one of our fittest and straightest men.

The rot now set in. With the arrival of the flying boats the sick-rate rose alarmingly. Some of this was plain malingering. Others, who had stiffened their weakening sinews to further resolves, now faced the fact that they were ill and quietly collapsed. Some fit men, seeing no reason or merit in fitness, slipped strangely into illness. One RAF officer became very odd and had to go off. By the lakeside there were big strong men whose minds were not big enough to match their bodies and they said to their bodies, 'Enough'. Little frail men with more reserves were left behind to carry on. Jock Yuille laughed at the men who flew away and said he would never be evacuated before his time. My gloomy sergeant could see that he would soon be sick and was almost making preparations to pack up. Stragglers, who had been eleven days in the jungle, came in from Blackpool, gaunt and wild-eyed. Their reason was partly gone and we sent them straight down to the lake.

We sat and waited in our regal *basha*, compiling the daily casualty returns and comparing the number of sick with the number of sorties available. There was still a deficit. Then 'Daisy' damaged herself on the Brahmaputra and 'Gert' gallantly carried on. Messages from Base were becoming daily more insistent: 'Re-equipment and evacuation must be carried out at all speed.' As both depended on supplies from Base we laughed it off and asked for more sorties. 6 June 1944 and news came over the wireless. Landings on the French coast. It was a strange place to hear the news. We cheered a little and felt that at any rate in one part of the world the war seemed to be going all right. But I am sorry to say that we were jealous. We had wandered into obscure places and had disappeared from the headlines of the world. Now we were completely out, we really were the Forgotten Army. Even the huge lake beside which we camped was unknown to any but ourselves. Frankie Baines let off some seditious verbal squibs. Mac said we had all had it, and that if Wingate had been alive the people of Burma would not have been let down like this. We argued with him in vain that under the circumstances we could do little else than what we were doing.

A rumour was spread about that the Chinese had arrived at Haungpa to the north-west and had constructed a Dakota strip. We were not particularly concerned with who it was that had arrived but the Dakota strip was most important, for Dakotas could fly you to India. A certain amount of measuring went on and it was decided that if we were going out that way there was a lot of marching to be done, but perhaps it was worth it. We believed this rumour because we wished to, and when it proved to be entirely false we were a little sad.

Where were the Chinese anyway? They were attacking Myitkyina after the airstrip had been captured by the Americans, and no doubt that would fall soon. That was target number one. But we were more directly concerned with Mogaung, which lay to the south-west of Myitkyina. The Chinese were advancing down the Hukawng Valley and should, so we thought, have reached the town of Kamaing. But they had not, indeed they were still some distance away. Reclining on our couches of bamboo we criticised them sharply for their inefficiency.

Our hopes were being further dashed by a series of very obscure messages, which appeared to promise release but turned out to mean no such thing. There were tentative allusions in the messages about marching north, and we remembered that to the north lay the regular forces who were advancing down Burma, and freedom. Then one day I deciphered a message which contained the unequivocal words, 'Prepare to march out.' Mac said, 'I know it's only a hoax,' but others were more impressed by it. It was certainly more definite than anything else we had received, and I hastened to take the news to Jack Masters. I caught him coming back from the lake with Scotty and passed on the message. He grinned and Scotty agreed that it was a good show. All seemed set and preparations were made with surprising speed considering the lethargy of yesterday.

CHAPTER THIRTEEN

INTO THE DEPTHS

The message reached us when we were preparing to pack up, and it read something as follows, 'A last task,' that was a dark beginning, '77 Brigade will attack Mogaung from the east, III Brigade from the west.' This was the brief plan and there followed the stirring order of the day which ended, 'You are Chindits. You can take it and make it.'

This was the last and bottom-most pit of disappointment. Mac said, 'I knew it was all a hoax.' Frankie said, 'They can have their glory' and more in a somewhat stronger vein. This meant to us a new beginning with an end so far away that we could not glimpse it. The future no longer had any significance and was merely a succession of discomforts growing daily less tolerable. We could not now look forward to the time of release. There was apparently going to be no release. For all of us there was a sharp jolt which in some cases turned into extreme bitterness. It said that sick men had been dissuaded from going down to the flying boats by the hope that the whole brigade would soon be going out; and when they returned to the column it was to pick up their packs for another job. Those who had just kept up the struggle now gave in and those who had already fallen by the wayside weakened further. There was a story in the 14th Army newspaper that we were 'the toughest of the bunch'. It was ludicrously different from how we felt. It was a very bad moment.

I think from this period dated our unwillingness to trust in anything that our higher command did or said. There seemed to us to have been a breach of trust somewhere in allowing us to continue to this state of physical decline. Our commander, General Lentaigne, was in fact in a fearfully difficult position. He knew our plight and he was anxious that we should not be allowed to endure more. But he was caught in a political maze from which he could find no escape, confronted by General Stilwell, now his superior, whose stock-in-trade was abuse, and Lord Louis Mountbatten, who was walking a politico-military tightrope where no rash moves could be made. We did not know this at the time, though we suspected it. And we never saw our commander. Why didn't he come to see us? Orde Wingate would have done so. Was Joe out of his depth? Had the spring gone right out of his step? So we could only exchange messages. It was a deeply unsatisfactory relationship.

Jack Masters was in a remarkable position. A major, thrust into the command of a brigade well above normal size, he had faced a desperate situation with energy and skill. Now, tired as any, he had to fight not only against the enemy but against the use of his men, who now numbered five and a half battalions, in intolerable situations.

For the odds were stacked against us. The weather was making air supply increasingly unreliable. The area in which we were to operate was quite unsuited to Long Range Penetration forces. We were being subordinated to American interests. And where was 14 Brigade, which was meant to be assisting us? With the best will in the world . . .

A study of the map showed two routes to Mogaung. One was over the pass we had crossed shortly before, then proceeding north up the railway valley. This we dismissed immediately as being too dangerous, as our experience of the railway valley had not been pleasant. The alternative route was north to the head of the lake to the village of Lakhren, then due east over the hills dropping down into the open country to the west of Mogaung. This open country looked very uninviting, and it was decided to take up a position at the village of Padigahtawng which was perched on top of the hills between Lakhren and the railway valley. From there it would be possible to spy out the land and decide on the most favourable approach to Mogaung.

At last we had to move and we did it with great reluctance, unused by now to the heavy weight of the pack with five days' rations stored away. Brigade headquarters hauled itself to its feet: Briggo and his wireless operators, those who were still on their feet; Mac, ready to plod on indefinitely with his sturdy hillmen; Ossie, fresh, with his Gurkha muleteers and their beloved animals; and myself, loaded with the books of my trade, and the ever-faithful Jock Yuille. We seemed to be starting all over again, learning the hard corners and the ill-fitting straps and the wet socks which were to become the bane of our lives. The way to Lakhren lay along the side of the lake in country which is usually marked 'liable to inundation'. It was not quite a marsh, but a succession of deep pools. The mud was a revelation to us. It was not merely lying in cakes on the path, as it was on the pass. It was the ground itself, bottomless, without a beginning or an end, rich, glutinous, all pervading, a brown stench that clutched at you and drew you down. The first evening saw us in a small patch of jungle being slowly bitten to pieces by mosquitoes. The next day we faced our biggest struggle.

We had not only ourselves to think of, but also our mules, who disliked the mud as much as we did and in addition were rendered quite helpless by it. While we swore and wrenched ourselves free the animals just stood there silent, and sank in until they floundered on their sides. Then a situation arose. First the mule had so to be manoeuvred that both the loads could be unhitched. These loads had to be carried across to firm ground, which was often hard to find. The mules had to be persuaded to rise and then led carefully across to their loads. This procedure was necessary every 400 yards or so, so that the rate of march slowed to a crawl and we at the back were content to see the column disappearing far ahead while we retrieved the loads. The fact that the Japs might try to ambush us did not occur to us, and we were concerned only with getting ourselves and our animals from A to B. A became increasingly near to B until a day's march consisted of only a few miles. There was no urgency about our marching, only a desire to see night harbour and get to a place where we could scrape the mud off our bodies and equipment and out of our eyes and mouths. Our webbing turned a rich brown and smelt; puttees stuck together and unwound in sticky clods. Only the boots seemed impervious to this brown onslaught, their part being to divert it onto all the other parts of our clothing. Mud became our life. We breathed it and on occasions spat it out, slept with the rich odour in our nostrils and on waking smelt it afresh in the warm mist of the early morning.

The march to Lakhren was only a short one, but it took us three days, in which we waded all day. The path was narrow and away from it there was nothing but bog and jungle so that we had no option but to keep to the track. At one point we were wading up to our knees in the brown liquid round narrow corners into the backs of struggling mules. Here one of my cipher books dropped out of my haversack in the mud and I had to bend slowly down balanced precariously under five days' rations until I could reach the book which was beginning to sink. There were loud oaths from the back, but we were all rather pleased to have a halt. The march was not completely awful. Although the way was very hard, we never troubled about hurrying and at night would light great fires in the dripping jungle. The mud would dry and we would knock it off in flakes onto the ground. We no longer took any precautions against the Japs beyond the flimsiest protective screen, and the Japs seem to have adopted the same policy, for we never clashed unless we went out to meet them. It was ridiculous, I suppose, as we were many miles behind the enemy lines, but we accepted it and had long ceased to fear about our position.

Some of those who had returned from the lakeside to the column discovered their mistake and fell out, until there was a line of men scattered along the side of the track. They were very weak and they staggered into night harbour very late.

On the third day we reached Lakhren, a deserted village set in the low-drainage area to the north-east of the lake. There was a river and a large number of involuntary streams; water from being a precious possession had become a pestilential surfeit. To the east the hills rose sharply to the village of Padigahtawng and fell again into the flat country west of Mogaung. We encamped in the scattered jungle which thrust from the hills into the flat country towards the lake. There were trees and wet jungle paths and open heath and mosquitoes. It was uninspiring country away from the enchantment of the lake and the broad vistas of the hilltops. It was also a place of insects, which filled the night with innumerable noises and filled themselves with our blood. Mosquitoes seemed to thrive in the low-lying swamps and they made much of us.

News arrived from 77 Brigade, who were now closing in on Mogaung and fighting a series of fierce engagements at the approaches to the town. Jack Masters sent off a reply to the brigade stating rather rashly that we were coming to their aid. Having sent this message, we proceeded to sit down at Lakhren and go through another of our periodical famines. Life became very easy again, but a bit sparse. Planes failed to arrive and the usual exchange of heated messages took place, with the usual result. But now we accepted short rations without too much fuss.

We did not bother too much about priorities; the first unit to be rationed would be the first unit to start the march up the mountain and we did not compete strenuously for this privilege. Days passed spent in idle speculation; we had accustomed ourselves to be content in idleness. Our attitude, had it been fully realised (and I think it was suspected), would have caused much exasperation in India. We were setting the pace and there was a general agreement that the pace would be a slow one.

The procession of sick to the lakeside continued. My gloomy sergeant finally gave up, a decision I had expected some time before. To assist in the evacuation and to provide a more convenient place of departure we constructed another strip. We had grave doubts as to how long it would last in the increasing rain, and our doubts were to some extent justified. The strip became a bog, but surprisingly a bog in which planes landed. They came down in a shower of mud and stones, careful not to stop too long in one place for fear of sinking in. It was a remarkable achievement and confirmed our faith in the American sergeant pilots.

It was as well that the strip was built, for a message arrived informing us that there would be no more flying boat sorties; 'Gert' was being taken away for another job. We could not understand why but accepted the fact and were thankful for the fine job she had done in evacuating our sick. Base 'regretted' and so did we. So the men waiting patiently by the lakeside came tramping back, disconsolate though a little better for their stay by the lake. The casualty staging post by the lake was in fact something of a health resort and many men were persuaded that they were fit enough to return. Some did so and in the heat of the march discovered their mistake. Across the other side of the lake a battalion commander who was assisting in the evacuation sent us an angry message, 'Do not send out fit men.' The battalion was not in our brigade and sending such a message to our brigadier seemed to us to be pure insolence. And it was a judgement on our own troops that we could not stomach. Doc Whyte, who knew what a deceptive condition the men acquired by the lakeside, was furious. The general opinion was that we should send a scorching reply, but Jack Masters with great restraint kept silent.

Once again our thoughts turned towards the Chinese and we grew more hopeful. They had captured Kamaing, the last town before Mogaung. This had a special significance for us, as it meant that we could at last get in touch with the outside world and end our isolation. The link was the Indaw River, which flowed south into the Indawgyi Lake, a somewhat turbulent stream at this time of the year but apparently unguarded by the Japs. Should we be ordered to march out there was a way open. Previously our hopes of India were always tempered by an uncertainty as to the means of getting there. Dakota strips seemed to be out of the question and with flying boats no longer available the way seemed barred. Now with the opening of a direct land route north-east to the regular forces our hopes became more substantial. For the present we were committed to an operation, but there was always a slight chance that this might be called off and an order come through to march to Kamaing.

The opening of the Indaw River brought one immediate advantage. With our thoughts constantly on the sick we were not slow to realise that here was another means of evacuating them. Boats took many more passengers than light planes and were far less dependent on the weather. There ensued a long interchange of messages about boats. Would we specify facilities available, further boats required, distances involved and any special equipment we might want. By good fortune there was at Kamaing a fleet of country boats capable of making the journey to the lake, and we did not require much in the way of supply drops. The fleet set off from Kamaing and we followed its progress with great interest, hoping for much. We were a bit disappointed, both by the boats themselves and the time taken for them to arrive, but we could only be thankful and long lines of sick men tramped west to the river. My sergeant, who was still waiting for a plane, went with them, grumbling incessantly and looking on life with such a jaundiced eye that even his fellow sick were compelled to ask him to desist.

One day we had to move, having no further excuse for delay, and one by one the battalions started the long trudge up the hill. First the Gurkhas, who were still reasonably fit, then the British troops, who were rapidly approaching exhaustion. The climb was steep and, although it left the bogged ground of the valley and the swarm of mosquitoes, it was exceedingly unpleasant. There was no attempt to hurry; for many people it was a struggle to keep going. The first night was spent halfway up the hill just off the track and as we sat down to prepare our evening meal we saw sick men returning to Lakhren, men who had misjudged their strength and attempted the climb. There were blazing fires late into the night and a comfortably late start in the morning. We reached the crest of the hill in the early afternoon. We were pleasantly surprised to see a dropping zone already marked out and supplies being collected in. Perhaps the only thing we did really well at this stage of the campaign was to arrange supply drops, knowing that on this depended our chances of keeping ourselves going. We insisted on supplementary rations to augment the inevitable K and usually got them, though more as a favour than a set practice.

In Padigahtawng we found at last some really good shelter and were able to gain immunity from the perpetual rain. I say 'we', but I mean headquarters, for the luxury of the village was denied to the troops, who most needed it. The *bashas* were large and commodious, though a bit verminous. The muddy track ran past the village down to the village of Mla in the valley, branches going off north and south along the ridge of the hills. All the tracks were a struggle, especially those running along the hills, which switchbacked madly over the crests and saddles of the range. Along the lower slopes of the mountains lay villages with strange names, so strange that for convenience of enciphering we had to devise a code. Few people lived in them, and no wonder, for they were miserable collections of *bashas* torn by the wind and rain into a state of decrepitude. On the hills themselves other and even less desirable dwelling places were found, usually deserted. The inhabitants fought their living from small patches of open paddy which they had torn from the jungle slopes, providing for us excellent dropping zones. We caught our first glimpse of the railway valley since our disastrous essay near Pinbaw and were able to look on it without fear. Mogaung was out of sight and there 77 Brigade was engaged in furious fighting. The mountain air was clearer than the air of the lake basin and the mosquitoes were below us.

The task set for us was to advance on Mogaung from the west in conjunction with 77 Brigade's drive from the south-east. That was the plan and it did not take us long to see that, as far as we were concerned, it was out. Between the hills and the town of Mogaung lay ten miles of open country. To a regular force this would have been a fairly easy proposition, but for us it was impossible. Our only artillery pieces were mortars which could fire a maximum of 3,000 yards, and the only other weapons of offence were our Vickers machine-guns. To expose ourselves on that stretch of flat country would have been to invite annihilation. We could not dig in and wait for our supplies to come up. Our supplies came from the air and in the open country they might well have been prevented from dropping by enemy action. There was no certainty, but in our game risks could not be taken with the supply system especially at this stage in the campaign. Our ability to operate depended on the ability of the planes to reach us and drop without interference.

Besides, we were being ordered into the open when the success of our warfare depended on our ability to conceal ourselves. Though we were physically uncomfortable in the jungle mentally we were at ease, for we knew that the enemy disliked the jungle-covered hills, preferring the clear decision of the valley. At least that was his attitude towards us, whom he had come to regard as a persistent bogey which should not be disturbed unless he threatened. He knew our weaknesses – Blackpool must have confirmed his experience of them – but he also knew our strength, our ability to roam at large behind his back and hit where we fancied. Admittedly at the moment our fancies were strictly limited, but we existed as a constant threat to his security of mind and position. Bearing this in mind the task now assigned to us appeared to be a gigantic folly.

Consideration of our new task brought to light one very obvious and disagreeable fact. Mogaung was one of the two objectives of Stilwell's Chinese troops before the onset of the rains. When the rains started we realised at once that the schedule was right out and we had to face a continuation of the campaign in the monsoons. Now we were going one step further and were being assigned the job that the Chinese had as yet failed to carry out, the capture of Mogaung. We found it hard to accept our redeployment.

To spy out the very uninviting land to the east Jack Masters sent out battalions to establish firm bases on the lower slopes of the hills and to push out patrols. The column of the 3/4 Gurkhas went off to the north-east, the King's Liverpool east, while the 3/9 Gurkhas remained in the area of Padigahtawng to defend the neighbouring peaks and passes over which the Japs in their retreat might wish to retire. First news reached us from the 3/4 Gurkhas, who had attacked a well-defended village in the dusk and had been compelled to hold off further attacks until the following day. Next day they attacked continuously until they finally captured the village. An SOS came in for more mortar bombs and small arms ammunition. Problem number one had already cropped up, namely, that a mobile column could not carry ammunition for more than a few hours' fighting. The answer to this is either to sit down in a block with continuous air supply or to desist from making any but lightning attacks. We sent down the required ammunition by mule, but it was too late and the Gurkhas were forced to withdraw from the village. The beginning of our grand offensive was not a happy one.

Reports came in one by one and each told the same story. There were Japs everywhere, not in large quantities but in small groups on the lower slopes. Patrols were continually bumping into them and, unable to inflict casualties on a very elusive enemy, proceeded until they met the next group of Japs. This kind of warfare is not pleasant, and I remember the feeling of strain and frustration in the officer who reported periodically to headquarters, 'The little —— are everywhere. You can't go a yard without meeting them.' Clashes were occurring almost hourly, indecisive and unsatisfactory. The sad news came back to us that Mike McGillicuddy had been killed; and on that windswept mountaintop we mourned a gay and gallant person. Jack Masters gave me a message to encipher telling of this news and drafting a personal message for Mike's mother. It was after this that we heard that Mike had been awarded the MC for his gallantry near Pinlebu. The patrols that emerged into the open country sent back reports that confirmed our fears. It was impossible to advance beyond the covering of the jungle without being seen and engaged. The paddy fields were flooded and the only routes lay along the *bunds*, providing an easy target for the enemy. If we could not advance a mile without being pinned down, what hope was there of covering the ten miles to Mogaung? Jack Masters signalled to Base to this effect and we confined our operations to continuous patrolling on the lower slopes of the hills. It must have been a blow to 77 Brigade, who were by now in difficulties, and to our General it must have been a bad setback to his plans. But we alone could judge the possible and insisted on our claim to be the final arbiters.

One day we met the Chinese. After capturing Kamaing they had advanced down the Indaw River to Lakhren. Our first meeting was involuntary and unfortunate. One day a message arrived from a battalion of 14 Brigade, 'Recce platoon engaged Japs for two hours in running battle.' Very satisfactory; but this message was shortly afterwards amended, 'For Japs read Chinese.' A major problem arose as to how to recognise each other, as the Chinese soldier in battle is not very careful to distinguish who is who. A system was evolved in which we were to wave our orange 'panic' maps on meeting the Chinese. A Gurkha and a Chinese patrol met one day and the leading Gurkha in accordance with instructions waved his map. He was greeted with a hail of fire and a lively little battle ensued. It was all very difficult. We signalled to Tactical HQ, a joint Chinese-American-British set-up in the Hukawng Valley, and asked for a wider circulation of the recognition system. For a time the situation was a little delicate but the Chinese soon came to realise what an extraordinary assortment of allies they had, British, Gurkha and West African. A Chinese regimental commander came to our HQ at Padigahtawng and exchanged views. He was a cheery fellow who spoke very good English. His men, like all the Chinese under Stilwell, were immaculately equipped by the Americans. We were impressed particularly by the care they took of their arms. Their weapons, even in the monsoon jungle, were spotlessly clean and always covered in a thin layer of oil. Modern weapons of war were a rarity to them and they treasured them. The commander said he had been given orders to take Mandalay by the end of the rains. We thought this was a very laudable ambition but wondered exactly who had given him these orders. It was a fantastic task, and maybe the Chinese commander was only trying to cheer us up. The Chinese seemed unquenchably cheerful and happy-go-lucky, an ideal attitude for this depressing sort of warfare.

The first task the Chinese had in conjunction with us was a welcome, if arduous, one. It was to hunt down the starving Japs still wandering about the north end of the lake valley. Earlier on our troops had patrolled the area and the operations were now enlarged in scope to include a Chinese battalion. Our side was taken care of by a battalion of 14 Brigade and between them there was a merry chase. The Japs were in a wretched condition on the verge of starvation and with nowhere to go. Periodical reports reached us of captures and killings. It was heartening to learn that physically the enemy was in an even worse condition than ourselves. But it is likely that they faced their state with quiet fatalism and with no bitterness. It must be good not to think too much.

For headquarters life became tolerable, and in the shelter of the *bashas* perched on the mountaintop we found rest and relief. In the big central *basha* Jack Masters held court, receiving messages from battalions and delivering orders in his concise, effective tone of voice. The messenger, usually an officer, would be asked to stay and share the luxuries of our rations. These were strictly limited, but tea can go a long way. After the business of the day, which was confined to no particular hours, the maps would be pushed aside, a fire lit on the floor and we would talk. Mostly our talk would turn to the future, which was not so uncertain that we could not hope sometime for a return to India. Bridging the discomforts of today and the trials of tomorrow we would reach into that far-off age when we would again be in civilisation. Pleasure came from imaginary delights, the vision of a mighty feast or the soft surrender of a bed; water which poured hot at your command and made your body glow. In the isolation of the mountaintop our imaginations took wings. There were two schools of thought, the gourmands and the gourmets. Some conjured mountains of food, others the delicate taste of exquisite cooking. I remember saying to Frankie Baines, 'You must spend your leave with my people in Quetta. We have long baths and hot water taps.'

We turned to the question of how we would spend our leave. Jack Masters announced his decision to walk through the Himalayas, and we said – as politely as we could – that he was mad. No, he said, not an arduous march but a luxury walk with a train of attendants stretching to the next night's halt, with one animal carrying a mobile whisky still. Briggo, our whisky expert, declared that the amount of whisky produced would be roughly one peg a day. He went on to say that he himself would get no nearer to the Himalayas than Kashmir, where his life would consist of late nights and uncertain days. It was a journey from the mists of our mountaintop to the equally obscure haze of alcohol.

My work still kept me busy far into the night. All my men were casualties except Jock Yuille. But sometimes the traffic would cease, the wireless sets would close down and I would be given leisure to ponder on the rain and the mountain mists and the men in the valley below. At one period business became very quiet and to occupy my mind, which was not used to idleness, I started on a course of self-education. Looking to possible campaigns ahead I decided to learn Malay. I sent out a letter by plane asking for a book on the language, and in a week's time it came tumbling through the trees. As these words were originally written in Kuala Lumpur, it is clear that my predictions were correct. My knowledge of the language did not advance far – when the time came I had to learn it all over again – but the study kept my mind marvellously comforted.

Once more there was famine and anxious days. The clouds swept against the mountainside and feeling their way up the slopes collected in a thick mass on the crest. Padigahtawng was shut off from the open sky and the air grew close and clammy.

From above in the clear sky came the drone of planes searching for us with their loads of food and clothing. They could not break through that mass of vapour and we used to pray for at least some gap in it to show us to the Dakotas, a brief glimpse in which they could judge their run. As sortie after sortie turned back without dropping its load we received urgent pleas to move our dropping zone to a lower level. We stubbornly refused to do any such thing, as there were big problems attached to such a move, and we sat down to wait out the weather. With the end of the rations in sight I embarked on an experiment. Taking a mess tin of mule's fodder I proceeded to pick out the grain and handed it to my orderly to cook. Unfortunately, he had procured a large quantity of fat and the result was nauseating. The Gurkhas watched my efforts with glee. So I turned to my emergency stocks of soup powder.

On the sixth day a plane shot out of the low cloud dangerously close to the side of the hill and dropped a load. I still remember the name of that plane, painted on its side, *Lucky Strike*. The American pilot flew with wonderful precision through the cloud right onto the tree tops, catching only momentary glimpses of the dropping zone as he turned into the cloud again for another circuit. It was a marvellously skilful piece of work, and it meant at least a promise of plenty. The planes that followed guessed their way to us. The breaks in the clouds were so small that the planes had to drop their 'sticks' in a few seconds. This resulted in some rather wild dropping, and laborious carries, but with the reorientation of the dropping zone the planes found the run-up less obstructed by cloud and hills. The dropping improved until we could reckon on each stick landing not more than thirty yards from the axis of the recognition signs on the ground.

One day a crowd of Kachins came into the village with strain on their faces and a tale to tell. Their women had been bayonetted by some traitor Burmans (whom we referred to as the BTA,

Burma Traitor Army) and were in a critical condition. Would we take them in? We had no choice and set up a separate hospital. These villagers had given so much in order to help us that we could only attempt to pay it back. Loyal to us, they had two sets of enemies, the Japs and their traitor kinsmen. While they had more to lose from the former, they feared and hated the latter with an uneasy fear and an intense hate. From all over the jungle Kachins came in to our camp, not only for medical attention but also for protection. They had so thoroughly compromised themselves in our cause that they had nothing to hope now from anyone but ourselves. They came to us not to beg but to live, and in the perimeter of our camp they lived in peace. Mac was delighted to see that we had at last stood by his beloved Burma people and he pressed for further relief. The food question became acute for the Kachins. While we could give some rations for their sick and wounded, we could not afford it for their fit men until we had fed our own mouths. An SOS was sent to Base for seeds with which to start new crops and our request was met quickly and imaginatively. It was good to think that we had space for the gifts for these villagers.

We made another, and to westerners rather strange, request. We asked for opium. The reason for this strange request was that most of the villagers were confirmed opium smokers and in order to obtain their opium they had to go down into the valley through the Jap lines. This was bad, both for our own security and for the safety of the men themselves. If we could have the opium dropped on the hilltop a lot of difficulties would be solved. The answer from Base was an emphatic no. Perhaps this was the only time when a supply drop depended on a point of ethics. At the time we did not appreciate the moral dilemma. Faced with a lot of opium-starved villagers the moral question did not loom very large, but for those who had to decide it was very real; there were bigger issues than the welfare of a few hundred Kachins. There could have been a very awkward moment when an inquisitive MP rose to his feet in the House of Commons and asked, 'Is the Minister aware that we are supplying opium to the inhabitants of Burma?' The villagers did not get their opium and I suppose they continued to go down into the valley for it.

With the villagers came strange, thin men who had suffered much. They were some of our troops who had escaped from the Japs and were living in the villages of the hill tribes in north Burma. Some of them had been taken in Singapore, others on the first Wingate expedition – these were Gurkhas. Though they were spare and hollow-cheeked their delight was wonderful to see. We sent them down the path to the strip at Lakhren and they were still chattering wildly as they left us. Contact with such people was strange. They were from another world, having suffered so much more than we, and we had a sort of fear that their sufferings had removed them far from us despite their smiles and cheers and shouts of greeting.

While we were watching the progress of the very desultory warfare being waged on the lower slopes of the mountain towards Mogaung, we received a very disturbing message from Chesty, who had stayed behind at the lake to organise the evacuation of sick and wounded up the river to Kamaing. The message came to us via Base, and because Chesty had forgotten how to do his ciphers it had taken twenty-four hours to break down. When it was finally deciphered it was a shock. I cannot remember the exact wording, but the gist of it was as follows:

'Situation at lakeside critical. Men dying daily and morale at very low ebb. Unless medical supplies and food dropped immediately there will be more deaths and complete collapse in morale.' That was the message, and in order to realise the full meaning it should be explained that Chesty normally adopted a harsh attitude to sick men. Being immensely tough himself he could not see why men should give in on what might appear to him to be a very slim pretext. In the earlier days he used to go to the lakeside and complain that we were evacuating fit men. This was the man who was now crying for help, and we realised the situation must indeed be critical. We could do nothing but reinforce his plea for instant help and hope that it would soon arrive. Our sick and wounded still burdened us.★

What was worse, the men we had officially to regard as fit were growing steadily weaker. With the onset of the monsoon proper weaknesses of a new kind appeared. Perhaps the most important was the foot problem. In the dry weather this had not bothered us, and we had been agreeably surprised by the lack of blisters. When the rains started things deteriorated, until after a month the men started to examine their feet and found them in a serious state. Wetness itself was bad enough; it softened the skin so as to render it less resistant to wear and abrasion. But the real trouble was the mud. It was impossible to keep the mud out of one's boots and it would work its way into the socks by constant pressure. After that there was no hope; the continuous rubbing of the mud against the soft wet skin reduced it to the state of raw pulp. I have never seen human feet reach such a state. They looked like raw steak, rubbed bare of all protective covering until the red flesh below was showing. How men walked with feet like this I do not know. We were told to wash our socks regularly to free them from mud, but most of the troops had gone too far to be able to

---

★ Chesty Jennings has since told me that the numbers by the lake rose to 450, most with malaria, dysentery or jaundice. There were few medical stores and it was some time before a doctor could reach them. For long periods there was little food except fish from the lake and what the locals could supply. Many died and at the end Chesty held a funeral service, without a book, commending the dead as best he could. Then, when the flying boat service stopped, he ran a boat service up the Namsun Chaung before he himself flew out on 27 July. It was by any standards a remarkable effort.

avail themselves of this remedy. The West Africans, though free of most physical troubles, suffered badly from lacerated feet, and I remember seeing them hobble through Padigahtawng, their fine strong bodies barely kept up by their festering feet. Once the trouble started there was no cure except constant applications of ointment and a dry climate, neither of which were available to us.

And there were the leeches. I had often heard of these parasites and I knew they sucked one's blood; but until you see them and sleep with them and feel their claws in your flesh you cannot appreciate how foul they are. Frankie Baines came in one day from patrol with fifty leeches on him and with his usual gusto he told me exactly what he felt like. The ground, he said, had moved with leeches, and in the area where he had camped they were inescapable. You cannot pull a leech off. There are only two methods of getting rid of it, either to burn it off or salt it off, and if you have neither a cigarette nor a supply of salt handy you must be content to watch the insect at work. One of Frankie Baines's Gurkhas had a very neat way of dealing with leeches. It consisted of a small bag of salt on the end of a string, the string being attached to a stick. Should a leech alight on his leg he would lower the salt on the offending insect until it curled up and dropped obligingly into the mud. There was one weak link in our defence which the leeches always went for, and that was the area between the top of the boot and the bottom of the trouser. Gaiters were not very effective as they seldom fitted tightly enough, and I found that puttees were the only real answer.

Sores appeared where leeches had been unwisely plucked away, but not ordinary sores. The dampness of the atmosphere and the weak condition of the men turned each sore into an ugly wound, which, if not properly tended, could bring total incapacitation. Cases occurred of men with jungle sores becoming paralysed and Frank Turner even went blind for three weeks.

A further cause of our weakness, which we had not fully

realised at the time, was the rations. For four months we had been existing on K-rations, which is, I think, a world record. These rations had been augmented to some extent, but the K remained the basis. Before going into operations we had been assured that the rations contained an ample reserve of calories and we believed it. The truth we afterwards discovered was something entirely different. The K-ration is only sufficient to keep up a man's strength for ten days at fighting pitch. What was more, a fair proportion of our ration was never consumed. The little round tins of meat, the cellophane packets, began to exasperate us until we longed for good plain food that was not wrapped up, hygienically prepared and guaranteed to contain all the necessary vitamins. The exotic American flavours began to nauseate us, until we cried for bully beef and the biscuits grew sodden in our pockets. It became increasingly necessary to camouflage and disguise, as we tried to lose the Corned Pork Loaf in a welter of rice or a handful of local spice. You could make a pudding by mixing biscuits and fruit bars, an imitation that fooled no one and finally turned my stomach. When a new recipe was discovered the news was eagerly passed from fire to fire. The troops weakened through unsuitable rations, and the process was accelerated by the fact that they could not make themselves eat all that was provided. Jaded appetites could be stirred by onions, and we always welcomed them. Rice, which we obtained locally, was our greatest standby; it filled our bellies and left us deeply satisfied, while it could form a solid basis for all kinds of foods. But there was not enough of it. The Gurkhas and Kachins had to have first priority, and the British troops got what they could. This was quite fair, but we missed it. Malnutrition grew apace, stealthily but really.

There came a time when our commander was compelled to state our position very forcibly. Jack Masters had continually reminded headquarters of our growing weakness and had received not very encouraging replies. He sent off a message which read as follows: 'Colonel Scott says his men in worse condition than in 1943 expedition. Suggest I hand over command.' Unable to find relief for the men under his command, Jack Masters had for the last few weeks been giving orders which he knew his troops could not carry out properly. Now that one of his COs had brought matters to a head he felt compelled to resign rather than carry on as an instrument of this merciless wearing-down process. It was a drastic message, and I was the only officer who saw it. But the situation demanded it.

The reply was non-committal, 'No question your resignation. Will send you all the help I can.' It was as well that the troops did not see this. They would have laughed themselves hoarse. What the help was I could not discover. We did not need help, but relief. We did not want aid for a fresh task; we wanted an end to tasks. There was obviously something going on 'behind the scenes', and it did not smell at all good. So thought the troops, and with good reason. I heard later what the General meant by 'help'. While we toiled up and down hills and slept damp and ate unwillingly, the powers that be were haggling over our future, and the arguments grew heated. There were two points of view. One was ours and our General's, that we were quite incapable of taking any further part in operations and had done enough already to ensure the successful outcome of the campaign.

This point was strongly reinforced when 77 Brigade entered Mogaung after heroic fighting. The General signalled, 'The most glorious day in the history of the brigade,' and it was. It was a quite remarkable feat of arms, sustained gallantry from very weary men. It was then announced that the Chinese had captured the town, and Brigadier Calvert sent his famous message, 'Chinese take Mogaung. We take umbrage.' Why should we go on fighting for the Chinese, who had been so slow in everything they did? The General signalled one day, 'Uncle Joe has sent third rocket to Chinese,' and we realised that our opinion of the Chinese was shared by others. Our fault lay in trying to synchronise our movements with theirs. Their actions were quite unpredictable, and they should have set their own timetable. But that was not clear to us at the time. Now that Mogaung was captured there appeared to be no reason whatever why we should be kept in Burma, as we had ceased to be operationally capable of anything of significance, and in a short time would become a shambles.

The other point of view was represented by General Stilwell and it was not always very clear to us. First, the Chinese had to be considered. They had been in operations for an even longer period than we had, though in a somewhat less arduous role, and they would take rather a poor view if we cleared out immediately. Secondly, there was a grave shortage of troops, and until fresh troops arrived we would have to stay, if only to maintain the present line across the Mogaung Valley. The fact that we were wasting away rapidly and losing heart could not count. There is a story that the senior medical officers at HQ pleaded with Stilwell to release us. His refusal to do so may be explained by simple bloody-mindedness and an inbuilt distaste for the British. He was a brave soldier but an impossible commander. We couldn't stand his guts.

The CO of a British battalion reported to Jack Masters that his men were mentally and physically incapable of any further effort. This was true and the CO had the courage to admit it. Our commander had realised this for some time, and he decided he had no option but to accept what he was told. The battalion was sent back to Lakhren to rest, a magnificent body of men whom we had always considered to be our best and who had been played to a finish. As I watched them picking their way down the track to Lakhren and joking over their good fortune I saw the final stage in the breaking-down process. Unfortunately, we could not afford ourselves the luxury of sending more troops to rest, and we continued operations knowing full well that most of our troops were now a liability.

Mogaung was clear, the road to Myitkyina was open and we continued to wander round the hills, watching the rain beat down against the mountainside and turn the paths into quagmires. We watched our feet rot and felt the leeches digging into our flesh. We also felt the damp chill of nights spent in the soaking undergrowth, and when we woke next morning to lift our packs weighed down with the night's rain we wondered why it was necessary. 'I promise you, you will be out before the rains.' The words of our dead leader mocked us more stridently than ever, as our expectations of adventure sank into a kind of dull despair. The marvel is that, when we were called on yet again, we could still obey.

CHAPTER FOURTEEN

THE LAST STRAW

In the dejection of our fifth month in Burma we received our orders for our final operation. After the disappointments of the past we could hardly take it as such, but this time it was true. The plan, briefly, was as follows. The West Africans, who had been re-formed into a brigade, were to advance south down the railway valley, while we were to proceed south along the hills and then descend into the valley to capture a village north of the town of Taungni. The mention of the valley did not please us, but now that we were in touch with regular troops it might be easier to extricate ourselves if the necessity arose. That the necessity should arise before we reached our objective did not occur to us.

We received the news without shock; we had ceased to react as sharply as we did. We were inured, rather dangerously I think, to disappointment. But we still had the strength to respond. Before moving off to our new job we had a first 'weed-out' to spare those who were too ill for the effort of another march. Doc Whyte, himself still remarkably fit, lined us up and inspected each man in the headquarters. The signallers, who had worked themselves into a shadow, were mostly put on one side, until Briggo had to protest that he must have some left to man the wireless sets. My corporal, Jock Yuille, was stubbornly and cheerfully fit and insisted on showing it. He said to me, 'I walked twice as far looking for a job in Glasgow as I have done here.' He was the only man I had left at HQ and while he was with me I felt able to withstand the flood of messages that continued to pour in. The unfit were placed on one side and left behind in the village along with the wounded and the Kachins. When ordering this weed-out Jack Masters knew that he was depleting his already weakened force, but numbers mean nothing when they are made up of decrepits. Some men who turned back protested their fitness, but for the most part they accepted Doc Whyte's decision.

Mac was deathly pale, as indeed he always was, but he refused to admit that he was not perfectly fit. His sickliness used to frighten me at times, and I expected him to fold up one day on the jungle track. But he never did so, and carried on, looking increasingly ill. Frankie Baines was also in a bad state. His struggle with the leeches left many ugly sores on his legs, which started to fester, and he walked around wreathed in bandages. His high spirits were by no means curbed by these trials; in fact he used to explain with peculiar heartiness how awful he felt.

As usual we queried our orders and judging by past experiences were uneasy about the task allotted to us. The advance to the edge of the valley would be easy enough tactically speaking, though of course uncomfortable. The trouble would lie in the attack on the village and the succeeding twelve hours. At Blackpool we had crept in unawares and had been able to dig in. We could not expect such luck again, and should we be attacked immediately on taking the objective, the position could be a very awkward one. Everything depended, as it so often did, on a supply drop. We needed picks, shovels and wire the moment we captured the position. One day's bad weather and there would be another Blackpool. Jack Masters signalled to Base explaining these difficulties and the elements of chance in the operation. The reply was terse and advised our commander not to haggle about difficulties but get a move on.

'Look what 77 Brigade has done.' We looked and were duly astonished, but the sight did not make us any more sure of ourselves, and the reprimand came hard to us.

The march started south along the hills, a leisurely stumble through the mud. A certain measure of comfort was afforded to us by the arrival of American jungle hammocks. They were, in fact, a wonderful relief. They were totally enclosed, the top consisting of a waterproof canopy and the sides mosquito netting with a zip at the bottom to allow you to get in. Underneath was a strap on which to hang your carbine. We had been told to order on the scale of one per sick man, but we did not obey our instructions; finally every officer and almost every NCO possessed a hammock. Perhaps the officers should have suffered with the men. One officer, a friend of mine, upbraided me for using a hammock when my men could not. It was a fair comment that went very deep. I remained dry but ill at ease.

The column of the 4th Gurkhas went on ahead, while behind came the 9th Gurkhas. The Gurkha troops were still remarkably fit, or so they seemed. Being unable to reason out the whys and wherefores of the campaign they were never haunted by doubts, nor did they question their leaders. They realised that conditions were bad but supposed that in the army bad conditions must be expected. Provided that they continued to get their food and to receive clear orders from their officers they were content. I often wondered what they now thought about the performance of the British troops.

The first night of the march was spent in a small clearing by some abandoned *bashas*. The *bashas* were stinking with vermin and we preferred our hammocks, though when it came to enciphering messages various problems arose. I finally compromised by sitting under my hammock and shouting numbers to my one remaining corporal. The messages that night contained plans for the coming battle and renewed doubts as to its outcome. It was emphasised that, if the plan was to succeed, the West Africans must be well down the valley to be able to link up with us. With a rather bitter experience of badly co-ordinated movements Jack Masters was insistent on this point, and I think the General took it as a sign of our increasing reluctance to carry out the operation. Perhaps he was right.

On the afternoon of the second day's march the column was stopped by the sound of firing ahead. There was the crack of small arms fire and the persistent thud of mortars. After a period of quiet on the hilltop the noise came hard on our ears and we were reminded again of the battle of Blackpool. The column halted, cleared the track and sat thankfully by the side. Jack Masters went on ahead to see what was going on and we opened our rations. Ahead, the column of the 4th Gurkhas had bumped into the enemy earlier than they expected. As the afternoon wore on the firing increased, but with the fall of night there was a pause and we sat down to consider the day's work.

The Japs were entrenched in a very strong position on a feature known by its height as Point 2171. It was tactically an important position as it overlooked the valley and commanded the approaches to the town of Taungni. The enemy strength was about one company and they were dug in. The only accessible route to the summit was a steep track running up the north-west face, which could easily be defended and allowed no deployment for the attacking force. If we captured this feature we could dominate the valley, and the Japs were well aware of this. At the bottom of the slope was a small patch of cleared jungle on the side of a steep rise, and when brigade headquarters was stopped just short of this clearing we could see parachutes falling. It was a well-timed supply drop which we had arranged beforehand to give us sufficient supplies for our bound into the valley. If we had met the Japs before we had reached the clearing we would have gone without supplies. It came at exactly the right moment. The

Gurkha supply party was picking up the parachutes, while the fighting troops were edging their way slowly up the track.

A forward platoon of the Gurkhas thrust up the path. There was a quiet piece of gallantry by a Havildar who took his platoon in single file along the path in the face of automatic fire. Not a man was hit and 300 yards were gained. Next day he was promoted to the rank of Jemadar. Captain Ellis with the forward company was doing very well with his usual air of complete indifference. The Gurkhas were holding and exerting constant pressure on the Japs. At headquarters we could hear only the rattle of automatic weapons and the thud of mortars. Messages flowed in and out, reports on our progress, queries from Base about our exact position, requests for more ammunition, Gurkha runners coming in from the battle. That night we turned in to the sound of spasmodic firing.

Next day Jack Masters formed a new plan. He ordered Lieutenant-Colonel Alec Harper's 3/9 Gurkhas to leapfrog through the 4th Gurkhas and assault the hill with two companies, one company going straight up and the other bringing in a hook from the flank. Major Thorpe was in charge of the frontal assault while Major Blaker had the responsibility for the flank. Blaker was an outstanding officer. He had won the MC previously in the Arakan, and his constant aggression was always getting him into scrapes. In any situation he would attack, and with such speed and vigour as to catch the enemy at a disadvantage. A short time before his position near Padigahtawng had been attacked and he had repelled the attack immediately with the aid of a bunch of Gurkhas and their kukris. His men, needless to say, worshipped him and referred to him as 'Blanket Sahib' – the Gurkha is a bad student of English names.

The mortars opened up and Blaker started on his very difficult flanking movement. There was a pause and a burst of automatic fire. A persistent machine-gun could be heard near the top of the hill, and news came by runner saying that the attack had been held up about 200 yards from the summit. If night fell with the position still in Jap hands our troops would be in a precarious predicament. The news went back to Base, though they could do little about it. Jack Masters sat by the wireless set chewing furiously and then went forward to visit the CO of the 9th Gurkhas. His fertile mind left behind him a pile of messages which I started rather wearily to convert into figures. Briggo was pleased because we were in touch with Base and conditions were good. Frankie Baines was plainly excited, and said so. The British troops with us were resting thankfully.

A short while later the news came through that the position had been stormed and the Japs had fled. It came surprisingly after the anxious situation of a few hours back, and we sat back feeling a sort of vicarious satisfaction in the fulfilment of the task. We had even at this stage of the campaign achieved something. Rumours came in about the details of the attack. They were confused, but one thing stood out and that was the gallantry of Jim Blaker. He had led the final charge and had been badly wounded, so badly that there was little chance for him. A few hours later, when we were preparing for the night, Briggo came and told me that Jim had died. He had also been recommended for the Victoria Cross.

This was all we learnt that day, but later the details became clear and we realised what a man we had lost in Jim Blaker. The initial stage of the attack, the approach from the flank, involved a march through very difficult country, in which it was almost impossible to maintain direction. Blaker arrived at the appointed place at the appointed time and started the assault. About 200 yards from the summit the attack was halted by a Jap machine-gun, which pinned our men to the ground. The situation was precarious, as our men had virtually no cover. Realising this Blaker charged forward toward the machine-gun firing his carbine as he went. The carbine jammed and a grenade struck him, but he carried on. He was hit a second time and finally fell a few yards from the gun. The Gurkhas rose up and charged the hill carrying all before them. Blaker was mortally wounded but raised himself into a sitting position to cheer his men on. 'Well done, C Company. I am going to die . . . but you will go on . . . I know.' He was carried gently down the hill but died when his wounds were being attended to.

The gallantry of Jim Blaker was a great tonic for the rest of us. The Gurkhas were sad at the passing of their 'Blanket Sahib', and we grieved that he had not lived to see the victory of his men. But his example pulled us up a bit from our apathy and made us realise that even in the wretched discomfort of our life there was still room for those virtues which in our weariness we had deemed impossible. We were rather ashamed of ourselves, I think, though this feeling lasted only a short time. Later we used to talk of Jim Blaker and, when we did, we forgot our condition and wondered at such a man.

The wounded were sent down the hill into a reception area near brigade headquarters. Major Thorpe was wounded in the knee and three Gurkhas had been sprayed with machine-gun bullets. Doc Whyte went through his usual procedure, which had now become a drill. *Bashas* were erected and parachute cloth was added to strengthen the waterproofing of the sides. This cloth also made excellent sheets and the wounded had surprisingly comfortable beds. They were miles from any evacuation point or airstrip, but they were very patient. All were treated with sulphonamide, and even in the dampness of the monsoon jungle the wounded remained remarkably fresh. There had been substantial casualties in the attack, but not crippling, and the survivors started to consolidate the hilltop position; something more elaborate than at Blackpool where the shelling had caused too many casualties; substantial bunkers with thick overhead cover on which grenades could bounce harmlessly. Digging is a strong point of the Gurkhas, being a task that requires effort but not overmuch thought, and the defences on Point 2171 were considerably more formidable than when we had captured it.

There was an uneasy lull, and it seemed that the enemy was husbanding his strength for the counter-attack. Down below at headquarters supplies were coming in fast. The weather had cleared and daily sorties were being made successfully. The little open stretch of mountainside with the broad recognition strips was unmistakable and very few failures were reported from the supply base. We used to bring in the planes on the wireless, and it was part of our rather strange game that we should call in as many as we could, whoever they were meant for. This was a game played by many columns. The pilots became suspicious and wanted to know more details when told to drop. In the north end of the Mogaung Valley there were several dropping zones, and it was easy for the pilot to be bewildered into dropping on the first column that got him on the air. The results of this game were not always satisfactory. Once we received several large rubber boats meant for 77 Brigade; on the mountainside they looked rather incongruous. On another occasion through no fault of our own we received a mail bag addressed to the 14th Army and for the next few days frantic messages came in asking us to send it on. This was all fun. Cheating the next column out of its food was a high achievement. To abscond with one planeload was good going, to divert all the sorties was a triumph. Our supplies accumulated rapidly.

One evening at brigade headquarters, when we were preparing our evening meal, a 75-mm shell came over and landed in our midst. It was quite unheralded and most uncomfortable. It landed in the middle of Frankie's platoon of Gurkhas, killing one man and wounding two others. Frankie's orderly was hit, an arm and a leg broken and a deep gash in his stomach. Poor Frankie was distraught; his orderly had been through everything with him and was a magnificent little fellow. He rushed up the path shouting for the MO and swearing his orderly was about to die. It certainly seemed so to me, but he was spared and lay that evening in parachute cloth in a little *basha* on the hill. A few more shells came over but without causing any damage. It was strange to have death strike so suddenly and then draw away.

Up on Point 2171 the column of the 4th Gurkhas relieved the 9th who had done so valiantly and prepared for the Jap attack. The 9th as they came down brought stories of unusually tall and fit Japs, and we presumed they must be fresh troops. An identity disc was brought down, but having already lost three intelligence officers at Blackpool we were not in a position to decipher it. Jack Masters had a brilliant suggestion. We tore up strips of parachute cloth and draped them across the clearing in the manner of Japanese characters. A message was sent to Base to fly an expert over in a light plane to read the inscription. As we were miles away from any airstrip this was the only solution. The plane never arrived, but we were pleased at our ingenuity.

After a few days the lull broke and down from the hilltop came the sound of heavy firing. It sounded like Blackpool all over again: artillery, mortars, grenade dischargers and small arms. The Japs were attacking in force and evidently meant to recapture the hill or be themselves annihilated. There was a telephone line laid from Point 2171 down to brigade headquarters and we heard the progress of the battle. The enemy was throwing in everything he had but was not inflicting many casualties; the defences were adequate. Finally the firing died down and there was peace. Next morning the casualties were carried down the hill and placed gently inside the *bashas*. There were mercifully few, but every wounded man meant another problem for us. Also we were having difficulty with the medical supplies and there were rumours of a black market at the supply base. We sent repeated signals for more drugs and received anxious inquiries from Base about the last lot they had sent. We had seen no last lot; it must have overshot into the dense jungle or been dropped on another column.

There came another attack against the hilltop, and this time in greater strength. The noise was louder that evening and the casualties rather heavier, though quite satisfactory. The *bashas* in our little hospital were filling up. HQ moved forward a few hundred yards up the hill to bring ourselves inside the defensive area; a few Japs could easily have scattered us. The sound of battle grew more frequent, but the Japs were unable to move our troops. Rations were ample and excellent, and there was a steady supply of ammunition. But despite all this the situation was beginning to cause anxiety. Jack Masters was again in a tight spot.

The chief trouble, as before, was our casualties. There was no possibility of constructing an airstrip and the only method of evacuation was north along the hills, then down into the valley west of Mogaung where a hospital had been set up. The carry was formidable, and as a permanent line of evacuation the work involved was cruel. We never used that route, because we heard that there were Japs in position on the track between us and the hospital. The King's Own who had been left at Padigahtawng to guard the sick and were now coming to join us reported Japs at a track junction. We were thus completely cut off from the first line of communication we had possessed, and there seemed no possibility of getting the casualties out unless the Japs on the track could be cleared. We at Point 2171 had not the troops to do the job. That was the reason why, although we were beating the Japs, we were ourselves facing defeat.

News came through, and it was very heartening; 36 Division was landing at Myitkyina and was starting the march down to Mogaung. This could mean only one thing, that we were going to be relieved. In the daily 'sitreps' we followed their progress with deep interest. They must at last have realised our position and were sending troops to take over. I used to have a sort of news conference of my own and give out the latest position of the various units of the division. Briggo said this was highly reprehensible and there were proper channels for disseminating information. But so many rumours were around that I thought the truth should go out by as many channels as possible. A rumour started that the West Africans had advanced down the valley and were almost due east of us. There were high hopes for a few hours, but the next message from the West Africans brought us down to earth. Men clung to any news that brought promise of relief and nursed it so as to gain comfort.

With the knowledge that our evacuation route was denied us we looked elsewhere for help; 14 Brigade, we were told, was marching from the area south of the lake to relieve us, and on the arrival of the brigade we would proceed north to the village of Mla preparatory to marching out. Here was another hope of release and it looked like the truth. Mac was as pessimistic as ever and Frankie made some rather crude comments, but I tried to persuade them that at last the end was near. Before we could leave our present position 14 Brigade must take over, but at present there were no signs of 14 Brigade. Was it going to be the story of Blackpool all over again? Once again the brigade was ordered to march through some foul country and once again our safety depended on their prompt arrival.

The British troops were now nearing the end, and the Gurkhas could not be expected to keep going continuously. My orderly told me that he would spend the rest of his life in Burma and apparently expected to do so. Reliefs for the position on the hilltop became increasingly frequent and the men less able to respond to commands. We hoped they did not realise that if they were wounded they would have great difficulty in reaching a hospital. They did realise that they were utterly weary. All this Jack Masters knew well enough and he kept the General informed. The ssages that went out were mostly headed 'Officer to decipher', d told of approaching exhaustion and mounting casualties. ter each attack the wounded would come down the hill in little oups, walking if they could or being carried down on the backs mules. The casualties incurred in each encounter were light, and compared with the enemy's losses almost negligible, but it was the cumulative effect that caused so much anxiety. We had 150 cases in the jungle hospital and each of them would have to be carried to safety. That safety lay the other side of danger and beyond the toil and jerking pain of a long jungle march. No news came from the King's Own and 14 Brigade had not arrived, though they were getting close. Rumours started that the brigade was in sight, but again the evening report squashed them. We asked for air support, but the weather and various other circumstances limited the sorties so that we could gain very little benefit from them. It was a ridiculous state of affairs; troops winning battles daily but losing the more vital battle of their own security. We knew that the wounded should reach hospital with the minimum of delay, and we knew that this was impossible. One day the doctors at Base excelled themselves and sent us the following message: 'To prevent foot trouble essential troops use dry socks.' We replied: 'Please arrange for rain to decrease from ten hours a day and the mud from six inches. Then we will be able to follow your advice.' Somehow the men in the *bashas* survived and the wounds did not fester.

Once again our commander was faced with the problem of clinging to his position at the risk of his wounded or retreating from what had been so hardly gained to ensure himself from complete isolation. It would be a sad anticlimax to withdraw and yield the position. There was a possibility that the enemy was tiring and might himself withdraw; there was also a possibility that the track behind us might be cleared. But unless these were probabilities the risk could not be justified. At Blackpool some of the wounded had been left and we still felt the guilt. While there was still a chance to get them out, that chance must be taken. To detach troops as an escort for the wounded would have deprived us of most of the little strength we had left to hold Point 2171. Jack Masters sent a message to the General requesting permission to withdraw before being relieved by 14 Brigade. His request was granted, and we were told to proceed to Mla 'preparatory to marching out'. Those magic words again.

Another day went by, and another battle. Then the order was given to prepare to move. In the distance came the sounds of battle from 14 Brigade and we hung back a little while hoping even now for relief. We were leaving behind a vast supply of food, a brand new 4.2-inch mortar and a host of other stores. It was our second withdrawal of the campaign, a failure not of our own making but once again fashioned by circumstance. Once again 14 Brigade had not arrived and we were faced with exhausted troops and roughly tended casualties. The way was blocked, or so we supposed, and the problem remained of how to transport our wounded safely to the hospital far north in the valley. The track junction must be avoided. In our present state we could not afford to risk an encounter with the enemy and must pick our way carefully down circuitous, unfrequented paths until we were once more safe behind our own rather thin lines. There was no line as such, only a series of isolated positions manned by troops who had had enough.

The end was nearer than most of us dared to think. Mac collected his men together and started off with the same weary gloom. We missed John Hedley's consuming zeal. Frankie Baines spilled out his hopes and talked of the Taj Mahal Hotel, Bombay. Jack Masters continued chewing his gum, piecing together messages of reasoned despair, and in his off-moments at night he let himself go. We turned north to march out, not daring to hope too much, but hoping more than we did as we squelched down the narrow track.

CHAPTER FIFTEEN

RETURN

It was clear that we would not be able to use the main track north for our withdrawal, as we were in no position to fight our way through. There remained a big loop to the west skirting a village that 14 Brigade had just captured, then through a maze of small paths by a flooded *chaung* meeting the main track north of the junction where the Japs had been reported. No one knew this way except the people who lived there, and Mac explained the situation to them. On these locals depended the fate of two and a half battalions and 150 wounded; for though we could keep a rough check on them with our maps only they knew the intricacies of the winding paths. It was the last bit of assistance given to us by the Kachins and as a farewell performance it was superb.

We plunged down a steep slope into a *chaung* with sheer sides which echoed to the sounds of our marching. Mortar bombs burst near, or so we thought, and there were crashes that echoed backwards and forwards among us. We found it uncomfortable; it appeared to be coming from behind and catching us up. There was congestion and we could not speed up. Our rate of progress was limited by the wounded, who were staggering along the path or swaying precariously on the back of mules. As well as the wounded we had a large crowd of Kachins – men, women and children – who were taking the opportunity of our protection to escape the wrath that would inevitably come if they stayed behind. Altogether it was a strange army. Frankie Baines went on ahead with one of his platoons to clear the way and reported back shortly afterwards looking very fierce with a grenade in each hand. There were Japs ahead. As they had not made their presence felt and would probably be in small numbers we took no notice as the wild-eyed Frankie, still firmly clutching the grenades, made his way forward again. Japs were now only real to us if we could hear their bullets through the trees, and until we met them face to face we must speed ahead with the wounded. The first night was spent on the side of the path in a huddled confusion. Darkness had fallen when we halted and there was no time to put up the hammocks. It rained heavily and we lay in pools of water shivering and squelching. Dawn came in a wretched drizzle and the march resumed in deep gloom.

Approaching a broad track next day we met with a burst of fire and there was confusion. On these occasions the animals were always the worst problem, as we could not hide them anywhere. After an exchange of shots and a few grenades a patrol of 14 Brigade emerged from behind the undergrowth. There was immense relief and a chat. If we had stuck it at the hilltop another day all would have been well and 14 Brigade would have taken over, but we had made the decision and hoped that our relieving force would find the supplies intact. After exchanging a few words we crossed the track and led by the villagers plunged into a deep-cut river valley. A few months ago the river would have been dry; it was now a raging torrent. We crossed and recrossed it standing with difficulty against the strong current. How the wounded managed the crossings I do not know. Night harbour was by the side of the stream in a rather congested area hemmed in by the hills. After a long day's march tempers were short. Again a make-shift hospital was built for the night and the wounded lowered gently onto the bamboo beds. A Kachin woman gave birth to a son after having complained of tiredness on the march, and it was duly christened 'Joe Chinthe'. Doc Whyte took time off from his wounded to assist at the birth and next day the astonishing woman carried on with the march. Indeed she was soon carrying her baby and most of her household belongings. A message went off to Base, along with some rather heavier ones, announcing the birth of a Kachin prince.

On the third day what we had dreaded occurred. A horse carrying a wounded Gurkha slipped on the narrow track and rolled down the slope. The little man's back was broken and he died a short while afterwards. This danger was always with us, especially in the monsoon months, and I am amazed that it did not happen more often. The horses were always the greater danger, as their strength was now no more than ours and their footing was not nearly as sure as the mules'. They were skin and bone with withered flanks and angular, gawky frames. The mules were much steadier, but the difficulty was to find suitable saddles. One moment they would be carrying a 3-inch mortar, the next a wounded man, and they could not both be accommodated equally well. We longed for Maggie and her huge patient body ready to carry a wounded man with such gentle care. But above all we longed for the end to all this when we could hand over our wounded and be able to look to ourselves.

Midday saw us at the village of Pahok – there were two villages of this name and this one we always referred to as 'Hill Pahok'. On a precipitous clearing parachutes were falling and there was a vast supply of food and clothing. This was one of the 14 Brigade supply points, and they were in no danger of going short. On the top of the hill there was a complete quartermaster's stores, and I took away socks for the men. We had lunch on a hillside dotted with parachutes; as we ate, more planes appeared. The afternoon march took us through the village of Pahok up a steep ridge to the north-east and then down towards the valley, which was our immediate goal. The last hour or so of marching was carried out in pouring rain. In harbour we lit gigantic fires, knowing that now for the first time we were behind our own lines. After putting up with two months of rain I caught a chill that night but took most of the effects away in a steaming brew of tea. Next day would see us in Mla and a resting place; at least for a while.

The final day of the march was short, but scorching hot. We were dropping down into the valley and with a pause in the rain there came an oppressive heat, sticky, persistent and very weary-ing. After the comparative freshness of the hills the humidity of the lower altitude hit us and drained us. The effect was like hav-ing strength clawed out of us, in flows of salt sweat that blurred our vision and set up little irritations. Now we had a real view of the valley, looking easily on what we had so long avoided and feared. We reached Mla at about midday and scared off a small party of Japs who had apparently been left behind in the retreat; their maps were in the *basha*. The village was deserted but pos-sessed some clean and commodious *bashas* which we occupied. They were dry in the rain and cool in the heat. We removed our equipment, breathless in the heat, lay gently down and for a few delicious moments forgot everything but peace and rest.

Things were beginning to happen. For weeks Jack Masters had been asking for permission to hold a medical inspection to assess our ability to continue the campaign. Now the permission came through to take a census of how many men were fit for another two months' operations. Then we would present the figures to Base and tell the powers that be to see sense. For several days men lined up and were appraised; thin and scraggy they looked except for a few who had stood it well and thrived. The figures were compiled and the answers given. It was approximately as follows: 6 officers and 120 other ranks, out of a total strength of about

2,500. That was the number of fit men in our brigade. Surely it would impress someone.

It did. But a message came back saying that the deciding factor was one month's further operations and not two. Perhaps they wanted better figures. If so, they were disappointed. We stuck to our figures and repeated them. Jack Masters realised the strength of his argument and sat back waiting for the General to come to a final agreement with Stilwell. The troops rested and only the signallers continued with their work, as they always did. Supply drops were easy in the broad valley and our immediate needs were satisfied. There was still rather a confusion between the different dropping zones and supplies would go astray, but there was no lack. An RAF officer spoke to an American supply dropping pilot and asked him to reserve a room in the Taj Mahal Hotel, Bombay, from 25 August. Our hopes ran high in those days.

And there was good reason. For orders were received for the two British battalions to start marching to Mogaung. This was the moment we had been waiting for through these months. And yet in a strange way the order took us aback. Faced with the real thing we could only wonder and hope that it was not all just a glorious dream. The troops packed up their kit, filled up with rations and set off towards the Mogaung Road. They were singing as they went, their tired faces lit up at the thought of release.

On the following day the General arrived. It was a strange meeting. For months now, since he had left us on the airstrip down south, he had been a name and a force transmitting orders and unable through lack of contact to transmit also his live personality. When he sent out a hard order, he did not come to us and explain why he had done so. We could not discuss matters with him; we could only criticise if an order was not to our liking. When the General met us at Mla and discussed the past with us, our attitude changed. It was quite like old times seeing Joe again. Those who were able to hear him speak and reveal the difficulties and confusion of higher policy came to realise that, while we were enduring physically, he was going through a time of great mental stress; worrying over men he knew could fight no more and trying to persuade those above him that we had had enough. We discussed decorations, and the General told us he had forwarded the recommendation for Jim Blaker's Victoria Cross. The future was passed over lightly. The immediate future was clear; what was beyond that we were not able to discuss, as there were hints of another operation. The General spoke to the Gurkhas in their own language – he had done all his service with them – and told them what they had done. He told them also that in a few months after leave and refit they would return again to Burma. Even the amenable Gurkhas found this a hard statement, and it was well that it was not passed on to the British troops, who had in fact given the General a not very friendly reception.

Even at this stage there were reservations about the plan. The tiny body of troops still considered fit enough to carry on were to be left behind while the others returned to India. It was a ludicrous idea and appeared to us to be extremely petty. Surely, we thought, the manpower situation could not be as bad as that; and what contribution could an extra 130 men make to the successful issue of the campaign? I believe it was part of the tortuous bargaining that was going on over our heads, but to us it made no sense at all.

Our casualties had gone ahead to the hospital several days before and the march to Mogaung was not hampered by wounded men. Once on the road we stepped out. It was the first metalled road we had walked on since we left India five months before, and in the last twelve miles of the campaign we developed our first blisters. We passed the other village of 'Valley Pahok', where the hospital was. Frankie inquired about his orderly and got reassuring news. Planes were landing on the road and drawing up at the hospital gates, American planes and American doctors. They did not fight with us, but they fought for our men's lives, men who had been wounded a week previously and had been lying in the jungle. An hourly halt found us at the gates of the hospital, and as we sat down we could see some of our men being carried into the little planes en route for India.

A few miles further on we passed troops of 36 Division, who were coming to relieve us and carry on the campaign in a rather more orthodox manner. The men seemed huge and fresh, their clothes spotlessly clean. They looked like new men. What we must have looked to them I can only guess. But in all our filth and scruffiness we felt superior. Their food was being brought up by wheeled vehicles, their pack loads seemed much less than ours. Their path lay not across mountains and down rushing streams but along the bottoms of valleys served by road and railway. It was a physical snobbery that affected all who came under Wingate, and in those moments of greeting on the road to Mogaung it became accentuated by the sudden contrast.

After a fast march and with blistered feet we entered the town of Mogaung. It had once been a town but it was now a shambles. Every house had some mark of war on it, and most were completely shattered. The ground was a swamp, and out of the swamp rose skeleton buildings, propped on the tops of wooden piles to keep out the mud and rain. Now there was precious little to prop up, only empty windows and roofless rooms and sodden bamboo floors. Headquarters bedded down in one of these gutted shacks. We could take our ease. Briggo's signallers had no messages to send nor mine to encipher, and Frankie Baines had no enemy to ward off; he could ease his warlike grimace and just laugh. We were continually trying to find shelter in the building, both from the intermittent rain and the breathless heat between the showers. In a nearby pagoda was a stack of shells with a large Buddha looking down on them disapprovingly. There were dud shells scattered about in the mud. One exploded and the fragments whistled over our heads plopping into a pool of water a few yards away. We thought we had escaped from all this. An officer of 77 Brigade was still in the town. The brigade had been evacuated, but he had been left behind to bring on the mules. He insisted on showing us round the battlefield where so many of his brigade had fallen. He pointed out the open ground in front of the railway embankment over which they had advanced under cover of a shower of grenades, the embankment itself riddled with foxholes, and the places where two VCs had been won (as yet they were only recommendations). Here was the scene of an open battle such as we had scarcely known. This brigade had marched out in the hour of their victory and they had the morale of victors. After our uncertain wanderings and unsuccessful battles we were going out of Burma a largely broken force. This tour of the battlefield, the scene of triumphs not our own, was galling.

The Chinese were in possession of the town, and just near our billet was the house of the Regimental Commander. At night it was unsafe to be abroad as the Chinese sentries interpreted their duties very sternly. There were shots heard in all directions, and sundry explosions. We sat tight in our little billet, sheltering under our hammocks which we had strung up to the tottering beams. An American came in to see us, straight from the States on a job that he neither liked nor fully understood. We sympathised. And could he spare some of his Lucky Strikes? He could and did. He told rather a serious-looking officer to 'take it easy'. It was the best advice he could have given us.

The next stage of the journey was by train to the airstrip at Myitkyina. The 'train' was a makeshift arrangement of jeeps and diesel trucks and goods wagons. Brigade headquarters split up, never to be an operating unit again. It was a very informal dispersal as we chugged off in our separate trucks to make our own way back to India. Jack Masters, Briggo, Frankie, Mac; we had seen much together which had changed our lives and which no one else would quite understand. For the moment we were content to be alive and eager to be at rest.

We chugged off. It worked and we were very willing to put up with its discomforts. Fortunately the distance was only thirty-five miles, and even allowing for breakdowns we could make the trip in reasonable time. It took us three hours and we were one of the last parties to go. Three times the train stopped and each breakdown afforded huge delight to the Americans running the train, a welcome break in a rather humdrum life. We reached the railhead as darkness was falling and we decided to spend the night right there. It was our last night in Burma, and about our worst. Rain fell in torrents and there were no hammocks. It was a dawn of soaking gloom and sodden packs and baggage. We had left our mules at Mogaung after their magnificent service to us; they had stood it far better than we had. Their loads had come with us in the train and had to be unloaded in the pouring rain. We would like to have thrown it all away, but that would never do.

The march to the airstrip was only two or three miles, but it took us a long time. The track was knee-deep in water. There was no marked way and our only means of keeping direction was to follow the telephone lines propped up on poles. The guns were firing in Myitkyina, though not as fiercely as they had been the night before. The airstrip came in sight suddenly and rose magically out of the filth and wet and our feet. There was a long gravel stretch and an endless stream of planes taxiing about. There were no sorties yet, but great activity. We reported at the Control Office and were promised a quick return to India. Inside the bare hut steaming tea was handed round. We looked anxiously up at the sky. No sorties yet, and bad weather reports from India. But the officer in charge of the evacuation was not unduly perturbed. Apparently the planes came through in any kind of weather. As he spoke the first plane circled and touched down, and the first load of troops piled into it. Lists were completed and we waited our turn watching each plane settle down and then asking the pilot if he happened to be going to Dinjan in Assam. It was all amazingly informal, and I suppose it is about the first time a formation has been evacuated by thumbing its way out.

When most of the day's arrival of troops were away there came a lull and a long wait. Planes were landing bound for everywhere in the world except Dinjan. Hospital planes drew up periodically beside the control tower; others said they were going to China. One pilot said he had orders to find a lost column and drop some food – shades of our yesterdays! This time it was the Chinese and not us. The airfield seemed to be run by a small group of American sergeants and everyone took their orders from them. Behind the control tower a touching reunion took place. A Burma rifleman was asking permission to fly to Chungking to find his sister. Dr Seagrave, the noted American missionary surgeon, who was there, said, 'She's here!' They met and talked and wept.

Finally, our turn came and a pilot was persuaded to take us aboard; like most on the evacuation he was American; it was our last taste of the splendid partnership that had made our enterprise possible. Muddy kit was strewn on the hard steel floor and there was a grating of boots. We circled up and swung out towards Mogaung, then Kamaing and Shadazup, names that meant nothing to any but us. Up the Hukawng Valley and over the crest of the huge hills to the north-west. Below us was the Ledo Road, winding frenziedly up and down the steep muddy slopes. This was a regular run and planes passed us every few minutes. There were fleeting glimpses of the hills through the hurrying clouds and a chill over our damp bodies. After an hour we saw ahead the plains of Assam and as we came lower the Ledo Road stood out very sharp as it curved round into the flat ground. The airstrip lay a few minutes south down the valley, and without further ado we landed. It was 31 July.

'Is this Dinjan?' Colonel Scott asked the pilot.

'No,' he replied, 'this is Chabwa.'

This sounded bad, like catching the wrong train, but it was not so. The reception camp was only a few miles away. When we alighted from the plane the heat of India closed in on us, the hot breath of civilisation after five months of isolation. The first bullock cart caused us to stop, and for perhaps the first time we found pleasure in the smells of an Indian bazaar. At the side of the road was a store of K-rations which struck rather a jarring note. The roads were firm and the houses sheltered from the rain. The sound of the lorry's engine was reassuring music, telling us with its shrill tones that we were really back again.

The lorry turned in to the reception camp, and we climbed out. Before us stood new men, or so they seemed to us. Twenty-four hours previously they had been like us, but now they were clean and clothed in spotless uniforms. After a cup of tea we went through a sanitary sausage machine, a complete but swift process which in a few minutes converted us from what we were to what we had to become before we could enter civilised society again. For once we really praised the base wallahs. They had prepared a wonderful reception for us. During the day there was rest and fresh food, no more cellophane packets and little round tins; at night music and singing, the expansive gaiety of a concert party or the grand solitude of a symphony played on the padre's gramophone. I heard Beethoven's 'Emperor' Concerto and wondered at all that I had missed in these last five months; though perhaps I had gained far more.

We clutched at comforts less eagerly than we had hoped. Food had once been a beautiful dream. Now we ate the food we had dreamed of and it lost its wonder. It was disappointing. Expectation and reality refused to merge, but we came to accept this, content with what we had and thankful for being where we were.

★

After another bout of malaria, a blissful convalescence at the Himalayan hill-station of Mussoorie, and leave with my parents in Quetta, relaxing, proud of what I had done but as yet unable to tell them, I returned to Special Force, which was starting to train for another operation. It was in the Central Provinces again, but otherwise all was different. Things were changing. Jack Masters, with a DSO, was commanding a battalion. He was shortly to become chief staff officer to General Pete Rees, the diminutive Welsh dynamo in command of the 19th Indian Division, which was advancing towards my birthplace, the town of Mandalay, and in which force my elder brother was serving. John Hedley, having recovered from his grenade wound, was with the undercover outfit Force 136 behind the lines in Burma – he seemed to prefer to see the enemy from behind. His adventures were to earn him the DSO. Doc Whyte, also with a DSO, went off to command a Field Ambulance. Briggo, still remarkably fit, was at Special Force HQ. Frankie Baines had been hastily recalled to the Camouflage Pool ('where the sedge is withered and no birds sing') to explain why he had gone into Burma without permission. But first they had to find him, which proved quite a task. Mac, who at last had to admit that he was a sick man, had been transferred to training. He went to Ceylon to prepare personnel of Force 136 for undercover operations. He had much experience to impart. Chesty Jennings had gone off to Air HQ in Delhi and was last seen drinking vast quantities of quinine with a temperature of 104 and declaring that he had never felt so fit in his life. He was awarded the MC.

And Frank Turner! It was amazing that he was still alive. He had had typhoid, pneumonia, been totally blind for thirty-one days and then had had hepatitis and recurrent malaria ('A hundred and ten times,' he told me). He was shipped home and was to get a disability pension. His successor, Ossie, was the only familiar face at our new camp.

The spring had gone out of my step. On the first field exercise I was violently sick and brought up the new rations they had devised for us, something that had never happened to five months of K-rations. And in the evening bivouac I put on my face what I thought was mosquito cream and found that it was Dubbin, a preparation used on boots for keeping the leather waterproof.

Our General, still Joe Lentaigne, came to visit us. 'Hello, R. J.,' he said, 'how are you?' We exchanged greetings and in a quick glance recalled those months of toil and fear. We had a new brigade commander, the marvellously energetic and ebullient Claud Rome. Then one day he fell out of his jeep, which was being misdirected by his Gurkha driver, and the following day he was told that he had broken his neck. He came to make his farewells, stiff and giraffe-like in plaster, smiling away much disappointment.

On 1 February 1945 we were declared 'ready for war' again, and on 2 February General Sir Oliver Leese, former Commander of the Eighth Army after Montgomery and now Commander Allied Land Forces South-East Asia, came to see us and tell us, as gently as he could, that we were no longer needed. The mooted plan that we should be landed by glider north of Rangoon was dead. We were to be broken up.

I suppose we should have been broken-hearted, special people becoming ordinary again. But somehow we were not. The momentum had gone out of the Chindits. Perhaps it was that very few of the originals were still there; the wastage of the last campaign had been prodigious. But perhaps after all it was that we had no Wingate. Whatever people felt about him, there was no denying his specialness and his power to stir the imagination.

So when I said goodbye to my new brigadier at the tented headquarters in central India not far from where we had first trained, and went off to a good posting that the kind General had engineered for me, I had many memories but no regrets.

I suppose that in the end Orde Wingate won.

POSTSCRIPT

On 23 June 1979 the Chindits met for a special reunion to celebrate the thirty-fifth anniversary of their airborne invasion of Burma.

We started with a service of remembrance at the chapel of the Royal Chelsea Hospital. As we gathered the Pensioners looked on at warriors not much younger than themselves. In the chapel we remembered our leader and the fallen. A small body of Americans had crossed the Atlantic to be with us. One of them leaned back and said, 'I piloted a glider into Broadway.' Then we fell in outside the chapel and were inspected by our old Supreme Commander, Lord Louis Mountbatten, who had words for many of us. After that we formed up and, as best we could with creaking joints and gently clanging medals, we marched past, turning our eyes to him as we did so. Age had not withered his bearing nor those firm, warm, commanding eyes. My mind went back to the lithe figure jumping from his jeep at our camp thirty miles south of Imphal to encourage us to battle.

In the evening we wined and dined and the past began to flow. Bernard Fergusson was there. Since we last met he had been Governor-General of New Zealand and he was now Lord Ballantrae. But he was just the same person, ready to dispense to all, colonel or captain or corporal, his expansive friendliness. Of the

III Brigade headquarters staff only Frank Turner and Mac were there. One I had last met desperately ill in Burma, the other very weak after it was all over. Now I was delighted to see two very fit men, ready to recollect, which we did.

There were many absent friends. There were, of course, no Gurkhas. The little men who had walked so far and so cheerfully with us – Ananda Bahadur, Budi Bahadur, Prem Lal, Kalu, Didi Ram, Chota and my faithful Birbal – were living out their declining years in their mountain kingdom and no doubt remembering much themselves. Jock Yuille disappeared from my life at Mogaung. Briggs was said to be still in Customs and Excise. Joe Lentaigne had died some years before; after the war he occupied a senior post in the Indian defence forces. Sadly, John Hedley had died four months before the gathering; he had lived so fully and so generously, latterly as a schoolmaster. Jack Masters just missed the show. He was now John Masters, world-famous novelist and American citizen. He flew in briefly to launch a huge new trilogy of novels, and I managed to catch him. Thirty-four years are not easily compressed into forty minutes, but we did our best. And then he flew off again.

And Frankie Baines? No one seemed to know where he was. His career since the war had included running a tea-chest repairing business in Calcutta, three years' silent meditation as a Hindu monk in the Himalayas, labouring at Waterloo Station, deep-sea trawling and writing two fine volumes of autobiography. The last news was that he had undertaken to write the history of a leading firm of building contractors. I remembered seeing him referred to some years ago in a paper as 'one of the few genuine eccentrics remaining'. How much he coloured our lives, and how much he strove to find a meaning to his own.

The evening wore on. Important men made speeches and others listened and dreamt. It is wholly fanciful, but comforting, to think that above the drone of speeches and the gruff bonhomie of ageing men we could make out faint traces of other sounds: the clank of mule harness, the sucking of boots out of mud, the swish and thud of a parachute, and rain in the trees. These were the sounds that came with the man we were especially remembering that evening; the strange man we followed because he had ideas and because, for a brief moment in our lives, he made us bigger than ourselves.

FURTHER READING

Three brigade commanders have written accounts of the 1944 Operation:

Calvert, M., *77 Brigade: Prisoners of Hope*, Jonathan Cape, London, 1952.

Fergusson, B., *16 Brigade: The Wild Green Earth*, Collins, London, 1946.

This contains some fine chapters on the techniques of Long Range Penetration.

Masters, J., *III Brigade: The Road Past Mandalay*, Michael Joseph, London, 1961.

A strikingly professional piece of storytelling.

For the campaign as a whole:

Bidwell, S., *The Chindit War: The Campaign in Burma 1944*, Hodder & Stoughton, London, 1979.

An acute and comprehensive analysis.

For an assessment of Wingate:

Sykes, C., *Orde Wingate*, Collins, London, 1959.

The definitive biography.

Tulloch, D., *Wingate in Peace and War*, Macdonald, London, 1972.

A vigorous defence of Wingate by his chief of staff. This is a reaction against the hostile assessment of Wingate given in the official publication:

Kirby, S. Woodburn et al., *The War Against Japan*, HMSO, London, 1961.

INDEX

Page numbers with 'n' after them refer to footnotes

ABOUT THE AUTHOR

Richard Rhodes James was born in Mandalay, Burma, in 1921, one of five children of an Indian Army officer. After his education in England, he returned to India in 1942 and joined the 3rd Gurkha Rifles.

Following the Chindit operations, in which he was mentioned in dispatches, he went on the expedition to repossess Malaya from the Japanese, and he ended the Second World War in Java with the British occupying force.

From 1947 to 1981 he taught at Haileybury College, Hertford, and subsequently in Cambridge. He broadcast and contributed to various journals. He died in 2012.

THE SANDS OF DUNKIRK
by Richard Collier

With a new introduction
by James Holland

The authentic account of the most
successful evacuation in history,
Dunkirk, told in the words of the
men and women who were there
on both sides of the conflict.

Coming summer 2022

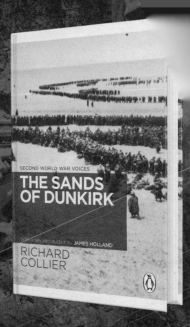

ECLIPSE
by Alan Moorehead

With a new introduction
by James Holland

An eyewitness account of the
Allied invasion of Fortress
Europe, detailing the collapse
of Germany, the wholesale
destruction, mass surrenders,
and the unimaginable horrors of
the concentration camps.

Coming winter 2022

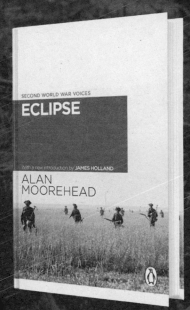